HISTORY OF ANCIENT EGYPT

HISTORY OF ANCIENT EGYPT

AN INTRODUCTION

ERIK HORNUNG

Translated from the German by David Lorton

CORNELL UNIVERSITY PRESS

ITHACA, NEW YORK

Grundzüge der ägyptischen Geschichte, © 1978 by Wissenschaftliche
Buchgesellschaft, Darmstadt.

English translation copyright © 1999 by Cornell University

First published 1999 by Cornell University Press.
First printing, Cornell Paperbacks, 1999.

Printed in the United States of America.

Library of Congress Cataloging-in-Publication Data
Hornung, Erik.
    [Grundzüge der ägyptischen Geschichte.   English]
    History of ancient Egypt : an introduction / Erik Hornung :
translated from the German by David Lorton.
      p.   cm.
    Translation of: Grundzüge der ägyptischen Geschichte.
    Includes bibliographical references (p.   ) and index.
    ISBN 0-8014-3471-8 (cloth : alk. paper).—ISBN 0-8014-8475-8
(pbk. : alk. paper)
    1. Egypt—History—To 332 B.C.   I. Title.
DT83.H5813   1999
932—dc21   98-44396

Cornell University Press strives to use environmentally responsible suppliers and
materials to the fullest extent possible in the publishing of its books. Such materials
include vegetable-based, low-VOC inks and acid-free papers that are recycled, totally
chlorine-free, or partly composed of nonwood fibers. Books that bear the logo of the FSC
(Forest Stewardship Council) use paper taken from forests that have been inspected and
certified as meeting the highest standards for environmental and social responsibility.
For further information, visit our website at www.cornellpress.cornell.edu.

Cloth printing

10 9 8 7 6 5 4 3 2 1

Paperback printing

10 9 8 7 6 5 4 3 2 1

CONTENTS

ILLUSTRATIONS

Maps

PREFACE

When we in modern times encounter ancient Egypt, whether as an exotic culture or as one ultimately related to our own, we never fail to be astonished by the tranquillity of things Egyptian, by the petrified and hierarchic organization the Egyptians imposed upon their world thousands of years ago. To anyone under such an impression, Egypt can easily seem like a land of rigid permanence whose superficial tranquillity and homogeneity conceal a lack of history, or at least a lack of "historic determinations of humanity," to use a phrase coined by the German philosopher Karl Jaspers. The task of the historian, then, is to disclose the ongoing, often stormy changes behind this rigid facade, repeatedly detaching them and fitting them back into the abundant flux revealed by the sources. To give but a single example, what a host of historical events and radical decisions took place in just the few years of the Amarna Period! If other periods seem poorer in historic determinations, that is often because of the difficulties presented to the historian by chronology and by the concept of history in the ancient Near East. (The general rubric "ancient Near East" designates the common history of Egypt and western Asia down to the Persian conquest, 539–525 B.C.E., a period comprising the first half of written human history.) With the refining of method and the acquisition of new sources, chronology can shrink an uneventful millennium into a lively century, while acquaintance with the ancient Egyptian concept of history warns us against understanding the monotonous repetitions and stock formulas of "histori-cal" texts as a reflection of real history. For people in those ancient times, history was not a social or economic process but rather cultic practice and ritual drama, with the result that their "historical" texts conceal rather more from us than they communicate.

The difficulties that chronology and the concept of history pose for any attempt to draw a picture of the history of the ancient Near East are the presuppositions of this book, not its content. I therefore omit them here and concentrate on historical events from Menes to Alexander the Great, touching only briefly on the prehistoric period. The dates the reader will find here are secure only for Dynasties 26–30. With regard to the Middle and New Kingdoms, I have sought to take into account re-cent revisions in datings; the dates for the Old Kingdom remain quite uncertain.

The references have been considerably expanded and updated in this new edition. I thank Thomas Schneider and Boris Schibler for their assis-tance in the incorporation of further literature in the American and French editions.

ERIK HORNUNG

TRANSLATOR'S NOTE

English-speaking scholars do not have a single set of conventions for the rendering of ancient Egyptian and modern Arabic personal and place names. Most of the names mentioned in this book occur in two standard reference works: John Baines and Jaromír Málek, *Atlas of Ancient Egypt* (New York, 1980), and *Civilizations of the Ancient Near East*, edited by Jack M. Sasson (New York, 1995). Wherever possible, the renderings of Egyptian and western Asian names follow the usages in those volumes. The only exception is the omission of the typographical sign for *ayin;* this consonant does not exist in English, and it was felt that its inclusion would serve only as a distraction.

The brief quotations from the poetry of Rilke are cited from Rainer Maria Rilke, *Duino Elegies,* translated by David Young (New York, 1978).

This volume fills the need for a concise history of pharaonic Egypt, both for general readers and for use in the classroom, and I am grateful to Cornell University Press for asking me to serve as its translator. I also thank Erik Hornung and Eckhard Eichler for their help and encouragement during the course of this project.

D. L.

CHRONOLOGY

What follows is an inventory of the more important monarchs, not a complete list. The Archaic Period is given more leeway here than in the text. Under Dynasties 18 and 19, I follow now an alternative resulting from recent proposals by M. L. Bierbrier, R. Krauss, and others, including fixing the beginning of the reign of Ramesses II at 1279 B.C.E., shortening the reign of Merneptah to ten years, and eliminating an independent reign for Amenmesse, though it cannot be regarded as definitive. The list is made up of the personal names of the kings, with the throne names added in parentheses from Dynasty 12 on; for Dynasty 11, the Horus names are added, and for Dynasty 1, the Greek forms as handed down in the epitomes of Manetho.

Dynasty 0

Irihor (?)
"Scorpion"   c. 3050 B.C.E.
Narmer

Archaic Period

Dynasty I   c. 3000–2800

Aha (Athothis)
Djer (Kenkenes)

Wadj (Uenephes)
Den (Usaphais)
Adjib (Miebis)
Semerkhet (Semempses)
Qaa (Ubienthes)

Dynasty 2   **c. 2800–2670**

Hetepsekhemwy
Reneb
Ninetjer
Peribsen
Khasekhem(wy)

Old Kingdom

Dynasty 3   **c. 2670–2600**

Nebka
Djoser   2654–2635
Sekhemkhet
Huni   2625–2600

Dynasty 4   **c. 2600–2487**

Snofru   2600–2571
Khufu (Cheops)   2571–2548
Radjedef   2548–2540
Khephren (Khafre)   2540–2514
Menkaure (Mycerinos)   2510–2491
Shepseskaf   2491–2487

Dynasty 5   **c. 2487–2348**

Userkaf   2487–2480
Sahure   2480–2468
Neferirkare   2468–2449
Neuserre   2443–2419
Menkauhor   2419–2411
Djedkare (Izezi)   2411–2378
Wenis   2378–2348

Dynasty 6   **c. 2348–2198**

Teti   2348–2320
Userkare

Pepy I (Meryre)	2316–2284
Merenre I	2284–2270
Pepy II (Neferkare)	2270–2205
Merenre II. Antyemzaf	
Nitocris (?)	

First Intermediate Period

Dynasties 7–8   **c. 2198–2160**

Several ephemeral rulers

Dynasties 9–10   **c. 2160–1980**

Kheti III
Merykare

Dynasty 11   **c. 2081–1938**

Inyotef I (Sehertawy)	2081–2065
Inyotef II (Wahankh)	2065–2016
Inyotef III (Nakhtnebtepnufer)	2016–2008
Mentuhotpe I (Nebhepetre)	2008–1957
Mentuhotpe II (Sankhkare)	1957–1945
Mentuhotpe III (Nebtawyre)	1945–1938

Middle Kingdom

Dynasty 12   **c. 1938–1759**

(Overlapping dates are due to coregencies)

Amenemhet I (Sehetepibre)	1938–1909
Senwosret I (Kheperkare)	1919–1875
Amenemhet II (Nubkaure)	1877–1843
Senwosret II (Khakheperre)	1845–1837
Senwosret III (Khakaure)	1837–1818
Amenemhet III (Nimaatre)	1818–1773
Amenemhet IV (Maakherure)	1773–1763
Nefrusobk (Nefru Sobek Shedty)	1763–1759

Second Intermediate Period

Dynasty 13   **c. 1759–1630**

(1) Wegaf (Khutawyre)	1759–1757
(12) Sebekhotpe I (Khaankhre)	

(14) Awibre
(16) Sebekhotpe II (Sekhemre-khutawy)
(17) Khendjer (Userkare)
(21) Sebekhotpe III (Sekhemre-swadjtawy)
(22) Neferhotep I (Khasekhemre)   1705–1694
(24) Sebekhotpe IV (Khaneferre)   1694–1685
(27) Aya (Merneferre)
and many others

Dynasty 14   c. 1700–1630

Nehesy and other minor kings in the delta

Dynasties 15–16 (Hyksos)   c. 1630–1522

Salitis (Sekhaenre?)
Bnon
Apachnan/Khiyan (Swoserenre)
Iannas/Yinassi
Arkhles/Sikruhaddu
Apophis (Awoserre)   1573–1533
Khamudi   1533–1522

Dynasty 17 (Theban)   c. 1640–1539

Inyotef V (Nubkheperre)   c. 1630
Tao I (Senakhtenre)   c. 1570
Tao II (?) (Seqenenre)   c. 1560/50
Kamose (Wadjkheperre)   1543–1539

New Kingdom

Dynasty 18   c. 1539–1292

Ahmose (Nebpehtire)   1539–1514
Amenophis I (Djeserkare)   1514–1493
Tuthmosis I (Akheperkare)   1493–1482
Tuthmosis II (Akheperenre)   1482–1479
Hatshepsut (Maatkare)   1479–1458
Tuthmosis III (Menkheperre)   1479–1426
Amenophis II (Akheprure)   1426–1400
Tuthmosis IV (Menkheprure)   1400–1390
Amenophis III (Nebmaatre)   1390–1353
Amenophis IV/Akhenaten (Neferkheprure)   1353–1336

Smenkhkare (Ankhkheprure)	1336–1333
Tutankhamun (Nebkheprure)	1333–1323
Aya (Kheperkheprure)	1323–1319
Haremhab (Djeserkheprure)	1319–1292

Dynasty 19 (early Ramesside Period) c. 1292–1188

Ramesses I (Menpehtire)	1292–1290
Sethos I (Menmaatre)	1290–1279
Ramesses II (Usermaatre setepenre)	1279–1213
Merneptah (Baenre meriamun)	1213–1203
Sethos II (Userkheprure setepenre)	1203–1196
Amenmesse (Menmire)	
Siptah (Akhenre setepenre)	1196–1190
Twosre (Sitre meritamun)	1190–1188

Dynasty 20 (late Ramesside Period) c. 1188–1075

Sethnakhte (Userkhaure meryamun)	1188–1186
Ramesses III (Usermaatre meryamun)	1186–1155
Ramesses IV (Heqamaatre setepenamun)	1155–1148
Ramesses V (Usermaatre sekheperenre)	1148–1143
Ramesses VI (Nebmaatre meryamun)	1143–1135
Ramesses VII (Usermaatre setepenre meryamun)	1135–1129
Ramesses VIII (Usermaatre akhenamun)	1129–1127
Ramesses IX (Neferkare setepenre)	1127–1108
Ramesses X (Khepermaatre setepenre)	1108–1104
Ramesses XI (Menmaatre setepenptah)	1104–1075

Third Intermediate Period

Dynasty 21 c.1075–945

Smendes (Hedjkheperre setepenre)	1075–1044
Amenemnisu (Neferkare)	1044–1040
Psusennes I (Akheperre setepenamun)	1040–990
Amenemope (Usermaatre setepenamun)	993–984
Siamun (Netjerkheperre setepenamun)	978–960
Psusennes II (Titkheprure setepenre)	960–945

Dynasty 22 (Bubastids) c. 945–715

Shoshenq I (Hedjkheperre setepenre)	945–924
Osorkon I (Sekhemkheperre setepenre)	924–889

Takelot I (Hedjkheperre setepenre)	889–874
Osorkon II (Usermaatre setepenamun)	874–850
Takelot II (Hedjkheprre setepenre)	850–825
Shoshenq III (Usermaatre setepenre)	825–773
Pami (Usermaatre setepenre)	773–767
Shoshenq V (Akheperre setepenre)	767–730
Osorkon IV (Akheperre setepenamun)	730–715?
(additionally, many local principalities)	

Dynasty 23   c. 818–715

Pedubaste (Usermaatre setepenamun)	818–793
Shoshenq IV (Usermaatre meryamun)	793–787
Osorkon III (Usermaatre setepenamun)	787–759
Takelot III (Usermaatre setepenamun)	764–757
Rudjamun (Usermaatre setepenamun)	757–754
Iupet II (Usermaatre setepenamun)	754–715 (?)
(additionally, many local principalities)	

Dynasty 24   c. 725–712

| Tefnakhte (Shepsesre) | 725–718 |
| Bocchoris (Wahkare) | 718–712 |

Dynasty 25 (Ethiopian)   c. 712–664

Kashta (Maatre ?)	?-740
Piye/Piankhy (?) (Usermaatre and others)	740–713
Shabaka (Neferkare)	712–698
Shebitku (Djedkaure)	698–690
Taharqa (Khunefertemre)	690–664
Tantamani (Bakare)	664–656

Assyrian Conquest   671–664

Late Period

Dynasty 26 (Saite)   664–525

Necho I (Menkheperre)	672–664
Psammetichus I (Wahibre)	664–610
Necho II (Wehemibre)	610–595
Psammetichus II (Neferibre)	595–589
Apries (Haaibre)	589–570

Amasis (Khnemibre)	570–526
Psammetichus III (Ankhkaenre)	526–525

Dynasty 27 (Persian Period) **525–404**

Dynasty 28

Amyrtaios	404–399

Dynasty 29 **399–380**

Nepherites I (Baenre merynetjeru)	399–393
Psammuthis (Userre setepenptah)	393
Hakoris (Khnemmaatre)	393–380
Nepherites II	380

Dynasty 30 **380–343**

Nectanebo (Nakhtnebef) I (Kheperkare)	380–362
Teos (Irmaatenre)	362–360
Nektanebo (Nakhthorehbit) II (Senedjemibre)	360–343

Second Persian Period **343–332**

Macedonians **332–305**

Ptolemaic Period **305–30**

Roman and Byzantine Periods **30 B.C.E.–642 C.E.**

HISTORY OF ANCIENT EGYPT

THE ARCHAIC PERIOD

We have no textual witnesses to the many thousands of years of the prehistoric period, during which the elements that supported and defined the historical culture of Egypt took shape. The first of these was the landscape, with its clear large-scale divisions. There was the narrow cultivable valley, full of luxuriant growth. Through it flowed the Nile, which was characterized by the yearly inundation. The valley was bounded by deserts that were flat and sand-filled in the north and marked by hills and cliffs in the south; desolate and immeasurable, these deserts were always life-threatening. Additionally, there was the fertile triangle of the delta, with its several Nile branches; the delta slowly gained in size as the sea of the Tertiary Period subsided.

Next, there was the climate, which down through the Neolithic Period had an equatorial African character, hot and humid with abundant rainfalls. Only after the Old Kingdom did it correspond to the dry, desert climate of the present day.

Lastly, there were the people, who had already made their appearance in the Nile valley in the Paleolithic Period and whose prehistory was dependent on climatic fluctuations. About 5500 B.C.E., the last great wet phase came to an end, making the Nile valley more attractive for human settlement. The earliest Neolithic cultures began a little later, at first in the Faiyum and then in the western delta at Merimda, from about 4800. In the later fifth millennium B.C.E., Upper Egypt assumed cultural lead-

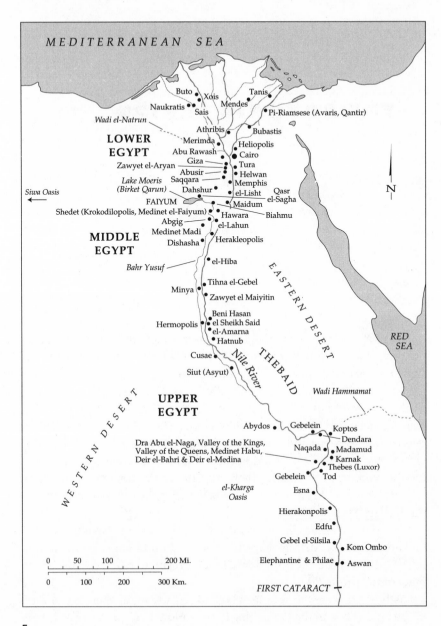

Egypt

ership, and probably political as well, especially with the Badarian and Naqadan cultures, the latter now divided by scholars into three phases (I–III) spanning the entire fourth millennium.

As they avoided the general desiccation by making a gradual descent from the desert plateau into the Nile valley, the early Egyptians made a gradual cultural ascent, becoming sedentary, practicing agriculture and animal husbandry, improving their tools, and providing their dead with grave goods for the journey into the next life. The provisioning of the deceased improved from one stage of culture to the next, increasing from a single pottery vessel to a whole burial treasure. The prevailing orientation of the deceased toward the west indicates that the realm of the dead was already located in the region where the sun sets. Gods revealed themselves, and the people discerned magical powers in both animals and objects. The desire to create order led to the first artistic works in stone, clay, and ivory, with stone early becoming the preferred material for the eternity of the afterlife. Chieftains made their appearance, accumulating political power and religious prestige, until one of them succeeded in shaping the Nile valley into a unified state.

According to later king lists and annals, the beginning of history was preceded by the reigns of gods along with those of very early kings who are mere names to us because they performed no deeds that were recorded. In picturing and explaining the origin of the world in which they lived, the Egyptians felt their task was to write not history, but rather myth. Historical deeds were supposed to repeat mythical events, restoring unsullied the perfect primeval condition of the world of creation recounted in myth; from such a point of view, they were nothing other than the performance of cult ritual. Later tradition also ascribed creative deeds to the legendary Menes, who from Dynasty 18 on was viewed as the founder of the Egyptian realm. He drained the original marshes; founded Memphis, the first city; and acquainted humankind with culture and civilization, which they had not previously known. Other polities and cultures have also placed such culture heroes at the beginning of their histories.

Nevertheless, the origin of Egyptian civilization does not vanish into the archetypal but instead can be traced to the historical reality of the late fourth millennium B.C.E. At that time, in the course of a few generations, a distinctive high culture grew out of the neolithic Naqada culture; kingship, administration, writing, art, and religion stepped fully formed into the light of history, already bearing their unmistakably Egyptian stamp. Two kings in particular seem to have accomplished, or at least completed, this act of historical creation: Narmer ("Sore Catfish") and Aha ("Fighter"). They already ruled over both parts of the country, and it was probably Aha who began the series of historical kings in the annals carved on the Palermo Stone and thus the first historical dynasty. Their predecessor, King Scorpion, to whom we give credit for the earliest writing of which we can be certain, had laid important foundations for their achievement. He already ruled over not only Upper Egypt, but also parts of the delta, whose western portion he perhaps freed from the hegemony of Libyan tribes. From recent finds in Cemetery U at Abydos, we know of several kings of a Dynasty 0, of which Scorpion and Narmer were the last but not the only monarchs. The later Naqada culture had already culturally united all of Egypt and extended its influence into Palestine. Political unification must have entailed a rather lengthy and complicated process.

The eastern delta, with its tribes of herdsmen, must have become a part of the new state at the latest under King Narmer. At the end of the prehistoric period, the sociological structure of the population in the delta and the valley was undoubtedly complex, as suggested by the traditional scenario that depicts the unification as the domination of tribes of Lower Egyptian agriculturalists by Upper Egyptian nomads. The role of Upper Egyptian tribes as political leaders during the process of unification is unmistakable, though we are not certain about the role of nomads. The situation in the historical period would lead us to expect much larger nomadic components in the population of the western delta than in the Nile valley with its narrow topography.

At the center of this new, historical world order was the institution of kingship. The falcon Horus, god of the sky, ruled the world in the form of each reigning king, just as the sun god Re illuminated it in the form of the daily changing and renewed sun. The king was thus divine but not a god, though this distinction might not yet have played a role in the beliefs of the Archaic Period, in which the magical powers at the king's command, by virtue of his divine nature, were omnipotent.

Of the five titles borne by Egyptian kings from Dynasty 4 on, only the Horus name, which identified the king as an incarnation of this god, is found at the beginning of history. Two further titles were added in the course of the Archaic Period. These designated him as king of Upper and Lower Egypt (*nisut-bit*) and connected him with the divine mistresses of the two portions of the land. This dualistic principle was characteristic of Egyptian thought; the doctrine of the Two Lands certainly did not derive solely from the political or sociological circumstances of the prehistoric period. The differentiated structure of ordered existence revealed itself to the ancient Egyptians through dualism, and also in groups of three or nine, all of which yield a whole in an additive manner; by way of contrast, the chaotic world before creation was for them a condition in which "there were not yet two things in this land." In historical reality, the doctrine of the Two Lands resulted from the fact that the high culture of Egypt and the elements that made it possible stemmed from a multiplicity of constitutive parts, and two is the simplest multiplicity. Around 3000 B.C.E., nomads, cattle breeders and farmers, Africans and Asiatics, Semites and Hamites had united to form the differentiated unity that was ancient Egypt. Ascending to the throne, each new king reunited the Two Lands and with that, the disparate elements of his realm.

In theory, the king carried out, in solitude, every cultic act and all historical deeds, for only he had the prerequisite magical capacities to do so. As late as the Roman Period, in the innermost chambers of every Egyptian temple, the king alone was depicted facing and serving the deities. Only in representations of festivals and battles did his agents appear: priests, officials, and soldiers. Since the king could not, in practice, celebrate every event personally, he delegated portions of his authority to others around him. The officialdom that thus arose can be noted on the earliest historical monuments, divided from the very beginning into two main groups: officials who were entrusted with the physical and cultic care of the ruler's person and insignia, and officials who mediated between him and the outside world as his spokesmen or carried out his direct orders throughout the land. Such orders were issued from time to time, and somewhat later this led to the establishment of administrative departments. At first, the actual office was less important than the rank of the official who held it, which was determined by his proximity to the king. In the earliest dynasties, important commissions and their related hierarchical status were probably given only to princes and their immediate descendants, for only close relatives of the divine king could withstand the sheer power of his presence. As "counts," these officials administered the various portions of the land, from which the nomes gradually developed. The distance between the king and his closest adherents seems to have been quite small at first; only when pyramids began to be built was the kingship decisively elevated to the apex of the social pyramid.

The sphere of influence of the earliest kings of the unified state seems to have stretched from the region of modern Edfu into the delta. Though these kings have not yet been attested at the First Cataract, the granite and diorite quarries at Aswan had been worked since the late prehistoric period, and the local deities Khnum and Satis often appear in the personal names of the Archaic Period. This region must therefore have fallen under the sovereignty of Dynasty 1 at a very early date. Expeditions to stone quarries had ventured into the mountainous eastern desert between the Nile and the Red Sea before 3000 B.C.E., under King Narmer. Trade relationships stretched as far as Palestine, where potsherds with the name of this king have recently been found. We know that during the reign of King Aha (c. 3000–2970 B.C.E.), there were trade links with the region of Syria and Lebanon, which delivered the precious coniferous timber that was lacking in the Nile floodplain. This was a continuation of relationships that had already developed in the prehistoric period, reaching as far as Mesopotamia. It remains uncertain to what extent the Egyptians set out to sea at this date; the hieroglyphic writing system contained no unambiguous sign for the maritime environment.

The royal Residence lay in southern Upper Egypt under Scorpion and Narmer, but Aha built an immense tomb nearly twelve and a half miles south of Cairo, near the modern site of Saqqara. Measuring about forty-seven by sixteen yards, its richly articulated superstructure of sun-dried mud bricks was erected above five subterranean rooms dug into the rock. It was the first tomb in the Memphite cemetery area, where kings, officials, and sacred animals would be buried during the ensuing three millennia. It is thus reasonable to ascribe the foundation of Memphis by the legendary Menes to King Aha, who moved the center of the state to the north where it could serve to link Upper and Lower Egypt. Aha constructed another Residence there, or at least a sort of castle. At Abydos, Upper Egypt retained a center that was religious rather than political. There, Aha and the remaining kings of Dynasty 1 built equally large tombs for themselves and the members of their households. The idea that Pharaoh, as king of Upper and Lower Egypt, had to have a tomb in each part of the land evidently lay behind this construction of two tombs. The actual burial site has been the object of controversy; since the art of mummification was not developed until after the Archaic Period, it might have made a difference in which one of his many castles the king died. As an old religious center, though, Abydos is more likely to have been the actual burial place. Important nonroyal cemeteries of the Archaic Period have been discovered at Helwan and Abu Rawash in the region of Memphis, where the administration was concentrated.

A second important innovation that seems to have occurred in the reign of Aha is the introduction of an official system of dating; this is probably the reason that the Egyptians began their first historical dynasty with Aha, though we know the names of a series of predecessors who are now counted as Dynasty 0. The Egyptian year was made up of three seasons, each of which had four thirty-day months; five epagomenal (i.e., additional) days brought the total to 365 days. The year, though it displayed a clear and constant arrangement, thus ran about one-fourth of a day behind the Julian year. New Year's Day, which was determined by the heliacal rising of Sirius and the nearly simultaneous beginning of the annual Nile inundation, thus moved through the actual seasons of the calendar. This Egyptian calendar, in which the moon also played an important role, was created at an unknown point in prehistory or the Archaic Period.

Under Aha, apparently for the first time, the individual regnal years were named after typical events, which probably occurred in the preceding year. Such a practice was maintained in Mesopotamia throughout the third millennium B.C.E., while in Egypt, it was soon superseded by a consecutive numbering of years in which taxes were collected, and then of regnal years. Thus, for example, one of King Aha's years was characterized by such events as "Smiting the Land of Nubia" (i.e., a military campaign in the area of the First Cataract) and "Fashioning" a divine statue, while another was the year of a "Visit" to the sanctuary of Neith. Notices of this sort were carved on tablets of wood or ivory that accompanied jars of oil to indicate their vintage year. Lists of such names make it possible to determine the interval between any two year-names. The famous Palermo Stone preserves such a list, though in a very fragmentary condition. Originally, it listed all the year-names of the Archaic Period, to which were added annalistic entries down to the end of Dynasty 5; it certainly does not stem from the Old Kingdom and perhaps was not created until the Late Period, though its compiler could have employed old and original records. Together with the small number of royal monuments, the annalistic tablets constitute the only existing contemporary historical tradition from the Archaic Period.

The means of recording this historical tradition was writing, whose invention immediately preceded Dynasty 1. Although it was never a pure picture writing, it also never developed into a purely alphabetic script. In the inscriptions, most of the signs simply represent the sequence of consonants; thus, they indicate not only the object represented, but also the pronunciation of the word, which was also determined by the vowels. Unfortunately, we are therefore unable to pronounce the words of the Egyptian language correctly. We know the vowels only from Coptic, the latest stage of the language, and this accounts for our various transcriptions of royal names, which are often based on ancient Greek renderings such as Amenophis. Alongside the hieroglyphs, which were themselves miniature works of art that captured some of the unbounded wealth of forms in the real world with their finite repertoire of signs, the Egyptians had from the very beginning developed cursive sign forms for use in everyday life. This cursive script, hieratic, and its corresponding medium, papyrus, are already attested at the beginning of the Archaic Period. At this early date, there were no continuous texts or arrangements of signs into rows; the signs of the writing system were at first used only for information that could not be expressed pictorially, especially the names of persons, places, and products.

The inscription at the Second Cataract attributed to Aha's successor, Djer (also read Sekhty, c. 2970–2950 B.C.E.), probably belongs to a later period. We thus lack proof that Egyptian expeditions crossed the actual frontier of the First Cataract at Aswan and penetrated deep into Nubian territory at this early time. On the other hand, there are textual confirmations of fresh battles during his reign with tribes in the Libyan region at the edge of the delta. The memory of this obviously important king was still alive in the Late Period, and from Dynasty 18 on, Djer's tomb at Abydos was revered as the tomb of Osiris. The more than 300 subsidiary graves seem to attest to the well-known Mesopotamian custom that members of the royal household follow their lord into death at his funeral. In Egypt, such mass burials of retainers were restricted to Dynasty 1.

Djer's successor, King Djet (Serpent, c. 2920 B.C.E.) is the most famous king of this earliest dynasty, thanks to his tomb stela (figure 1), now in the Louvre, which is an artistic masterpiece. Though its decoration consists of nothing more than the Horus name of this king, it attests to the heights attained in relief sculpture within a few generations. The falcon, previously depicted crouching and still fully a bird of prey, was now elevated to a symbol of majesty. Egyptian style is characterized by its restriction to the essential and the important and by its compression of models drawn from the world of nature into arrangements that were concise yet typical and unmistakable. Space was ordered and captured on the surface of reliefs by means of register lines and the hierarchical scaling of figures. In Dynasty 1, foreign artistic elements, such as the

1. Tomb stela of King Djet. Louvre E 11007. Photo courtesy of the Musées Nationaux.

heraldic style that continued in use in Mesopotamia, were eliminated so as to emphasize that which was specifically Egyptian with ever greater purity and elegance.

There was a prominent female figure in the reign of King Serpent, one of several we shall encounter in the course of Egyptian history. She was Queen Merneith; though her precise chronological and political positions have not yet been established, she was presumably the wife of this king and the mother of his successor, Den. Like the kings, she possessed two funerary monuments—one in Abydos and one in Saqqara—but she bore no royal titulary. That she ruled for a time as regent while her son remained a minor presents itself as the likeliest scenario. The equal status of women was always respected in ancient Egypt, even in legal practice; its continuation is perhaps seen in the matrilineal traits of neighboring peoples in Africa.

King Den (or Dewen, c. 2880 B.C.E.) was the first to bear the title King of Upper and Lower Egypt. Annalistic tablets mention the "Smiting of the East," referring to battles with Bedouin tribes in the Sinai peninsula. The king had his tomb at Abydos provided with diorite stelae and a floor of red granite. Up to this time, only vessels had been fashioned from these valuable hard stones; now, by employing them as architectural elements, Egyptians were able to accumulate experience upon which the architects of the pyramid age would build. The variety of forms taken by stone vessels would decrease steadily in Dynasty 2, after the invention of the potter's wheel. The Egyptians of the Archaic Period worked only two metals, copper and gold. Technologically, they thus remained in the Chalcolithic age, which had begun at the outset of the fourth millennium. Even the builders of the pyramids still did not use implements of bronze.

The cultural and technical heights attained up to this point were interrupted by political turmoil during the reigns of the last three kings of Dynasty 1 (down to c. 2800 B.C.E.). For the first time we encounter the erasure of royal names as a magical and political weapon, reflecting disputes in the royal house that prepared the way for a change in dynasty. Theriomorphic elements, which had been favored up to this point, disappeared from the royal names, revealing an important development in the religious thought of the Archaic Period that has been dubbed the "anthropomorphization of powers." In prehistoric thought, divine powers dwelled in animals or fetishes; in the Archaic Period, they also revealed themselves in human forms, often represented with animal heads that hieroglyphically indicated their former bestial nature. With this anthropomorphization, the gods became persons, and this enabled the recounting of divine destinies through the development of myths.

At the beginning of Dynasty 2 (c. 2800 B.C.E.), the tradition of a second tomb at Abydos was temporarily abandoned. The royal tombs of this period, only some of which have been discovered, were situated in a new section of the cemetery of the Residence at Saqqara. This signifies a neglect of the former Upper Egyptian center, and the consequence, a few generations later, was an Upper Egyptian reaction that threatened the national unity that had been achieved. Before this happened, King Ninetjer reigned nearly half a century (c. 2760–2715 B.C.E.). A statue of him in *sed* festival garb, provided with a royal name, has survived to us; considering the length of his reign, we may presume that Ninetjer in fact celebrated the *sed* festival one or more times, though we know of more or less exact rules for the celebration of this festival only from the New Kingdom on. From the very beginning, this festival was connected with the Egyptian concept of kingship. The magical, creative power of the king, which was exhausted in the course of a long reign, had to be ritually renewed through the ceremonies of this festival. The "old" king was buried in the form of a statue, and the "new," rejuvenated king once again ascended his throne. The statuette of Ninetjer depicts him wearing a tight-fitting mantle, the vestment typical of this festival, and in this respect it is a precursor of the famous statue of Djoser that marks the beginning of the large-scale sculpture of the Old Kingdom. In the case of Ninetjer's statue, the size (a little over five inches in height) and the level of artistic expression are still modest.

After Ninetjer's death, there arose a reaction to the prevailing concept of kingship along with a brief threat to the unity of the state. Earlier kings had considered themselves to be incarnations of the falcon god Horus, but Peribsen (c. 2715–2700 B.C.E.) now placed the fabulous animal of Seth above his name, thereby indicating that he was the incarnation of this mighty god of the desert. With his construction of a royal tomb at Abydos, he returned to the long-since-abandoned custom of Dynasty 1. Though in fact we do not yet know of any tomb of his at Saqqara, a mortuary cult there lasted into Dynasty 4, so this might again be a case of a second tomb at Abydos. The stress on Seth and the old cult center of Abydos afforded Peribsen's reign a rather strong orientation toward Upper Egypt, and it seems that at the same time, there also reigned a Lower Egyptian Horus king.

At the end of the dynasty, after an evidently confused period marked by strife, there stood the important figure of Khasekhemwy (c. 2690–

2670 B.C.E.), who restored state unity. Fragments of an alabaster vessel bearing his name found at Byblos represent the earliest secure attestation of Egyptian trade relations with this port city that was to represent the center of Egyptian influence in the region of Syria and the Lebanon from the Old Kingdom on. Khasekhemwy distinguished himself through several buildings he constructed in Upper Egypt in which he employed stone to a greater extent than before, thereby helping to prepare the way, albeit on a modest scale, for the monumental architecture of the pyramid age that followed. During his reign, royal and private stone sculpture also improved in quality and in confidence of execution. His Horus and Seth name, which the king probably assumed upon elimination of all his opponents, portrays the Horus falcon and the Seth animal above his royal name, whose Two Powers (*sekhemwy*) also allude to Horus and Seth. With this, the conventional notion that the king united and balanced these two inimical forces in his own person found its first figurative expression. This balance once again secured the unity of the state and its basis in religious belief, enabling that unity to become the Archaic Period's most valuable legacy to Dynasty 3, which was to inaugurate the first flowering of the high culture of ancient Egypt.

THE OLD KINGDOM

In the transition from Dynasty 2 to Dynasty 3, we encounter—as we frequently do in Egyptian history—a queen who was descended from the old dynasty and thus of divine origin, and who lent legitimacy to the new dynasty by her connection with the old. At the beginning of the Old Kingdom was Queen Nimaathapi, evidently a daughter of Khasekhemwy and the mother of Djoser. It is possible that her husband was King Nebka (c. 2670–2654 B.C.E.), who reigned between these two monarchs and whose Horus name is still the subject of debate.

No political break between the two dynasties is visible, yet we are correct in beginning a new era with Dynasty 3. In the course of a single generation, Pharaoh's architecture experienced a transition from its modest beginnings to monumental stone construction. Around the Step Pyramid at Saqqara, the royal palace made of brick, wood, and woven mats was transformed into a mighty stone edifice in which the king was to reside in death. At the same time, the first life-size statuary was created in the royal workshops, and the technique of relief sculpture was refined. Thus was Djoser (c. 2654–2635 B.C.E.; figure 2), the royal sponsor of this technological and artistic wonder, referred to as "the one who opened up the stone" in a graffito made by a visitor during the New Kingdom, ascribing to him the invention of building with this new, eternal material.

Djoser was thus viewed by the ancient Egyptians themselves as the creator of a new era. Among other monuments, the Famine Stela on the

2. Statue of Djoser. Cairo
Museum. Photo by Nancy J.
Corbin.

island of Sehel, which traces Egypt's claim to sovereignty over the region of Lower Nubia (the region between the First and Second Cataracts of the Nile) back to his reign, demonstrates that memory of and reverence toward him remained alive into the Ptolemaic Period. It is certain that in his day, Egyptian expeditions once again traversed this area, just as they also worked the copper deposits in the Sinai peninsula. Fragments of an offering table in the style of this period have been found at Byblos, showing that Egypt's impact in the region of Syria went beyond mere trade relations and extended into the areas of art and religion.

High above Djoser's Residence in the cultivated land, on the desert plateau of Saqqara, south of the royal cemetery of Dynasty 1, a rectangular area 596 yards long and 306 yards wide was surrounded by an enclosure wall of glistening white limestone about 33 feet in height. In its midst, at the end of a great open court containing two altars, a six-stepped pyramid more than 195 feet high rose over the subterranean tomb of the king (figure 3). This Step Pyramid was a stone replica of the "primeval mound" that emerged, at the moment of creation, from the

3. Step Pyramid of Djoser, showing early mastaba beginnings. Photo © 1992 by Al Berens, Suredesign Graphics.

chaotic primeval waters to serve as the basis for the ordered cosmos, and it was also a monumental improvement on a grave tumulus. To the southeast of this first of the pyramids lay a festival court surrounded by chapels, where the deceased king was supposed to celebrate a never-ending series of festivals of renewal (śed-festivals). A life-size statue, which was walled up in a chamber on the north side of the pyramid and is now in the Cairo Museum, depicts him, with its archaic, blocklike form, in the regalia of this festival. Notwithstanding considerable damage, the statue's visage gives some hint of the controlled sense of purpose that enabled the nearly superhuman accomplishments of the age of the pyramids. The dead king's spirit, which could move about freely, possessed not only a tomb, a temple, and a festival court, but a whole Residence of imperishable stone, though it consisted for the most part of massive false buildings filled with rubble. Even ceiling beams and half-open doors were translated into the new material. The engaged ribbed columns are not load-bearing but rather serve as further examples of earlier construction methods using wood and reeds transformed into stone.

Djoser's funerary enclosure served as a new and highly visible symbol for Memphis, which, as implied by its name "Balance of the Two Lands," was situated at the juncture of Upper and Lower Egypt. There was, however, no permanent capital of the realm, any more than there had been in the Archaic Period; during the Old Kingdom, the earthly Residence of the king continually changed, and with it its associated cemetery. Not far from the Step Pyramid lie the tombs of the officials of this period, whose inscriptions and reliefs supply a welcome supplement to our scanty sources for the history of Dynasty 3. The first of the innumerable biographies of officials, which began at this time and were recorded in tombs down into the Late Period, stems from the tomb of Metjen, who died in the reign of Snofru. This oldest biography consists of juridical documents—more concretely, royal edicts—which testify to this official's posthumous claim to his property.

The reliefs on the wooden plaques from the tomb of Hezyre, now in Cairo, display what became the enduring conventions for the representation of the human body in two-dimensional art. Sharing only some essential traits with its model in nature, the human figure is an aesthetically satisfying unity of the various parts of the anatomy, typically shown frontally or in profile. In Dynasty 3, in the workshops of the royal Residence, artisans created a rich variety of stone statues for private persons, including the archetypal seated scribe, which was to enjoy considerable popularity down into the latest periods. Indeed, every official was first and foremost a royal scribe, and he thus could commemorate this function in his tomb statue, which was intended to enable his vital essence, or *ka*, to live on after his death. At this time writing began to be used for continuous texts in addition to brief annotations; nevertheless, an actual literature did not emerge until the Middle Kingdom.

Among Djoser's officials, his architect, Imhotep, attained such paramount importance that in later periods he was revered as the "patron saint" of scribes and eventually as a god of healing; the Greeks identified him with Asclepius. Because his name and titles were found on the base of a statue of Djoser in 1926, he is also a tangible, historical personage. His high titles make it likely that he was closely related to the king and that he directed the work on Djoser's mortuary complex. Tradition revered him as a great architect, physician, and sage and ascribed to him the authorship of the earliest—and, unfortunately, lost—work of wisdom literature. Among his titles appears that of high priest of Heliopolis, though we cannot infer from it that there was a priestly school of Heliopolis at this early date. There was no independent priesthood in this period; from time to time, the king would delegate his own priestly functions to officials, and even in the Late Period he reserved the right of nomination to the highest priestly offices.

It remains uncertain whether the divine Ennead of Heliopolis, around whom an early creation myth sprang up, was already worshiped under Djoser. Several gods (of these, only Geb and Seth are identified) appear on a fragmentary relief of this king that is now in the Turin Museum; later, they, along with Isis, Osiris, and other deities constituted the Ennead. Djoser's Horus name, Most Divine of the Corporation (*Netjerykhet*), indicates that as early as Dynasty 3 the Egyptians may have ordered their deities into groups—"corporations"—and perhaps a little later into enneads, though triads did not become popular until the New Kingdom.

We know almost nothing about the immediate successors of Djoser, except that they began building pyramids but did not finish them. Southwest of the Step Pyramid of Saqqara completed by Imhotep, King Sekhemkhet (c. 2630 B.C.E.) began a similar complex. Its enclosure wall surrounds a rather smaller area than Djoser's, but it is built of larger blocks of stone, thus preparing the way for the even more monumental architecture at Giza. Another step pyramid was supposed to arise in its midst, but at the early death of the king, only the subterranean galleries and a twenty-three-foot-high portion of the superstructure had been completed.

The initiation of the construction of the pyramid located at Maidum (figure 4), about thirty miles south of Saqqara, was once ascribed to Huni (c. 2625–2600 B.C.E.), the last king of this dynasty, and it was thought that he left it uncompleted to his successor, Snofru. But it was not customary in any period for a pharaoh to complete the tomb of his predecessor, for he had to concern himself immediately with his own tomb. It is therefore now presumed that Huni's tomb is at either Zawyet el-Maiyitin or Saqqara. According to an inscription found on the island of Elephantine, Huni established a fortress there, thus securing the southern boundary of Egypt at the First Cataract. This information is practically the only insight we have into the political history of this period, during which were made such great strides in spiritual and technological developments.

Snofru (c. 2600–2571 B.C.E.), whose wife, Hetepheres, was probably a daughter of Huni and thus a vehicle to royal legitimacy, inaugurated not only a new dynasty, but also a new period of radical change. After the colossal achievements made within a few decades during Dynasty 3, it

4. Pyramid of Snofru at Maidum. Photo © 1992 by Al Berens, Suredesign Graphics.

seems nearly impossible that further rapid advances could have occurred, yet the creative momentum continued unhindered until the middle of Dynasty 4, when an abatement finally became perceptible.

Snofru began construction of the pyramid at Maidum, but before it was completed, he halted it in favor of his other pyramid complexes. At Maidum, a true pyramid was planned for the first time, one with a stepped nucleus covered by a smooth, sloping outer casing of finely polished limestone of the highest quality. Snofru brought this plan to fruition twice at Dahshur, between Maidum and Saqqara, with the Bent Pyramid (figure 5) and the Red Pyramid, which were erected under the guidance of Prince Kanefer, their architect. The royal mortuary complexes at Dahshur differ considerably from those of Dynasty 3 and served as the model for all the Old Kingdom pyramid complexes that were to follow. Though the upper and lower portions of the Bent Pyramid slope at different angles, so that its sides have an oddly bent appearance, it was actually planned as a true pyramid, if we can rely on the determinative after the name of the monument. In any event, it was built at a very steep angle, which perhaps could not be maintained dur-

5. Bent Pyramid (south pyramid) of Snofru at Dahshur. Photo © 1996 by Al Berens, Sure-design Graphics.

ing construction. The pure and consistent geometrical form of a pyramid with a less-steep slope was achieved for the first time with the Red Pyramid. Additionally, instead of the rectangular, closed complexes of Dynasty 3, a looser arrangement of the cult places appears at Maidum and Dahshur; these were situated in front of the east side of the pyramids, while the enclosure walls left only a narrow open space around the square bases of the pyramids. The mortuary temples, in which rituals were celebrated and offerings made on behalf of the deceased kings, were connected to valley temples by causeways that were open at first and later roofed over. The valley temples were often situated at the boundary between the cultivated land and the desert. The mortuary temples at Maidum and Dahshur were extremely simple, consisting basically of an altar and two tall stelae bearing the royal titulary, thus recalling the cult places of the royal tombs of the Archaic Period. By way of contrast, the valley temple of the Bent Pyramid was amply provided with statues and relief decorations. Statues of the king, somewhat larger than life-size, stood in niches, and the walls of the entrance hall bore carvings of a procession of female figures who personified the royal estates in the various nomes. Cult ceremonies are represented on the columns, including foundation rituals and scenes of the *sed* festival, along with the earliest scenes of the king being embraced by a deity, an image that would become standard in the decoration of temples and tombs in the Middle and New Kingdoms.

It remains uncertain in which of these pyramids, built simultaneously, Snofru was actually buried; no sarcophagus was found in any of them, though traces of fire speak in favor of the Red Pyramid as the most likely site. What is definite is that the two pyramids at Dahshur were planned as related complexes. They bore the same name, Epiphany of Snofru, and were distinguished only by their relative positions as the "northern" one and the "southern" one. In addition to these three large pyramids, a series of small stone pyramids lacking burial chambers were erected by Snofru (or Huni) throughout the land, from the delta to Elephantine, perhaps as symbols of the royal presence.

In later works of literature, Snofru was recognized as an "excellent" and affable monarch whose genial manner contrasted sharply with the tyrannical nature of his son Khufu. The historical kernel of this positive portrait might have lain in his patriarchal relationship with his subjects, to whom he remained, in the royal ideology of his day, the Greatest God and the absolute Lord of the Cosmic Order (*Maat*). The meaning of his name, which can be rendered as Benefactor, surely also played a role. In the Middle Kingdom, he was worshiped as a god at Dahshur and in the Sinai peninsula, and his cult was renewed in the Late Period.

The high officials during Snofru's reign, usually princes, were allowed to build their tombs, still mostly constructed of brick, close to the pyramids of Maidum and Dahshur; they thus surrounded their royal lord in the afterlife as they had surrounded him in this world. The court workshops prepared exquisite life-size statues for them; the statue pair of Rehotpe and his wife, Nofret, now in Cairo, has been preserved with the colors of the paint as fresh as new. The accidentally discovered burial treasure of Queen Hetepheres, which can be seen today in the Cairo Museum, demonstrates the taste and skill with which even everyday objects were created.

The name of this queen, who was the mother of Khufu, has also been found at Byblos, with which Dynasty 4 continued to have active trade relations. The annals report the arrival of forty ships laden with coniferous wood during one of the years of Snofru's reign; this wood was indispensable as a building material for palaces, mortuary complexes, and boats. The construction of ships one hundred cubits in length is mentioned several times, so we must assume that in this period, maritime trade flourished between Egypt and the Lebanon; King Khephren is also attested at Ebla. The Egyptian harbors presumably did not lie on the Mediterranean coast itself, but rather inland, in the delta, along the eastern branches of the Nile. The annals also report campaigns, whose goals were chiefly political and economic, against Nubia and Libya; the Egyptians brought back rich booty consisting of prisoners of war and cattle. These raids brought a welcome increase in the royal treasury, which administered the in-kind taxes of the land and the tribute from neighboring peoples, as the colossal building projects and the corresponding large number of expeditions to the stone quarries had led to hitherto unprecedented increases in the state's expenditures.

Throughout the age of the pyramids, the administration confronted new tasks and growing demands. Because of the increase in the number of responsibilities, individual administrative positions developed into whole departments, and the former patriarchal order of the royal household gave way to a bureaucracy. At its apex was the vizier (*tjaty*), who, with his long list of titles, replaced the former individual holders of the offices. He directed not only the entire administration but also the judicial system and the state-run economy, and he alone was responsible to the king for proper order in the land. The vizierate was apparently created at the beginning of Dynasty 3, though a continuous series of important viziers first began with Snofru's sons Kanefer and Nefermaat. For a long time, this highest office would be reserved for members of the royal house, and princes only rarely occupied other administrative posts. The large number of titles encountered especially in the Old Kingdom can be explained by the lack of permanent departments in the administration; officials were entrusted with commissions as needed and were then provided with corresponding titles. Proximity to the king was revealed by titles indicating high rank.

The list of domains supplying offerings to the king in the valley temple of the Bent Pyramid is arranged by nomes, showing that this division of the land into administrative districts had in the meantime assumed what was to be its enduring form, at least in Upper Egypt; in the delta, many changes would take place before the classical sum of forty-two Egyptian nomes was arrived at. For the most part, the nomes were administered from a royal estate, which stored what was delivered as taxes and then passed it along to the storehouses of the Residence. The administrator was appointed by the king and was often transferred from one estate to another. From time to time, the royal court sent authorized representatives into the provinces on precise, clear-cut commissions; only with the end of the Old Kingdom can we speak of an essentially independent nomarchy, that is, office of nomarch. Nevertheless, important tombs of officials made their appearance in the provinces as early as Dynasty 4—according to recent finds, even in distant Thebes.

After the premature deaths of his older brothers, Khufu (c. 2571–2548 B.C.E.; figure 6) succeeded his father, Snofru, on the throne. His name is associated for all time with the Great Pyramid (figure 7), the largest of all the pyramids and the mightiest work of all ancient architecture. Under the direction of the vizier Hemiunu, who was a cousin or nephew of the king, it was erected according to a unified plan (it was earlier thought that there were several phases of construction) on the desert plateau of Giza, eight and one-half miles north of the Step Pyramid of Saqqara. When it was completed, this mighty monument reached 480 feet in height and contained 2.3 million limestone blocks, each of them about one and one-third cubic yards in size and weighing two and one-half tons. It had an exterior casing of finely polished, high-quality limestone from Tura. The actual sarcophagus chamber was no longer subterranean but rather situated in the center of the pyramid's mass. There are now only scanty remains of the mortuary temple on the east side, which was provided with reliefs and was architecturally more elaborate than the simple cult places of Snofru. Khufu's pyramid is surrounded by three small subsidiary pyramids, as well as by five pits hewn into the rock. The latter were intended to contain the boats in which the deceased king was to traverse the waters of the sky; from inscriptions in the tombs of officials, we know that this was also expected for more ordinary deceased persons. One of these boats, discovered in 1954, is 143 feet long and proved able to be completely reassembled, revealing the considerable ability of Pharaoh's master shipwrights.

In later periods, people imagined that armies of slaves had worked on Khufu's immense construction project, and even in ancient times, writers recalled his twenty-three-year reign as a period of tyranny and oppression. Though we learn from the annals that prisoners of war were brought to Egypt in the reign of Snofru, it has yet to be proved that slavery existed at the peak of the Old Kingdom. Even if prisoners of war participated in certain tasks, as we must assume, there could not have been enough of them to complete the Great Pyramid by themselves. The necessary labor force could easily have been recruited from the overwhelmingly agricultural population during the inundation season, when work in the fields was suspended. In this period, it was possible to transport the blocks of stone on barges from the loading ramps of the stone quarries to the foot of the desert plateau; with manpower, draught animals, and the simplest technology—such as brick ramps and wooden sledges and rollers—the blocks could be hauled up the structure as it rose and positioned with the most remarkable precision. Since the an-

6. Statuette of Khufu. Cairo Museum. Photo by Nancy J. Corbin.

7. The Great Pyramid of Khufu at Giza. Photo by Sara E. Orel.

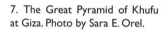

cient sources are silent regarding technical details, the specifics of how it was built remain unclear to us, and nearly every year brings fresh hypothetical reconstructions.

The immense expenditure entailed was intended not for the glorification of a king but rather for the welfare of the state, which in any case depended on the monarch: his creative powers, which held together the very order of the world, had to be preserved even beyond death's doorstep. The construction of a pyramid was thus a communal religious effort on the part of the Egyptians of the Old Kingdom, who were certainly not "free" in our sense of the word but rather were in various ways bound to and dependent on the king and the other divine powers. The period of Dynasties 3 and 4 has justly come to be characterized as the "age of the pyramids": the clear structure, the firm order, and the tight organization of the state, which made it possible for all its energies to be concentrated on a single cultic task, found symbolic expression in the form of the pyramid.

The architect Hemiunu and the members of his staff were assigned private tombs on the west side of Khufu's pyramid. Thus begun, the western cemetery of Giza (figure 8) developed into an impressive place in the course of the Old Kingdom, and stone made its breakthrough as a material in the construction of private tombs as well. Only the king had the right to use the stone quarries and mineral resources, and it was his grace alone that assigned these stone tombs to worthy officials and their wives. Such tombs are called mastabas, Arabic for bench, because of the benchlike form of their superstructures. Tomb statues, which were also bestowed upon the officials by the grace of the king, were temporarily replaced by the so-called reserve heads in the reign of Khufu; though not actual portraits, they impressively characterized the most important part of the human anatomy and kept it alive for the eternity of the hereafter. It seems that this was an economic measure by Khufu, intended to minimize his officials' expenditure on tomb decoration and statuary.

The effective basis for mummification as a means of preserving the body was laid at this time; in the case of Queen Hetepheres, we already encounter the separate burial of the viscera. For the material survival of the deceased, there was also the ongoing delivery of the "thousand of bread (loaves) and beers, thousand of cattle and fowl, and thousand of ointments and clothes" of the traditional mortuary offering formula. Mortuary foundations established by the king for his own tomb, as well as for those of his officials, served as the material basis of the supplies for these cults and the salaries of the priests who were needed to carry them out. Since the land

8. The western cemetery of Giza. Photo by H. Hauser.

belonged to the state, only state property and the yield thereof were used for these mortuary foundations, which, for all practical purposes, thus passed over into private usufruct.

Khufu doubtless had construction work done not only at Giza but also in many other places in Upper and Lower Egypt; later tradition credited him with building the first temple of Hathor at Dendara. Since nearly all the cultic constructions of the Old Kingdom have disappeared or were built over at a later date, we have no tangible traces of this building activity and can reconstruct the cults of gods and goddesses in this period only from the titles of priests, personal names, and other things mentioned by chance in tombs. Such sculpture as has been preserved is just enough to correct a one-sided picture based on the monument at Giza. The royal statuary of Khufu's reign is represented only by a tiny ivory figurine from Abydos that likely stems from the Late Period, while of the reliefs that decorated the royal mortuary temple at Giza, only scanty remains have been recovered. Since we lack the annals of his reign, its political history remains shrouded in darkness, but recent research has made it increasingly apparent that far-reaching religious and political changes, and perhaps even clashes within the ruling dynasty, lie hidden behind the architectonic unity.

Khufu had a series of capable sons, among whom Djedefhor was especially outstanding. Tradition ascribed a work of wisdom literature to him, as it did to Djoser's architect Imhotep, and fragments of it are preserved in a manuscript dating to a later period; he was worshiped as a god at Giza as early as the late Old Kingdom, and two thousand years later, his name still had a good reputation with scribes. Although an isolated inscription from a later period encloses the names of Djedefhor and other sons of Khufu in cartouches, he nevertheless does not seem to have exercised the rulership.

After Khufu's death, his son Radjedef (c. 2548–2540 B.C.E.) ascended the throne. His name has been found on blocks that sealed the boat pit discovered beside the pyramid of Khufu, so it is certain that it was Radjedef who celebrated the most monumental burial in history. To surpass the funerary monument of Khufu in size must have seemed an impossible feat, so Radjedef's plans soared to an equal height in boldness. He chose as the location for his pyramid the rocky eminence of Abu Rawash, which lies nearly five miles north of Giza; at a height of over 490 feet, it towers above the 260-foot plateaus of Giza and Saqqara. The pyramid was provided with the fitting name "Radjedef belongs to the firmament," and it would have towered over the Nile valley, far above the monuments of his predecessors despite its modest dimensions, but the early death of the king put an end to his bold plan.

The changes made by Snofru and Khufu to the ground plan and decoration of the pyramid temple changed the rectangular, closed complex of Dynasty 3 into a long processional ramp, and with that, we can recognize that a change occurred in the royal burial ritual. Under Radjedef, further signs of far-reaching religious change are visible. His name contains the name of the sun god (Re, or Ra), who until this time had played no role in royal names, aside from one passing occurrence in Dynasty 2. Now, however, this god began to surpass the other deities—even Horus, god of the sky and the kingship—in importance, and he assumed a place as an active power in the world, a position previously reserved for the king. This is shown first in the royal title "son of Re," which Radjedef was the first king to bear, though not yet in his official titulary. The sun god had, meanwhile, acquired such importance in the life of the people and the state that the king's relationship to him had to be clearly determined in some way. His relationship to

Horus was characterized as an incarnation, while his relationship to Re was set forth in dogma as that of a son. This formulation implied no diminution in the divinity of the king but rather a subordination to a power that was, as myth had it, older. The consequences first manifested themselves in a further development: the "emergence of the transcendent god," as Siegfried Morenz has described the phenomenon. In this, however, it was in no way believed that a single, almighty deity confronted the king and humankind; in the consciousness of pious Egyptians, a whole series of divine figures assumed ever more responsibility for the functioning of the world, overshadowing in the process the rational decisions of the divine kings.

None of Radjedef's sons, whose tombs also lie on the ridge of Abu Rawash, proved to be his successor, rather it was his brother or half brother Khephren (c. 2540–2514 B.C.E.), whose name as prince had evidently been Khufukhaef. His new name was also formed with Re, the name of the sun god. Additionally, like his predecessor, he bore the epithet "who lives forever like Re," which would be used again and again by the pharaohs down into the Roman Period. With the title "son of Re," the development of the ancient Egyptian royal titulary was essentially completed, though the employment of its full fivefold form did not begin until late in Dynasty 5. The definitive titulary begins with the Horus name of the Archaic Period and ends with the name the king received at birth; like the prenomen, this last name was enclosed by an oval ring, a cartouche.

Khephren also erected a mortuary complex at Giza, to the immediate southwest of Khufu's pyramid. His pyramid (figure 9) is a little smaller than that of his father, but it lies on higher ground so that it towers above it. A roofed causeway, nearly two thousand feet long, connected the mortuary temple with the valley temple, which even today impresses visitors with its huge granite ashlars. Originally, twenty-three diorite statues stood on alabaster bases in front of the finely polished granite surfaces of the walls and columns. In a bold but successful visualization of the royal ideology, the most famous of these statues portrays the falcon god Horus embracing the head of the king with his wings, protecting him and endowing him with his power—a type of representation that would subsequently be realized many times in the history of Egyptian art.

The Great Sphinx of Giza, which dates to the reign of Khephren, is another important portrait of the king with similar symbolic force. In a quarry next to Khephren's causeway, from which the blocks used in con-

9. Sphinx and Khephren pyramid, Giza. Photo © 1992 by Al Berens, Suredesign Graphics.

structing the core of the pyramid were extracted, there remained a nucleus of rock that Khephren's artists (though there has recently also been an attribution to Khufu) transformed into the sphinx. As a powerful guardian of his own pyramid complex, the king lies in the form of a lion, an embodiment of the magical beliefs of the prehistoric period that was supposed to ward off inimical forces, with a human head that wears a headcloth from the royal regalia. In the head of this portrait, which though damaged in the course of the millennia nevertheless remains filled with majesty, the poet Rainer Maria Rilke saw, in his tenth Duino Elegy, "a human face to be weighed on the scale of the stars." The Egyptians venerated the sphinx as the god Harmakhis ("Horus in the horizon"), and already in the Old Kingdom built a cult temple in front of its paws. Since the lion's body was ever and again covered by drifting desert sands, astonished visitors would for the most part have seen only the royal head.

The diorite for Khephren's statues was quarried in Nubia, at Toshka, and royal sealings of this period have been found at the fortress of Buhen at the Second Cataract. The territory of Lower Nubia between the First and Second Cataracts, with its valuable stone quarries and veins of gold, was thus securely in Egyptian hands at this time. Nubians are first

attested as household servants in Egypt in Dynasty 5, and they have remained indispensable to the present day; they were also constantly in
demand as soldiers and policemen.

The transition from Khephren to his son Menkaure (c. 2510–2491
B.C.E.; figure 10) might have been preceded by a brief period of internal
turmoil during which the sons of Radjedef and Khephren struggled over
the kingship; the evidence is too sparse, however, to arrive at more than

10. Statue triad depicting Menkaure flanked by the goddess Hathor (left) and a nome goddess. Cairo Museum. Photo by Nancy J. Corbin.

hypotheses. The northern pyramid at Zawyet el-Aryan, between Giza and Abusir, might belong to this transitional period; it bears many similarities to the monument at Abu Rawash, and like Radjedef and Khephren, its unknown builder exhibited a preference for huge blocks of granite. Menkaure also encased the lower portion of his pyramid in granite rather than limestone. On the whole, with its height of 218 feet, this third and last of the Giza pyramids (figure 11) is rather smaller than those of

11. The pyramid of Menkaure at Giza. Photo by Sara E. Orel.

Khufu and Khephren. Economic, political, and religious factors combined to diminish visibly the previous, literally "towering" significance of the royal tomb, thus betraying the reduction in the divinity and power of Pharaoh that the new title "son of Re" had made possible. Perhaps it had in the meantime become clear that a colossal construction project like the Great Pyramid could not be erected in every reign without soon exhausting the economic and administrative potential of the realm. The accent shifted from flat-featured monumental constructions to richer decorative features in the reliefs of the royal monuments and the tombs of the officials: a turn, thus, to detail. There was also a clear decrease in the rate at which new royal domains were established, in contrast to what occurred during the period from Snofru to Khephren, and thus development in this regard was less expansive as well.

But there was no holding back the loss of power on the part of the central royal authority that was now just beginning, a process that would end, after some centuries, in the collapse of the Old Kingdom. This development deprived the Egyptian world order of its previous center, but it lent people a greater measure of individuality, strengthened the self-consciousness of officials and priests, and led to the first beginnings of a middle class. The growing autonomy of the nomes vis-à-vis the Residence is tangible already under Menkaure, in the first provincial rock-cut tomb at Tihna el-Gebel. High dignitaries who worked in the provinces on commission of the king no longer had themselves buried at the Residence but rather in the areas where they served, with which they now came to have closer ties than with the distant center. Thus arose the nomarchy, which placed itself under the protection of local divine powers and gradually asserted the automatic inheritance of acquired office, as opposed to the king's right of appointment.

King Shepseskaf (c. 2491–2487 B.C.E.) broke with what was already a century-and-a-half-old tradition and built his tomb in the southern cemetery at Saqqara, not in the form of a pyramid, but rather as a huge mastaba with a vaulted roof. He thus also abandoned the royal cemetery at Giza, where in Dynasties 5 and 6 only priests who served the mortuary cults of the deceased monarchs were still buried. His sister Khentkaus brought the first king of Dynasty 5, whose father remains unknown to us, into the world. Later tradition, as recorded in the wondrous tales of Papyrus Westcar, made his father out to be Re of Sakhebu, and thus a form of the sun god. This old myth, which probably antedates Dynasty 5, is clearer to us from several sequences of scenes in temples of the New Kingdom: the sun god sires the heir to the throne with an earthly woman of royal descent, thus endowing him or her with a twofold legitimacy for the future office. Along with the sun god, in this time of radical change, we catch our first glimpse of the important divine figure Osiris; his emergence must have immediately followed that of Re.

The sun temples of Dynasty 5 lent an architectonic expression to the solar deity's preeminence over his earthly son, the king. To date, only two of them, those of Userkaf and Neuserre, have been excavated; the rest are known only through their names and their priests. Presumably all of them, like those that have been uncovered, lie in a previously unused sector of the Memphite necropolis north of the modern village of Abusir. Like the pyramid complexes, these sanctuaries consisted of a valley temple, a causeway, and a cult temple, but behind this last stood not a pyramid, but at first a pillar on a high, sloping podium and later a huge, masonry-built obelisk. Along with the pyramid, the sphinx, and the column, the obelisk is yet another of Egypt's gifts to the history of art and architecture. At daybreak, the first rays of the sun would fall on its tip, which was gilded, at least from the Middle Kingdom on. Offerings were made on an open altar to the god, whose "cult image" was always present in the sky. But the king, as the son of the god, must also have participated in the cult activities that were celebrated there; only thus can we comprehend the fact that each monarch had a temple of his own laid out, and that the cults continued to be carried out in these sanctuaries long after the custom of erecting such temples had been given up.

Royal tombs retained their pyramid form, but they became increasingly less important. This can be seen from their scale alone: with its height of only 160 feet, the pyramid of Userkaf (c. 2487–2480 B.C.E.), the first king of Dynasty 5, is far smaller than that of Menkaure. The tombs of his successors, some of whom ruled considerably longer than he, are scarcely any larger. Their associated cult places are also on a less monumental scale than those in the cemetery of Giza, though in their details, they are more richly decorated. Userkaf's mortuary temple served as a model for those of his successors. Red granite pillars (beginning with Sahure, columns with floral capitals) rose from the black basalt paving, the white limestone walls were richly decorated with painted reliefs, and statues of all types of stone further enlivened the gloriously colored picture. In the court of Userkaf's temple rose a statue more than sixteen feet in height, one of the earliest colossal statues we know from ancient Egypt.

While Userkaf erected his tomb close to the Step Pyramid at Saqqara, his brother Sahure (c. 2480–2468 B.C.E.) moved the royal cemetery to

Abusir, in the area of the sun temples. The annals of the Palermo Stone ascribe to him the first known expedition to the legendary land of Punt, the source of incense on the Somali coast. Under Sahure, the boundaries of Egypt's trade were also extended in the north. Reliefs from his mortuary temple depict the return of a trading fleet from the Syrian coast, bringing, among other things, Syrian bears for the royal zoo. Relationships probably reached beyond Syria and Asia Minor and into the Aegean, touching even Crete. Already at this time, the Egyptians, who were not enthusiastic seafarers, tended to take Asiatics into their service as sailors. Next to state trade, private trade could have developed only to a modest extent, for transport over longer distances was possible only by royal ship or royal caravan. Dynasty 5 left scant record of military undertakings. The victory over Libyans that Sahure had represented in his mortuary temple was copied several times (by Pepy II and Taharqa, for example) during Egyptian history and perhaps harkens back to an even earlier original. Also copied (by Wenis) was a scene of starving bedouins, which has only recently been found at the causeway leading to the mortuary temple of Sahure, along with another scene depicting the transport of his gilded pyramidion.

Considering the frequent mentions of his sun temple and the relatively large size of his mortuary complex, Neferirkare (c. 2468–2449 B.C.E.) must have been the most important ruler of the first half of Dynasty 5. Since only his mortuary temple has been excavated and his sun temple still awaits archaeological investigation, and because the annals of the Palermo Stone break off with his reign, little is known about his day and age. An archive of papyri from his mortuary temple, which has recently been published and contains inventories and other lists as well as letters, belongs to the reigns of Izezi and Wenis. The office of overseer of Upper Egypt, directly subordinate to the vizier, was probably first established at this time to provide more effective control and stronger royal authority in the provinces. This attempt did not have a lasting result. In the "Hare" nome around Hermopolis, a dynasty of nomarchs was already ruling at this time; they founded their own family cemetery in the steep cliffs at el-Sheikh Said on the east bank of the Nile. The importance of the provinces can also be seen in the royal decrees in favor of the temples located there (in the reign of Neferirkare, for Abydos); they exempted the personnel of the temples from being called away to perform tasks for the state.

During the second half of the twenty-fifth century B.C.E., a religious development took place that was similar in scope to the advance of solar worship a hundred years earlier. This time, in a development that be-came ever more tangible under Neferirkare and Neuserre, it was the god Osiris who stepped into the forefront of beliefs regarding the afterlife. From the outset, the nature of this god was highly complex, with royal and naturalistic traits combined in the myth of his murder at the hands of Seth and his resurrection, which also reflected the yearly revival of plant life. While the other Egyptian deities were also mortal, Osiris's vi-olent and deeply human fate especially qualified him to be the god of the dead and assured him a lasting place in the hearts of the faithful. In the course of Dynasty 5, he became increasingly prominent in the mor-tuary prayers inscribed in private tombs, at the expense of Anubis, while at Memphis and Abydos, he merged with Sokar and Khentamen-tiu, the local gods of the dead.

As soon as Osiris became the ruler of the dead, the problem was posed of his relationship to the deceased king, who in the process was made subject to his rulership. The solution that was found again stressed the human aspect of the king. In dying, he repeated the mythic fate of the god, becoming ruler in the hereafter as "Osiris NN" (e.g., "Osiris Wenis"); but this induction into the essence and role of the god could occur only through ritual, which actualized the myth. The king was made into a divinity through ritual; funeral rites made him into Osiris just as coronation rituals had made him into Horus. Outside this framework of ritual, he bore a human countenance. From the middle of Dynasty 5 on, officials laid ever more emphasis on their close relation-ship to the king, who considered himself responsible for their welfare. A new sense of ethical obligation defined the attitude of the king and his officials, and the doing of good works steps into the forefront of inscrip-tions in the tombs: "I saved the weak one from the one who was stronger than he. . . . I gave bread to the hungry and clothing to the naked, I ferried the one who had no boat. . . ." On this ethical basis, the old concept of a court in the afterlife that brought desecrators of tombs to justice was transformed into a Judgment of the Dead to which all were subject, one that judged all deceased persons according to the de-gree of their participation in *Maat*, the order of the cosmos. The less this order was believed to be guaranteed on earth, the more the Judgment of the Dead gained in importance as a source of requital.

After the death of Neferirkare, there followed some dark years upon which light is beginning to be shed by new finds; since 1980, numerous statues (including again the "king and falcon" motif), figures of cap-tives, seals, and administrative documents have been discovered in the unfinished pyramid complex of his son Raneferef at Abusir. Notwithstanding the growing importance of the beliefs concerning Osiris, the latter's brother Neuserre (c. 2443–2419 B.C.E.) steadfastly held to the worship of the sun as well. Reliefs from the Room of the Seasons in his sun temple vividly depict the life of nature during the seasons of the year, and thus the beneficent effect of the sun god on nature, as it would later be portrayed in the solar hymns of the New Kingdom. The same joy in the richness of life, in which even the deceased were supposed to share, is also evident in the private tombs of the time, such as the Saqqara tomb of Ty, who served under Neuserre as priest and administrator in the nearby sun temples at Abusir. With loving attention to natural detail, daily life on the estates of this worthy gentleman are displayed in the reliefs as though in a picture book. One room in these tombs, the serdab (Arabic for cellar), received an ever-increasing number of statues of the tomb owners and the members of their families. To this period belong the statue, now in the Louvre, of a scribe, alert and radiating a keen intelligence, as well as the lifelike Sheikh el-Beled in the Cairo Museum. As the tombs, with their increasing number of cult chambers, developed into family sepulchers, so the statuary also displayed a preference for family groups. The terseness and rigidity of the Giza period yielded to an increasing wealth of artistic forms, which continued to increase through the course of Dynasty 6 until the ultimate disintegration of the state.

Menkauhor (c. 2419–2411 B.C.E.) was the last king to build a sun temple. His successor, Izezi (c. 2411–2378 B.C.E.), abandoned not only this custom but also the royal cemetery at Abusir. The last two pyramids of Dynasty 5 were again situated at Saqqara, south of Djoser's complex, though the cults in the sanctuaries at Abusir were continued for a time. It seems certain that this development was connected with the increasing importance of Osiris; since the deceased king was transformed into Osiris, it no longer seemed crucial that he be equipped for the afterlife with a solar sanctuary of his own. It must be stressed, however, that this shift in the relative importance of Re and Osiris was not the result of a "religious war" or a power struggle between two rival priestly schools. An independent class of priests, separate from the bureaucracy, could develop only after service to the king had become less important than service to the gods. The king's right to appoint priests considerably circumscribed their power, and in this period, if there was to be a religious policy at all, it could be conducted only by the king and his closest associates. Primeval figures such as the deities of ancient Egypt have an existence and a development of their own in the religion of a people, one that priests and kings alike must take into account. With the appearance of the beliefs regarding Osiris, magical concepts once again rose to the surface out of deeper layers, concepts that had no meaning in solar belief. In the officialdom, old titles that had been given up because of their presumed magical power were once again popular; as Wolfgang Helck once put it, "They decked themselves out with them as with amulets." The bureaucratic order thus began to break up not only through decentralization, but also through an inflation in titles; with the beginning of Dynasty 6, it becomes ever more difficult to distinguish between functioning viziers and those who were merely titulary.

King Wenis (c. 2378–2348 B.C.E.), with whom Dynasty 5 ended, had spells from the royal burial ritual carved in the subterranean chambers of his pyramid. Many of these spells had undoubtedly been recited at the burial of his predecessor, and many might even have dated back to previous dynasties. But one cannot help suspecting that a fundamental revision of the ritual coincided with the decision to immortalize these spells, previously handed down on perishable papyrus, by carving them in stone and thereby also endowing them with greater magical power. This decision on Wenis's part has provided for us the earliest collection of religious texts, not only of Egypt, but of all humankind: the Pyramid Texts. It would be dangerous, though, to try to draw a picture of the religion of this period around 2350 B.C.E. from the Pyramid Texts alone. These spells were collected, in accordance with the thinking of the time, first and foremost on the basis of their magical effectiveness and their ritual goal: they were supposed to make the king independent of the ever more questionable care of the living; to deify him as Osiris; and to enable him, through the power of magic, to ascend unhindered into the celestial realm of his father, Re, the sun god. The hereafter thus lay in the sky with Re, but also in the depths of the earth with Osiris. The resolution of this paradox, which would be reduced to a brief formula in the New Kingdom, was already presaged in the Pyramid Texts: the body of the deceased belonged to the tomb and the netherworld, while his spiritual powers belonged to the sky, the realm of the heavenly bodies. (The Egyptians did not know the western opposition of body and soul; rather, they thought that a human being consisted of a multiplicity of components—body, heart, shadow, *ba*, and *ka*.) The problematic relationship between Re and Osiris was resolved with a similar clarity, perhaps as early as the First Intermediate Period: since the dead king, and soon every deceased person, became Osiris, the "deceased" seemed to be the evening sun, setting into the netherworld in the form of Osiris. Such syncretistic mergings of deities were the very stuff of ancient Egyptian theology.

Since the Pyramid Texts revolve around death and the afterlife, deities belonging entirely to this life make only rare appearances. The Memphite creator god Ptah is seldom mentioned, while the Memphite Theology, which places him at the center of a spiritual doctrine of creative utterance and was once dated to the Old Kingdom, actually belongs to a much later period. Even the god Amun, who was destined to enjoy a great future, finds his first mention in the pyramid of Wenis, though in a very indefinite context. It is significant that at nearly the same time that inscriptions were placed in the royal sarcophagus chamber, they also began to appear in the subterranean burial chambers of officials. We see in this practice an expression of the same skepticism as that felt by kings regarding the effectiveness of ritual texts that had received only oral expression.

Next to the Pyramid Texts, wisdom literature constitutes a second important source for the intellectual history of this period. These texts are concerned with this world, with how individuals should adapt themselves to the circumstances of an earthly lifetime. As in later eras, the wisdom literature of this period did not attempt to formulate moral laws but rather offered practical advice regarding how to conduct oneself in the presence of superiors, colleagues, and subordinates. In the advisements of these texts, we can discern not only a pragmatic experience of life, but also a sense of ethical and social responsibility. The texts were placed in the mouth of a leading individual in public life and addressed to his son or his pupil; thus, the most important wisdom text from this period was ascribed to the vizier Ptahhotpe of the court of king Izezi.

The valley temple of Wenis, with its palm-shaped columns of red granite, was connected to the temple in front of his pyramid by a roofed causeway nearly 2,300 feet long and whose high side walls bore both traditional and highly unusual representations. Along with scenes of hunting, agriculture, and market life, the technically impressive transport of the huge monolithic columns is depicted, as well as a much-discussed scene in which starving Bedouins are shown with crass realism; to them, Egypt probably already seemed like the "land of fleshpots." (As noted previously, an earlier version of this scene from the reign of Sahure has recently been found.) Another representation depicts campaigns against Asiatic Bedouins, whose home we must suppose to have been in the Sinai peninsula or southern Palestine. The storming of an Asiatic fortress depicted in the tomb of a nomarch at Dishasha shows that at the end of Dynasty 5, Egyptian attacks were directed not only against wandering Bedouins, but also against the sedentary culture of the cities of Palestine. Trading expeditions continued to be sent to Byblos and Punt; under King Izezi, an expedition to Punt brought back a pygmy, whose appearance very much impressed the people of his day.

Wenis evidently did not leave behind an heir; two sons predeceased him, and several princesses were buried in the vicinity of his pyramid. At his death, therefore, the crown fell to Teti (c. 2348–2320 B.C.E.), who founded Dynasty 6 and presumably owed the throne to his marriage to the princess Iput. The change of dynasty perhaps also brought a change in the Residence, but Saqqara remained the royal cemetery, and the chambers of the royal pyramids continued to be provided with spells from the burial ritual until the end of the Old Kingdom, though the selection of spells and their order constantly changed. Around the pyramid of Teti is an important cemetery of officials; the family tomb of the vizier Mereruka especially impresses visitors with its thirty-two chambers and rich relief decoration, though it does not match the artistic perfection of Dynasty 5. In the provinces, the power and influence of the nomarchs continued to grow unchecked; certain of them, such as Izi of Edfu and his later colleague, Heqaib of Elephantine, achieved such importance for their districts that they were worshiped as gods until the end of the Middle Kingdom. Under Izi, the local rulers' right to inheritance of office was again confirmed, and he was succeeded by his son Qar. On the other hand, the successors of King Teti seemed to experience difficulties; to begin with, there was the rather short reign of a king named Userkare, and there are also vague hints at conspiracy and regicide.

Teti's son Pepy I (c. 2316–2284 B.C.E.) altered his titulary several times during the course of his long reign, in particular at the celebration of his festival of renewal. As already in the latter half of Dynasty 5, kings were not averse to including a nickname (Teti, Pepy) in their titularies; quite some time earlier, private people had begun using them in addition to their "official" names. Along with this vulgarization of the kingship, the institution was now visibly yielding to new ruling powers, both deities and feudal lords. Pepy I was the first king to have himself represented making offerings to the gods in a kneeling position, in a statuette now in the Brooklyn Museum; and following a harem conspiracy, he entered into marriage with two daughters of the Upper Egyptian nomarch Khui, whose family from Abydos now gained a strong influence over the affairs of state. Djau, a brother of the two queens, later rose to the vizierate, and he is the first nonroyal person to be attested, under Pepy II, with a statue in a temple. The kingship had become dependent on the loyalty of powerful lords in the provinces, and it was forced to rely to a certain extent on a policy of alodium.

The growing importance of the provinces manifested itself not least of all in Pepy I's active building program in a number of the nomes throughout the land; since the king still had control over the most important stone quarries, the nomarchs could not act as their own architects, so that in this respect, at least, they remained dependent on good relations with the kingship. The king paid special attention to the goddesses Bastet and Hathor and to the fertility god Min, the tutelary deity of the eastern desert, divinities who had played an important role at court and in the land since the Archaic Period. But Montu, a deity of the Theban nome and later a god of war, also acquired a conspicuous position, both on a cylinder seal and in the burial ritual of Pepy I; in this, we see a first indication of the cultic importance of this region that was to assume the political leadership two centuries later. Though the Residence seems to have diminished in importance under Pepy I, it received its lasting name, Memphis, from the abbreviated name of his pyramid complex, "Lasting and perfect (is Pepy)." Vessels bearing the king's name found at Byblos and the north Syrian city of Ebla testify to far-flung trade relations.

In his provincial tomb at Abydos, the expedition leader Weni reports on military undertakings during this reign; these were directed against the "sand dwellers," that is, the Bedouins of the Sinai region, though tribes in southern Palestine were also overcome by Egyptian troops through a combined operation by land and sea on the enemy's rear. We meet the same Weni under Pepy's son Merenre (c. 2284–2270 B.C.E.), in the office of Overseer of Upper Egypt; a little later, this office would cease to serve as a means of controlling the nomarchs as the most powerful nomarchs incorporated its name into their lists of titles. In this new capacity, Weni was responsible for all expeditions to the eastern desert and Nubia. Rock inscriptions commemorate personal inspections by the young king at the First Cataract, where he received the tribute of the Nubian chieftains. During his reign, the nomarch Harkhuf of Elephantine ventured out on three expeditions over the caravan routes of the western desert deep into Nubian territory, to the region of the Third Cataract. This advance might have been connected with the formation of a rather large political entity in Nubia, which corresponded culturally with the penetration into the area of a new people, whom we call the C-Group.

After the early death of Merenre, his half-brother Pepy II (c. 2270–2205 B.C.E.; figure 12) ascended the throne. The incredibly long reign of ninety-four years ascribed to him by Manetho is confirmed, at least in its order of magnitude, by the New Kingdom Royal Canon of Turin. Preserved dates and the succession of several generations of nomarchs dur-

12. Statuette depicting Pepy II and his mother. Brooklyn Museum, Charles Edwin Wilbour Fund (39.119). Photo courtesy of The Brooklyn Museum.

ing his reign also attest to a long period of rule. It is certain that he came to the throne as a child. There had not been a child on the throne for a long time, if at all, and Egyptians surely felt reminded of the mythic model of the child Horus, who had been called to the rulership as a boy. Childlike joy and curiosity are expressed in the king's concern for the well-being of a dancing pygmy from Nubia of whom he had been informed by Harkhuf, the seasoned expedition leader. On the other hand, representations of Pepy II as a royal child probably belong to the end of his reign, when a manifest rejuvenation of the aged king was hoped for.

During the nine decades of this long reign, the way was paved for the collapse of the Old Kingdom. It did not result from outside stimulus. Attacks on Egyptian expeditions seem to have become more frequent, to be sure, but no serious dangers threatened Egypt from western Asia or Nubia. A few expedition leaders recorded in their rock-cut tombs at Aswan detailed accounts of their undertakings. One of them, Pepynakht, was deified shortly after his death and received a sanctuary at Elephantine, which was later decorated with statues by monarchs of Dynasties 11 and 12. Another, Sabni, reports on bringing back his deceased father from Nubia and on the transport of two obelisks to Heliopolis. Journeys to faraway places, such as Byblos and Punt, had become routine; one official, Khnumhotpe, took part in eleven such journeys.

Internally, however, the long period of rule, during which the king's mother and her nomarchical family determined policy, brought about a further weakening of the central administration and the institution of kingship. A folk tale of the New Kingdom even depicts the adult king not as a strong personality, but rather as someone embroiled in dangerous situations because of his abnormal tendencies. But the decisive factor was that the archaic, patriarchal structure of the administration was no longer adequate to meet the more specialized demands of the era and thus not suited in all respects to the tenor of the times.

Because of this ongoing weakening of the kingship, the perfect organization of the body politic that characterized the height of the Old Kingdom and enabled its astounding achievements could no longer be maintained. The increase in the number of cultic endowments freed by royal decree from taxes and other obligations put a strain on the economy of the state and placed an increasing burden on the remaining taxpayers as well as on the royal treasury. A weak central administration could no longer provide the state-conducted trade with the rational planning or the armed protection it needed. The consequences were economic difficulties and ultimate catastrophe, famine, and struggle for life itself.

Economic need, only occasionally overcome, occupies the center of attention in biographical inscriptions. In literary texts depicting upheaval, which appeared later, famine and the consequent dissolution of traditional social bonds are depicted in drastic terms. The national organization achieved in the Archaic Period now reverted to its opposite, and the country sank back into a chaotic state—on the mythic plane, into the world before creation. The struggle against this frightful experience, this return into a chaos that supposedly had been banished along with its destructive forces, led to a flowering of literature such as Egypt had never before known. This literature developed at the beginning of the Middle Kingdom, when it served as a reminder of the chaos that existed at the end of the Old Kingdom and in the subsequent Intermediate Period, from which the newly won order radiantly arose; in the New Kingdom, many of these works would still be among the texts read by schoolboys.

While art sank to a provincial level for lack of support from a central Residence (figure 13), the intellectual elite of the land took pen in hand and even held the creator and sustainer of the world, now called "God," responsible for the collapse. It seemed as though the divine shepherd had forsaken his human flock, which he had previously guided in safety, and even the promise of a blessed afterlife was called into question. Writers now sought the consolation of words and took comfort in finding new expression that could break through the formulaic style of the mortuary literature and the biographies; they were now discovering the power of the word as well as the power of the individual.

The Coffin Texts, which replaced the Pyramid Texts in the twenty-first century B.C.E., also bear traces of this intellectual debate. Older material is handed down in the Coffin Texts, but for the most part, these consist of newly formulated spells that were supposed to accompany deceased persons on their journey in the afterlife, equipping them with the magical power they would need, for this afterlife seems to have been a world more fraught with danger than in the Pyramid Texts. Since there were no more pyramids, the spells were written on wooden coffins. Nomarchs and officials took over the royal burial ritual, and in time, every deceased person laid claim to becoming an "Osiris NN" and thus divine. Economic and political conditions, however, necessitated a modest scale; large monuments like those of the Old Kingdom were no longer possible, and decoration necessary for the afterlife was shifted from tomb walls to stelae and coffins.

With the collapse of the central administration, the economy, and the

13. Stela depicting Maaty (center) and his wife, Dedwi. Brooklyn Museum of Art, Charles Edwin Wilbour Fund (39.1). Photo courtesy of The Brooklyn Museum.

social order, local potentates turned to self-help to procure the necessary foodstuffs for themselves and their subjects. This often took the form of raids on neighboring regions and the collection of food by force from the peasants, who were thereby obliged to form armed bands. Thus grew the general lack of safety in the land. In the walled Residences of the nomarchs, an urban middle class was formed, devoted to the acquisition and accumulation of private property. *Nedjes,* a pejorative word for small, became the positive self-designation of these "bourgeois." Now the cities became political centers, and those in power lent them their special attention.

After the death of Pepy II (c. 2205 B.C.E.), his son Merenre II Antyemsaef, himself already well on in years, occupied the throne for only thirteen months. In similar rapid succession followed at least a dozen kings, who still resided in Memphis and nominally ruled the entire land, though they held increasingly less real power in their hands. The Royal Canon of Turin, Herodotus, and Manetho agree in placing a queen, Nitocris, at the end of the dynasty; she cannot be verified from contemporary sources, however, and she perhaps owes her existence in the king lists to an error on the part of a copyist. After Merenre II, there evidently reigned only one further monarch from Pepy II's family; he was followed by Dynasty 7, whose kings succeeded one another so rapidly that Manetho mentions seventy kings who each ruled for only one day, while the Royal Canon of Turin refrains from mentioning all but six of them, and those only by name. The four or five kings of Dynasty 8 ruled for a total of only a decade, and there is mention of an Overseer of Upper Egypt from a family of nomarchs in Koptos that allied itself by marriage with the short-lived royal house. The kings of this dynasty built modest pyramids at Saqqara, enacted decrees of tax exemption for the temple of Min at Koptos, and acted as rulers over the entire country. Only with the end of Dynasty 8 did the unity of the land finally come to an end and Memphis lose its function as the royal Residence. The king lists mark an end to Dynasty 8 with a Neferirkare, at the same time indicating a deep rupture: the end of the Old Kingdom and the beginning of a first Intermediate Period.

What happened in Memphis around 2160 B.C.E. must unfortunately be left to speculation. The capital quickly fell to a family of nomarchs residing in Herakleopolis, south of the Faiyum, who now had no hesitation in taking over the royal office. The Ptolemaic priest Manetho (c. 280 B.C.E.), to whom our division of the kings into dynasties dates back, counted these as Dynasties 9 and 10 (c. 2160–1980 B.C.E.). His Dynasty 9 perhaps enjoyed a period of sole rule over all the land before the founding of Dynasty 11 in Thebes, though we do not know how far south the sphere of influence of these kings stretched at the very beginning of the dynasty. Koptos, which had been so closely tied to Dynasty 8, apparently sided with Thebes, a second power center that had sprung up in the fourth nome of Upper Egypt. The local dynasty there seems to have originated with a "god's father," Mentuhotpe, and had close family ties to the nomarchs of Elephantine. Statues of the Theban rulers were set up in the temple of Heqaib on the island of Elephantine, and we must assume that because of this tie with the south, the Thebans had at their disposal, from the very beginning, seasoned Nubian soldiers who would lend considerable combat strength to the Theban army in the warfare that ensued to reunite the land.

At first, in the last decades of the twenty-second century, the "count" Ankhtifi appears acting independently in the two nomes of Hierakonpolis and Edfu, which separated Thebes from Elephantine. The inscriptions in his tomb at el-Moalla show the narrow scope in which the "high" policy of the time was obliged to operate; overcoming ongoing economic difficulties, obtaining the grain necessary for sowing, and caring for the most elementary needs of his subjects occupy the foreground of the texts. Within his small territory, Ankhtifi assumed the royal role of "good shepherd," and he did not shy away from comparing his solicitousness to that of the gods. Indeed, he considered himself to be a unique personality: "For no one like me has ever been born or will be born for millions of years." Under such circumstances, there could be no thought of an Egyptian foreign policy; journeys to Byblos and Punt ceased, while Nubia, left to itself, was penetrated by a new social stratum, the so-called C-Group.

The Theban ruling family assumed the royal titulary at about the same time as the nomarchs of Herakleopolis, though in an abbreviated form. With his Horus name, Sehertawy ("he who calms the Two Lands"), Inyotef I, the first king of this Dynasty 11, already laid claim to the whole country, but even his brother Inyotef II (2065–2016 B.C.E.), who guided the fortunes of the Theban mini-kingdom for an entire half-century, had possession at first of little more than the Theban nome. Only with the death of Ankhtifi could he unite the southern nomes, all the way to the First Cataract, securely in his grasp. To the north, the eighth (Thinite) nome stood at the center of the first known battle between the two petty kingdoms; during the reign of Inyotef II, it changed hands several times. In this nome lay Abydos, which was gaining greater importance as the Upper Egyptian cult center of Osiris.

A powerful counterassault, which brought Inyotef II north beyond Abydos in response to an attack, succeeded as far as the Serpent nome but it foundered in the realm where the nomarchs of Siut (in the thirteenth nome, modern Asyut) held sway; to the very last, these people remained loyal vassals of the northern kingdom. After these early battles, relatively friendly relations ensued between the rulers in Herakleopolis and Thebes; both were much too occupied with internal problems to involve themselves in long-term, wearing conflicts. From Minya to the eastern delta, the Herakleopolitans attempted to establish a line of defense against raids by Asiatic Bedouins, and they even reestablished maritime trade with Byblos.

An instruction for his son Merykare, which in reality was a sort of inaugural address of this son, was ascribed to one of the kings of Dynasty 10; it established a new literary genre, one that clothed political intentions with a literary mantle and that would especially flourish in Dynasty 12. The "Instruction for Merykare" is also important as a witness to the growing currency of the Judgment of the Dead, which guaranteed for the next life, at least, a justice missing from this one. Doubts regarding the powers that governed the world and their inner ties to *Maat* run through the complaints of the "Eloquent Peasant," whose tale of woe was also set in the northern realm. It is now assumed, however, that both these works belong to Dynasty 12.

In the southern kingdom, whose vitality would eventually win out over the cultural refinement of the north, the brief reign of Inyotef III (2016–2008 B.C.E.) ran its course essentially in peace. One of his officials was the first to have what would be the programmatic name of four kings of Dynasty 12: Amenemhet, which means "Amun is at the forefront." Amun, whose origin and original nature can no longer be ascertained with certainty, had developed into the leading deity of the Theban nome, along with Montu, and thus of the southern kingdom; he is attested at Karnak, his preferred sanctuary, beginning with the reign of Inyotef II. In the process, he took on the characteristics of other gods, such as the fertility aspect of Min of Koptos, but especially the creative role of the sun god, whose divine abundance enabled him to become Amun-Re, guider of the cosmos. With Amun's assumption of this role, the Egyptian pantheon achieved the form it was to maintain for the long term.

After some early years of peace under Inyotef III's son Mentuhotpe I (2008–1957 B.C.E.; often counted as Mentuhotpe II) came the decisive struggle with the northern realm, which was ruled by Merykare. Its immediate cause seems to have been an attempt by the north to reassert control over the Thinite nome, which by now had long been within the Theban sphere of control. The attempt was thwarted and in the course of a counterattack, Siut was conquered; only a few years earlier, King Merykare had personally participated in the installation there of the new nomarch, Khety II. With Merykare robbed of his most powerful vassals through the loss of Siut, the leaders of the adjoining nomes to the north, the Hare nome and the Antelope nome, attempted to keep their regions out of the hostilities through diplomatic skill. The Thebans were thus able to advance past Hermopolis to the Residence of Herakleopolis without encountering any resistance worthy of mention. Merykare's successor, whose name has not come down to us, lost his capital and his throne. Of the officials of his realm, some were imprisoned while others were accepted into the service of the victor along with the artisans and craftsmen of the northern Residence. Many also probably fled to western Asia; the Story of Sinuhe makes mention of Egyptian émigrés there. The severity of the battles preceding the reunification of the land is attested by a mass burial of sixty Theban soldiers discovered in 1923. After the fall of Herakleopolis, the Memphite area and the delta fell into the hands of the Thebans with no serious struggles. Thus, around 1980 B.C.E., all Egypt was again in the grasp of a single ruler after a century of disunity.

THE MIDDLE KINGDOM

Even in ancient times, posterity would recall that under his throne name Nebhepetre, Mentuhotpe I was the second to unite the land, along with Menes and, later, Ahmose. For his part, the actual re-union of the separated portions of the land was grounds for changing his Horus name a second time: for the remainder of his fifty-one-year reign, he was called Horus Sema-tawy, "He who united the Two Lands." To connect the north of the country more closely to the new center at Thebes, the king created the office of Overseer of Lower Egypt. The borders were secured, and once again ships fared out from the delta to Byblos to bring back wood, the much-sought-after building material. Royal building activity was revived in Upper Egypt, at least, and was crowned by the construction of a double tomb in the cliff-bound inlet of Deir el-Bahri on the west bank of Thebes (Figure 14). The impressive construction, called "Transfigured are the places of Nebhepetre," combines elements of pyramid tombs and Upper Egyptian rock-cut tombs, and the unity thus achieved is striking. The actual tomb lies in the cliff while the modest pyramid (or rectangular superstructure) rises above a royal statue that was ritually buried in a hypostyle court. Though expressively carved, the sandstone statues of the king are still coarse and blocklike in shape, while the reliefs of his mortuary temple, compared to their awkward beginnings before the reunification of the land, find a new sureness and fineness of line. Mentuhotpe I also had rock-cut tombs pre-

14. Mortuary temple of Mentuhotpe I (Nebhepetre) seen from cliff walk. Photo © 1992 by Al Berens, Suredesign Graphics.

pared for his higher-ranking officials at Deir el-Bahri, in the vicinity of the royal tomb; with their broad, perforated facades, they are distinct from the tombs of later officials.

At the end of his long reign, the reuniter of the kingdom bequeathed to his son Mentuhotpe II (1957–1945 B.C.E.) a state that was politically and economically stable, along with capable officials and superb artisans. The new king continued his father's ambitious building program, extending it to the delta as well, for throughout the land it was necessary to fulfill the cultic requirements of deities who had now stepped into the foreground for the first time. Since temples otherwise were located in the Nile valley, the small sanctuary he erected for Montu-Re on Thoth Hill on the west bank of Thebes is unusual.

In the eighth year of the king (1950 B.C.E.), one of his officials, Henenu, equipped an expedition to distant Punt, the first to that land in a long time. Discovered in the tomb of another high official of the time, the chancellor Meketre, was an especially rich hoard of models of the sort that Egyptians were fond of giving to nomarchs and other dignitaries of the First Intermediate Period for the afterlife. The chancellor's garden, house, workshops, boats, and herds are all reproduced in a lifelike manner, along with servants performing their various tasks as they were supposed to do for their master in the realm of the dead. The colorful richness of life in the country, which had been captured in relief in the tombs of the Old Kingdom, is here recorded in sculpture in the round. Such scenes of daily life find their written counterparts in the letters of Heqanakhte, a small landowner and mortuary priest. Both finds are now dated a little later, to the beginning of Dynasty 12.

The last king of Dynasty 11, Mentuhotpe III (1945–1938 B.C.E.), was not a legitimate successor to the throne and was omitted from the later king lists. At the beginning of his reign, however, he also undertook large building projects, and he dispatched his highest official, the vizier Amenemhet, to head a whole army of workers at the quarries of the Wadi Hammamat in preparing a sarcophagus for the intended royal tomb. This presumably was the same Amenemhet who founded Dynasty 12, though we have no reliable tradition regarding the detailed circumstances of this succession and change of dynasty. In the Prophecies of Neferty, the change is depicted according to a stereotyped pattern: after upheaval and general affliction in the land, the new king, Ameny (his nickname), the "son of a woman from Nubia," appears as a savior who restores order. There is considerable reason to think that in reality the succession did not take place by force, and the way might even have been paved by a period of coregency.

Amenemhet I (1938–1909 B.C.E.; Figure 15), the new king and the founder of Dynasty 12, seems to have been the son of a "god's father" named Senwosret and a member of the house of the nomarchs of Elephantine. The remaining kings of this illustrious dynasty also bore either his personal name or that of his father. For the first three names of his titulary, Amenemhet I aptly chose the expression "Repeater of births (that is, of the creation)," thus rightly characterizing his reign as the beginning of a new epoch. From its modest beginnings, Dynasty 11 had restored Egypt to an ordered, functioning state, and with Dynasty 12, Egypt commenced its second great period of cultural flowering.

At the beginning of the dynasty, the Residence was moved from Thebes, with its altogether too remote location, to the old center of the land—not to Memphis itself, but rather eighteen and a half miles south of it, where a new capital was built near the modern town of el-Lisht and named "Amenemhet, who has taken possession of the Two Lands."

15. Upper portion of a lintel depicting Amenemhet I (center) and four deities. The Metropolitan Museum of Art, Rogers Fund, 1908 (08.200.5). Photo courtesy of The Metropolitan Museum of Art.

The pyramid age, whose stony witnesses lay within the range of eyesight, served the new Residence as a model, and old forms were invested with new meaning. Amenemhet I returned to the traditional form of the royal tomb and erected a pyramid near his Residence. In front of it rises a mortuary temple decorated with fluted columns; among other things, its reliefs once again depict ceremonies of the royal festival of renewal. In the vicinity, and also decorated with reliefs, lie the tombs of his high officials, which revive the mastaba form of the Old Kingdom. In their technical execution, however, the pyramids of the Middle Kingdom were more modest and less enduring than those of the Old Kingdom. Many layers of mud bricks, of the kind used for building houses and enclosure walls, were laid around a skeleton of stone walls, the spaces between which had been filled with sand and rubble; when possible, the pyramid rested on an existing core of rock. The layers of brick were originally concealed by an outer casing of stone that was crowned by an inscribed capstone. The casing has not survived, and the fact that the perishable mud bricks are still preserved is due solely to the grace of Egypt's dry climate.

Thebes remained the center of Amun worship, though it lost its political importance during Dynasty 12. At this time, only a few members of the royal court and the ranks of officials had themselves buried in the Theban necropolis on the west bank of the Nile. On the east bank, though, zealous building activity took place at Karnak, the temple of Amun near the present-day city of Luxor; Amenemhet I donated statues and a granite altar. Memphis also enjoyed the attention of the king; its creator god, Ptah, who had not been very prominent in the Old Kingdom, now gained a growing influence throughout the land, an example of which can be seen in his mention on stelae at Abydos. With Amun,

Re, and Ptah, a leading constellation of gods had been formed, one that would be intensified into a trinity in the New Kingdom, in the hymns to Amun on a papyrus now in Leiden. Osiris also assumed a special prominence as the enduring center of beliefs concerning the afterlife.

Notwithstanding the unification of the land, the nomarchs were at first able to maintain their power undiminished and even to acquire the additional privilege—normally reserved for royalty—of dating according to their own years of rule. Feudalism, along with the middle class and private property, thus outlasted the First Intermediate Period. Amenemhet left in office the families of loyal nomarchs, while in other nomes he appointed new "dynasties." Under the first kings of Dynasty 12, the nomarchs of Hermopolis and Elephantine were especially prominent; the former were responsible for the coveted alabaster quarries of Hatnub and the latter for the territory of Nubia and its products.

Amenemhet I evidently initiated the construction of the fortress of Buhen at the Second Cataract, whose astonishing fortifications were excavated in the 1950s. The walls, which were nearly thirty feet high and more than sixteen feet thick, provided optimal firepower by means of a complex system of embrasures, and the walls would be further strengthened by bastions in the New Kingdom; defense was enhanced by a wide moat. For a time, it was believed that the earliest skeleton of an Egyptian horse had been found in the Middle Kingdom stratum at Buhen, but the find has since been redated to the beginning of the New Kingdom. The mighty fortification at Buhen marks the beginning of a deliberate colonial policy on Egypt's part. In the Old Kingdom, expeditions had penetrated Wawat (Lower Nubia) from bases on Egyptian soil; now, a chain of fortified bases assured permanent possession of the area and thus unhindered access to its quarries and gold mines. Only seldom do we hear of armed Nubian resistance to this Egyptian takeover of their territory; an inscription near Korosko dating to the penultimate year of the king commemorates a military expedition against Wawat.

In the north, Amenemhet I strove to secure the open borders with Asia and Libya. On the eastern edge of the delta, he constructed the Walls of the Ruler, a system of fortifications that secured the few passages to the Sinai peninsula and were thus supposed to control raids by Asiatic Bedouins, who now had "once again to ask for water when they wished their cattle to drink," as stated in the Prophecies of Neferty. The Sinai region with its copper and turquoise deposits was brought under control, but no extensive colonial policy like that in Nubia was planned for the region of Asia, especially since the trade routes to Syria were almost en-

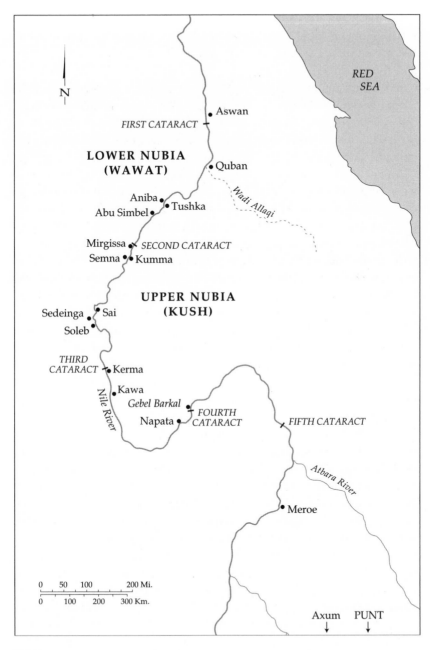

Nubia

tirely maritime. The securing of the northwestern border against the warlike Libyan tribes remained difficult; here, it was not easy to establish a continuous system of fortifications like that in the eastern delta, and the endangered western edge of the delta therefore had to be secured by means of frequent military expeditions. As reported in the Story of Sinuhe, when the king died, his coregent and successor, Senwosret, was on just such an expedition in the vicinity of the Wadi el-Natrun. But this undertaking also had a ritual task, that of obtaining valuable cattle for the planned festival of renewal of the elder monarch.

Amenemhet I had elevated his son Senwosret to the coregency in 1919 B.C.E., and for nine years they had conducted the affairs of state together. The remaining kings of Dynasty 12 would also follow this custom of appointing their successors as coregents during their own lifetimes. The system assured a special continuity for the royal line and endowed it with an unusual number of important rulers. A harem conspiracy, however, threatened the king's plans. While his coregent was far from the Residence on the expedition to Libya, the conspirators attempted to do away with the elderly king so as to place another prince on the throne. In order to strike the king at a low point in his effective powers, they chose a time immediately before his planned *sed* festival, or festival of renewal, which was supposed to replenish the power of the aged king for a new period of rule. The assassination attempt, which took place at night, evidently succeeded, but the swift reaction of the legitimate successor thwarted the remainder of the conspirators' plans.

Two important works of literature afford us an unusually deep insight into what happened during this change on the throne, though some questions remain unresolved. The adventure-packed Story of Sinuhe, mentioned previously, was placed in the mouth of a harem official named Sinuhe; it is in the form of an autobiography, though there is considerable reason to think that it is not the story of the life of a historical person but rather a political work commissioned by the ruling dynasty. It begins with the exact date of the king's death and then depicts the immediate reactions of the successor to the throne and of the hero: the former speeds off to the Residence to assume the reins of power, while the latter, fearing the coming strife, furtively leaves the expeditionary force and pursues a complicated route of flight that ultimately takes him to a tribe of Bedouins in Palestine. There, for many years he leads the life of a highly respected Bedouin sheikh, establishes a family, and experiences many adventures. The depiction of life in Palestine in the twentieth century B.C.E. is not an eyewitness account but rather reflects the conceptions regarding Asia and its inhabitants entertained by the Egyptians of that time. Nevertheless, by the New Kingdom, this lively depiction was viewed as the main attraction of the story; scarcely any other work of Egyptian literature has been handed down to us in so many copies as the Story of Sinuhe. But the conceptual and political kernel of the work lies in its conclusion, which consists of a decree of amnesty from the new king and Sinuhe's safe return to the royal court from his exile.

The other literary-political document is the Instruction of King Amenemhet, composed for Senwosret I by the writer Khety. Khety was also the author of the Satire of the Trades, which enjoyed a wide circulation; it praises the scribal profession, and in the New Kingdom it was one of the standard texts read in scribal schools. His less important Instruction, which was widely read down into the Late Period, is a fictitious communication by the assassinated king to his son to "establish the truth"; in reality, it is an "inaugural address" of Senwosret I that allows us a deep insight into the changed concept of kingship and its role in the world. This role was still divine, but its burden of responsibility weighed heavily on the human person of the king. What would later be said of the office of vizier was now true for that of the king: it was "not sweet, but bitter." Since its breakdown at the end of the Old Kingdom, the institution of kingship was no longer sustained by a natural trust on the part of the people. The era of patriarchal community was over, and distrust, vigilance, and self-preservation were required in a king. Placed on his own, he had to justify his kingship through deeds that surpassed human standards. This requirement endowed him with the heroic trait that distinguished the monarchs of the Middle Kingdom and that survived in the late Senwosret Legend. Superhuman effort, energy, and insight were needed to protect the vulnerable world order from yet another return into chaos; more than human, too, were the responsibility of the king and the solitude of his decision making. The Instruction of King Amenemhet thus anticipates in literary form what royal portrait statues of late Dynasty 12 would express in features worked in stone—the kingship as a rich, intensified instance of the human condition, one that, having gone through many trials, knew its very depths.

According to recent research, the great flowering of literature previously associated with the radical changes of the First Intermediate Period had its beginnings at this time. The social class to which these literary works were directed was supposed to be loyal to the kingship, which accounts for the works' eminently political character; their priority was to legitimize the new dynasty. An anonymous instruction of this period, known as the Loyalist Instruction, unequivocally demands adherence to the king: "Worship the king inside yourselves, pray to him in your hearts"—in this manner was one to avoid the king's wrath.

As his father had done, Senwosret I (1919–1875 B.C.E.; Figure 16) resided at el-Lisht. There he received Sinuhe when he returned from exile, and there he built, during his sole reign, a burial place (Figure 17) whose cult complex emulated Old Kingdom models, especially that of Pepy II. The life-size Osirid pillars lining the causeway were new, but the causeway of Wenis served as the model for the decoration of its walls; even giraffes as part of the tribute of Nubia had already made their appearance under Wenis. An inhabitant of Punt appears in the reliefs of the mortuary temple, but he too might have had an Old Kingdom model. In their technical perfection, the statues and reliefs created by Senwosret I's artisans can make us forget that the deep breach of the First Intermediate Period ever occurred, though in their reserve and detachment they testify to an altered sensibility.

It is not just the hazards of preservation that cause the temple cults to seem much more prominent in the Middle Kingdom than they had been earlier. During the upheavals of the First Intermediate Period, notwithstanding doubts that surfaced, the divine realm had proved reliable as a calming influence on what was happening in the world. Deities afforded refuge and consolation to people when earthly institutions failed, and even the kingship now recognized a need to stress that its actions were in agreement with divine will. Senwosret I's patronage was directed to the cults of all the important deities in the land, and he would be first surpassed as an architect only by the great kings of Dynasty 18. During his coregency, he had already had important buildings constructed at Karnak and Heliopolis. A tiny kiosk for the barque of Amun at Karnak, which has been reconstructed from its disassembled and reused blocks, is distinguished by the fineness of its relief decoration; it contrasts sharply with the coarse mass production that took place much later in the Ramesside Period. At Heliopolis, the cult center of the sun god, the great temple was entirely renewed, and it was provided with two granite obelisks for the celebration of the royal *sed* festival; the Ramesseum Dramatic Papyrus preserves the cultic drama that formed part of the ritual of this renewal festival. In the Faiyum, the granite pillar at Abgig bears witness to a growing interest in this fertile area.

As a place of pilgrimage, Abydos was a virtual mecca in this period, and the city also profited from the king's zealous building activity. From Dynasty 11 on, inscriptions mention the annual celebration of the great

16. Wooden statuette of Senwosret I. Cairo Museum. Photo by Nancy J. Corbin.

17. The pyramid of Senwosret I at el-Lisht. Photo by Sara E. Orel.

mysteries of Osiris, a ritual drama that actualized the death and resurrection of the god. To have a lasting share in the holiness of the place, Egyptians sought to secure an eternal presence by means of a stela or a small chapel located along the processional way; in the course of the Middle Kingdom, thousands of these stelae were set up at Abydos. A similar goal was served by the now widespread custom of placing statues of kings and officials in temples. Most of our Middle Kingdom statues of private people come not from tombs but from temples, where they were supposed to share not only in the holiness of these places but also, more concretely, in the cult offerings.

Senwosret I successfully continued the vigorous foreign policy at Egypt's southern frontier, completing the colonization of Nubia. The nomarch Sarenput of Elephantine was especially active there as a royal representative, but Middle Egyptian nomarchs were also involved, such as Ameny of the Antelope nome and Djefaihapy of Siut; the latter's contracts with his mortuary priests constitute an early and important source for our knowledge of law. Access to the gold mines of the Wadi Allaqi was secured by mighty fortresses at Quban and Aniba. Beyond Buhen at the Second Cataract, where stelae of the king have been found, Egyptian influence already stretched well to the south, as far as the trading center of Kerma, south of the Third Cataract; it thus penetrated the area of Kush (Upper Nubia), which finds its first textual mention at this time. Chieftains who resisted Egyptian penetration or threatened the caravan routes of Nubia and Asia were magically eliminated by means of Execration Texts: their names were written on statuettes or pots that were then ritually smashed. The means to political ends thus ran the gamut from literary propaganda to performative magic. As the founder of Egyptian rule in Nubia, Senwosret I enjoyed divine worship in this area for as long as it remained under Egyptian influence; it has been demonstrated that he also had a posthumous cult in the area of his Residence at el-Lisht in the New Kingdom.

In the pacified desert areas on either side of the Nile valley, expeditions set out for the gold mines, the stone quarries, and the distant oases. Their leaders and the scribes who accompanied them often left behind comprehensive inscriptions regarding the size and goal of their expeditions, as well as events that occurred along the way (Figure 18). Thus, we learn that in year 38 of the reign of Senwosret I (1882 B.C.E.), the royal herald Ameny journeyed into the eastern desert at the head of an expeditionary force numbering 17,000 men to procure sixty sphinxes and 150 statues for the king's building program. The provisioning of such a large

18. Rock inscriptions in the Wadi Hammamat. Photo © Guillemette Andreu.

number of men in the uninhabited, rough desert terrain was a challenging problem that was superbly resolved by the organizational talents of Egyptian officialdom; from the Ameny's inscription, we can glean the exact amounts of the rations, which differed according to rank, allotted to those who took part in the expedition. Since the camel was not yet known, donkeys were used as beasts of burden; under Amenemhet II, more than a thousand donkeys were allocated to an expedition to the diorite quarry at Tushka. But expeditions were doubtless normally smaller in size, seldom surpassing a thousand men.

Three years before his death, Senwosret I appointed his son Amenemhet II (1877–1843 B.C.E.; Figure 19) as coregent to assure a smooth transition on the throne, which this time was evidently not threatened by a conspiracy. While the new king was still prince, he had taken part in an expedition to Nubia along with his namesake, Ameny of the Antelope nome, and an annalistic inscription from Memphis reports a campaign to Asia that brought back 1,500 captives. An inspection of the fortresses of Wawat, carried out by one of his officials, demonstrated the king's vigilance with regard to the established borders. The peace that

19. Wooden statuette of
Amenemhet II or Senwosret II.
The Metropolitan Museum of
Art, Museum Excavations,
1913–14; Rogers Fund
supplemented by Contribution
of Edward S. Harkness (14.3.17).
Photo courtesy of The
Metropolitan Museum of Art.

reigned for half a century under this king and his successor did not stem
from weakness in Egypt's foreign policy but rather from the strength of
the position that Senwosret I had won in Nubia and Asia.

Commerce and trade could flourish in such a climate, and the reign of
Amenemhet II offers impressive examples of the extent of world trade at
that time. The products of the African interior were regularly imported

via Punt, the incense-producing land on the Somali coast. More important still, for both partners, were Egypt's economic relations with Asia. A shipment of trade goods from Syria at this time has been preserved to us in the famous Treasure of Tod, four copper chests discovered in the foundations of the temple of Montu at Tod, near Thebes. The chests contained precious metals and semiprecious stones that had been imported in part as raw materials and in part in the form of finished products; Egypt depended above all on Asiatic imports for silver and lapis lazuli. Along with Cretan and Babylonian works of art, Babylonian cylinder seals of the Third Dynasty of Ur (2050–1950 B.C.E.) made their way into Egypt as part of this treasure. On the other hand, Egyptian artworks of Middle Kingdom date have been excavated at Byblos and Ugarit, in Asia Minor, and on Crete, while Minoan ceramics (kamares ware) have come to light in tombs and dwellings of late Dynasty 12. How trade can also stimulate art is shown by the adoption of Cretan ornamentation, such as spirals and herringbone patterns, by Egyptian artists. Finally, unlike the Old Kingdom, we can distinguish a brisk trade in slaves in this period; there were not enough military undertakings to explain the ever-growing number of Asiatic slaves in Egypt.

The fragment of an annalistic inscription from Memphis contains further information about these steady trade relations. Goods from the Lebanon were brought in two ships, and Nubian tribute was delivered; the inscription reports numerous religious donations and also mentions a campaign to Asia.

Amenemhet II built his mortuary complex east of the pyramid of Snofru at Dahshur, much nearer to the old metropolis of Memphis; perhaps in doing so he also temporarily abandoned the Residence at el-Lisht. After his death, his son Senwosret II (1845–1837 B.C.E.), who had already been coregent for some years, became the sole ruler. During his reign, the focus of interest turned from Nubia to an area located within Egypt: the Faiyum. This large Egyptian oasis lies in the western desert, in a depression that at that time was mostly filled by a huge lake, Lake Moeris of the Greek authors. Today called the Birket Qarun, this lake, which has no outlet, covers only a portion of its original area; its water surface lies 144 feet below sea level. During the inundation season, a tributary, the Bahr Yusuf, carried large amounts of water into it from the Nile; Senwosret II and his successors regulated this water by building dams and canals, thus enabling a regular irrigation of the Faiyum. It also seems that a portion of the lake area was drained by means of dams and thus won for agriculture. Thus, during Dynasty 12, this unimportant district of lake water and swamps was transformed into one of the most fertile provinces of Egypt. Its chief deity, the crocodile god, Sobek (called Suchos by the Greeks), whose name had already been included in theophoric personal names in early Dynasty 12, now received a number of new sanctuaries.

Senwosret II laid out his pyramid tomb at a commanding site near the place where the Bahr Yusuf breaks through the hills at the edge of the western desert, at the modern town of el-Lahun. A settlement of officials, priests, and workers was established in its vicinity; its excavated remains constitute one of the few towns preserved to us from ancient Egypt. The Kahun papyri, which were found there, yield important insights into the religious and economic life of the period, though only a small portion of them has received publication and commentary. The Sothic date (the term for the heliacal rising of Sothis the rising of the star Sirius just before sunrise) on one of these papyrus fragments is of decisive importance for the chronology of the Middle Kingdom. This closely compacted settlement once contained more than a hundred houses, of which even the smallest, intended for workmen and priests of lower rank, had four to six rooms and an area of 1,022 to 1,819 square feet, thus affording ample space for a large family. The unique temple at Qasr el-Sagha on the northern edge of the Faiyum apparently also belongs to this reign.

With Egypt protected by mighty fortresses at its northern and southern borders, the reign of Senwosret II was a peaceful one. Internally, the nomarchs were becoming increasingly powerful. Thus Djehutihotpe II, master of the Hare nome with its capital at Hermopolis, had a colossal statue prepared for himself in the alabaster quarry of Hatnub, which lay within his jurisdiction, and in his rock tomb he commemorated its transport from the quarry (Figure 20). The statue is lost, but fragments of a statuette of this same official and other statuettes of the period have been found at Megiddo in Palestine, showing that the nomarchs were also active outside their jurisdictions as royal emissaries, as had been the case earlier. In the cemetery of Beni Hasan, the tomb of another nomarch of the period, Khnumhotpe II of the Antelope nome, contains a famed representation of an armed trading expedition of Semites, whose donkey caravan was led by the Bedouin sheikh Abishar.

Around the middle of the nineteenth century B.C.E., a crucial change seems to have taken place in Egyptian beliefs concerning the hereafter, entailing a definitive shift in stress from a celestial afterlife to a subterranean one. Senwosret II abandoned the traditional orientation of the

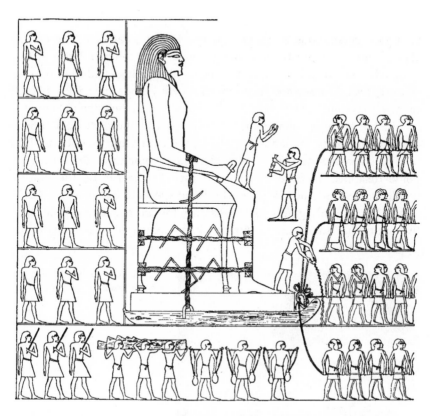

20. Transport of the colossal statue of Djehutihotpe II. From his tomb at Deir el-Bersha. After C. R. Lepsius, Denkmaeler aus Aegypten und Aethiopien (Berlin, 1849–56), pt. 2, pl. 134.

pyramid entrance to the north, the region of the circumpolar stars, and he replaced the straight axis of its underground passageway with a winding one that reflected the routes through the netherworld in the kingdom of Osiris. The scarab beetle, an important symbol of the hoped-for regeneration in the depths of the netherworld, became the most popular form of amulet at this time; the numerous block statues probably also refer to the desire for resurrection in the netherworldly realm of the afterlife, while the charming figurines of animals from this period, especially the hippopotamus, are a clear expression of the hope for regeneration.

Senwosret II died in his ninth year of rule, after a reign that was brief considering the stable conditions of Dynasty 12. It seems that a short time earlier, he had remembered to elevate a coregent, who now ascended the throne as Senwosret III (1837–1818 B.C.E.; Figure 21) and, after two generations of peace and quiet, inaugurated a new era of change in both domestic and foreign policy. The independence of the nomarchs, which had begun to assume royal trappings with the colossal statue of Djehutihotpe and the nomarchs' own year datings, was obliged to yield to the authoritarian will of the new king. In the reign of Senwosret III, the tradition of nomarchal families with their rock-cut tombs came to an end in the land as a whole, with very few exceptions. The mighty dynasties of Elephantine, the Hare nome, and the Antelope nome disappeared from Egyptian history. In the future, the nomes would be centrally administered by three special bureaus at the Residence. We can only guess what resistance this far-reaching administrative reform had to overcome, but it took as strong a ruling personality as

21. Statue of Senwosret III. Cairo Museum. Photo by Nancy J. Corbin.

Senwosret III to bring it to a rigorous and successful conclusion. The results can be seen in a clear strengthening of the kingship and an increased prominence of the middle and lower levels of the bureaucracy.

If Senwosret III was one of the most important of Egypt's ruling figures in the eyes of his contemporaries and of posterity as well, he owed this renown not least of all to his energetic foreign policy, which brought Egypt's standing in the world to a new high. In Nubia, he strengthened Egypt's position at the Second Cataract and secured it by means of a string of fortresses stretching thirty miles farther to the south. To enable a better and faster provisioning of the border fortresses in Nubia, he had a canal dug through the granite barrier of the First Cataract in 1830 B.C.E.; more than twenty-six feet deep, it afforded passage to still larger supply ships. In addition to the previously existing fortresses, there was now Mirgissa just south of the rapids, and also, in this advanced line of defenses, the important double fortress of Semna-Kumma. Here, in the eighth year of the king's reign (1830 B.C.E.) and again in his sixteenth year (1822 B.C.E.), the new southern boundary of Egypt was solemnly proclaimed by the erection of stelae. No Nubian was to pass by traveling north, whether by water or on land, without strict border control, and the king commanded his heirs to preserve the border, employing a double "blessing and curse" formula conferring a blessing on succeeding kings who maintained the border and a curse on those who might not. In his year 16, a statue of the king was set up at Semna to guarantee the enduring presence of the kingship as guardian of the realm; at the same time, yet another fortress was constructed on the nearby island of Uronarti. An inscription in this new fortress reports a campaign against the land of Kush, which was brought to a standstill by low water, in year 19 (1819 B.C.E.). Senwosret III was worshiped as a god in Nubia until the end of Dynasty 18, and Tuthmosis III built him a temple at Semna.

Senwosret III also penetrated farther than any of his predecessors at the other end of the realm, in Palestine. Military bases secured the trade routes in southern Palestine, and a small unit of Egyptian troops even reached the city of Shechem in the region of Samaria. A fresh series of Execration Texts mentions Jerusalem, along with other cities, revealing the wide geographical horizon of the Egyptians in this area. Further north, in the region of Syria and the Lebanon, Byblos remained the point from which Egyptian influence emanated; its prince bore titles that designated him as an Egyptian administrative official, thus distinguishing him from the "chiefs" of the other Asiatic cities. The Egyptian writing system and calendar were used at Byblos, and Egyptian deities were worshiped there, while names of Byblite princes even appear on scarabs.

It was only as an architect that Senwosret III did not prove the equal of his predecessors or successors. In the eastern delta, he enlarged a temple of Amenemhet I near Qantir, in the immediate vicinity of the later Residence of the Hyksos and the Ramessides. He built a temple in honor of Montu, the god of war, at Madamud, near Karnak. As his grandfather, Amenemhet II, had done, he chose the vicinity of the pyramid of Snofru at Dahshur as the site of his pyramid. In the realm of art, his reign is especially important because of its expressive royal sculpture, which for the first time emphasized a personal portraiture stamped by age, lending quite human and individual traits to the concept of kingship, which had previously been characterized by its timeless and sublime divine aspect. It is surely not coincidence that this new concept appeared at nearly the same time that far-reaching changes were occurring in beliefs regarding the afterlife; immediately transformed into a stereotype, its influence continued past the end of Dynasty 12.

Senwosret III's son and perhaps also coregent, Amenemhet III (1818–1773 B.C.E.; Figure 22), was scarcely less important than his father. In both his domestic and his foreign policies, the new king safeguarded what had been achieved. In the double fortress of Semna-Kumma, the southern boundary established by Senwosret III was kept under careful surveillance; daybooks of the border control, preserved in the Semna Despatches, carefully record border crossings in both directions. Egyptian influence continued to extend farther south, beyond the Third Cataract to the trading center of Kerma. The bases in southern Palestine assured that work continued uninterrupted in the copper mines and turquoise quarries of Sinai, where Amenemhet III's officials left innumerable inscriptions; the expedition leader Harwerre vividly recorded how he penetrated desolate valleys in the blistering heat of summer without having to mourn the loss of any of his men.

Pressing tasks of a different nature had caused an abatement of efforts in the Faiyum under Senwosret III. Amenemhet III now resumed his grandfather's colonization policy, which culminated in a large-scale building program. At Shedet (Greek Krokodilopolis), modern Medinet el-Faiyum, the king erected a great hall of granite pillars for Sobek, the chief god of the newly won province, and at Medinet Madi a small temple for Renenutet, the serpent-goddess of the harvest, who had so obviously blessed this new land wrested from the lake. On the new shore, at Biahmu near the capital, two colossal statues embodied the continuing

22. Statue head of a king, perhaps Amenemhet III. The Metropolitan Museum of Art, gift of Dr. and Mrs. Thomas H. Foulds, 1924 (24.7.1). Photo courtesy of The Metropolitan Museum of Art.

presence of the king. On the south side of the pyramid of Hawara, on the northeast edge of the depression, the remains of his mortuary temple lie under much-ransacked heaps of rubble and potsherds; Herodotus (*Histories*, book II, chapter 20) and other Greek writers described this huge layout, consisting of many courtyards, halls, and chambers, as a labyrinth. The rich burial of the king's daughter Nefruptah was discovered in its immediate proximity. It is thus highly likely that Amenemhet

III was buried not in the Black Pyramid at Dahshur, which was abandoned because of the threat of collapse, but rather here in the Faiyum, where he was still worshiped in the Greco-Roman Period as the protective deity of this depression around Lake Moeris.

The development of the Faiyum was the last great achievement of Dynasty 12. For six generations, this heroic line had produced capable and important ruling figures, but with the death of Amenemhet III, its creative powers ran dry. Compared to his illustrious predecessors, Amenemhet IV (1773–1763 B.C.E.) seems a colorless personality, though the brevity of his reign may contribute to that impression. Though a period of decline was just commencing, the condition of the realm remained fully safeguarded. The yearly Nile levels continued to be recorded at the Second Cataract, the southern boundary, while in the north, a diorite sphinx of the king has been found at Beirut, and the turquoise quarries and copper mines were worked with undiminished intensity. It is still not clear where the last king of this glorious dynasty was buried. He evidently had no male heir, for after the death of Amenemhet IV, his sister Nefrusobk (1763–1759 B.C.E.; Figure 23) assumed the titulary of a reigning monarch and ruled the land for the brief period of four years. In contrast to the historically unattested Nitocris at the end of Dynasty 6, the short reign of Nefrusobk left tangible traces from the delta to the Second Cataract.

With this first woman on the pharaonic throne, a dynasty that had led Egypt to unprecedented political and economic heights came to an end. Intellectually, the Middle Kingdom drew much from the foundations laid by the Old Kingdom and the stormy First Intermediate Period, but we must not undervalue its own achievements. Its art lent perfect expression to a new, more complex portrait of the human condition, and especially of the ruler. Literature developed and flowered for the first time, yielding a series of works that were to become classics, such as the Story of Sinuhe and the Book of Kemyt, a summa of the knowledge of the schoolboys of the time. Unfortunately, only modest fragments of these works—such as the Story of the Shipwrecked Sailor and Papyrus Westcar's tales of wonder—have been preserved out of what must have been a rich store of popular literature and folklore. Artful hymns to deities and kings laid the foundations for the great hymnic literature of the New Kingdom. The theology and philosophy of the Middle Kingdom have scarcely been investigated, but the doubts and debates of the period of upheaval seem to have led to fruitful reflections on many problems and to new formulations. Egyptian science, which was able to

23. Upper part of statuette of Queen Nefrusobk. The Metropolitan Museum of Art, Rogers Fund, 1965 (65.59.1). Photo courtesy of The Metropolitan Museum of Art.

yield notable achievements in medicine and mathematics, is better known to us from this period than from the Old Kingdom. Mathematics, worked out in a practical fashion through the building of pyramids and the measuring of fields, remained geared to practical uses; the known rules were never supported by theoretical proofs. Practical demands, those of the calendar, also determined Egyptian astronomy, leaving no room for astrological speculations. Medicine had already developed into a specialty with its own technical terminology in the Old Kingdom. The surgical Papyrus Edwin Smith surgical papyrus contains excellent diagnoses, and it recognizes the heart as the center of a system of "vessels"; when treating their patients, though, Egyptian physicians often resorted to magical practices. A papyrus fragment from the pyramid city of Senwosret II shows that the diseases of animals were also noted and studied. In the religious literature, special reference must be made to the Book of the Two Ways, which supplies the first exact representation of the realm of the afterlife, graphically depicted in diagrams that prepared the way to the Books of the Netherworld in the New Kingdom.

The political picture we have of Dynasty 13, which was founded by Khutawyre Ugaf in 1759 B.C.E., bears a close resemblance to that of the end of the Old Kingdom after the death of Pepy II: a rapid succession of rulers who might have risen from the bureaucracy and whose brief reigns, seldom lasting more than two to four years, did not allow for political stability; a weakening of the central administration; insecure borders; and a drop in the level of culture. Most of these short-lived kings of Dynasty 13 are no more than names to us, transmitted to posterity by the later king lists. Dominant in their personal names is Sobek, god of the Faiyum, who by that time had gained prestige throughout the realm.

The power of the nomarchs had dwindled permanently since the reign of Senwosret III, so that now, two to three generations later, the weakness at the center did not result in the revival of any thirst for power in the provinces. Instead, political power passed into the hands of the viziers and was transmitted through several generations of a single influential family. The office was divided, though, into an Upper Egyptian and a Lower Egyptian vizierate.

At Semna on the southern border secured by Senwosret III, the annual Nile levels continued to be recorded, and sealings of kings and officials of this period have been found at the nearby fortresses of Uronarti and Mirgissa. But the evidence eventually breaks off, and we must assume that by about 1750 B.C.E., the southern boundary had already been pulled back from Semna to the Second Cataract, where it could be defended by the mighty fortress of Buhen. Traces of fire indicate that this base was also eventually conquered and destroyed. In the latter part of Dynasty 13, the southern boundary again lay at Elephantine, the starting point of the conquests of the Middle Kingdom; later kings of the dynasty, such as Neferhotep I and Sebekhotpe III, continued to leave rock inscriptions in its region. In the north, Egypt was able to maintain its position of power for a longer time. Under Neferhotep I (c. 1705–1694 B.C.E.), Byblos and its prince, Yantin, still belonged to the Egyptian sphere of influence, whereas a short time earlier, Hetepibre had sent a ceremonial mace as a coronation gift to Prince Immeya of Ebla. Since Egypt gains no mention in the large archive of cuneiform tablets at Mari, though, Egyptian influence seems scarcely to have reached beyond the coastal area of the Lebanon. A short while later, the Egyptians also pulled back from this region, and there have been almost no Egyptian finds in Palestine from the latter half of the dynasty.

The chain of fortifications erected by Amenemhet I in the eastern delta proved capable of penetration during Dynasty 13, and we must reckon with a steady infiltration of nomadic tribes of Semites; these settled especially in the eastern delta, where they identified their god Baal with the Egyptian Seth and built a cult center for him at Avaris, the later Residence of the Hyksos. The ranks of the Semitic immigrants were swelled by a considerable number of Asiatic slaves and freedmen. A papyrus in the Brooklyn Museum mentions that a single Theban family possessed ninety-five slaves, most of them Asiatics. From this numerous Asiatic stratum, which was not confined to the delta or to the lower classes of the population, certain strong personalities had already ascended to the office of kingship by early Dynasty 13; they were probably able to wrest it for themselves as military leaders. These Semitic rulers, among them one named Khendjer (Boar) and another actually called Asiatic, erected pyramids of brick at Dahshur and Saqqara, as did other kings of Dynasty 13. It can no longer be doubted that nearby el-Lisht remained the preferred Residence until the end of the eighteenth century B.C.E. The kings of Dynasty 13 were attentive to the mortuary cults of their great predecessors who were buried there, but their building activity was especially evident in Upper Egypt, and Manetho therefore designates the dynasty as Theban. From Papyrus Boulaq 18, an account book of the royal court that affords us a modest cross-section of affairs at the court, it emerges that Sebekhotpe III (c. 1710 B.C.E.) came to Thebes only for a festival of the god Montu, though he otherwise resided at el-Lisht. As the Asiatic intruders in the delta made themselves generally independent of the central government and various kinglets began to reign there (Manetho's Dynasty 14 of Xois), Upper Egypt became the ultimate refuge of Dynasty 13. The last kings of the dynasty left monuments only in the area between Abydos and Aswan.

In the first half of the seventeenth century B.C.E., movements of peoples in western Asia, which had been triggered by migrations of Indo-Aryans, also affected Egypt. The Egyptians called the foreign leaders *hekau-khasut*, "rulers of foreign countries," a title that had been applied to Bedouin chieftains in the Middle Kingdom and that ancient Greek writers would later reproduce as Hyksos. The Hyksos were certainly not a people, but rather a small ruling class, evidently west Semitic, that had wrested for itself the political leadership of the tribes of Syria-Palestine by means of their dynamic policies as well as their new, superior weapons and battlefield tactics; later, they also overran the delta, founding a dynasty of their own at Avaris around 1630 B.C.E. This was the first Egyptian dynasty to consist entirely of foreigners. The Hyksos monarchs claimed sovereignty over all of Egypt and apparently also over adjoining portions of Palestine, though they allowed dependent kings to remain as vassals in certain places, most notably in Thebes. Dynasty 16, the lesser Hyksos whom Manetho lists alongside Dynasty 15, probably consisted of such vassal kings. The actual Hyksos dynasty consisted of only six kings, among whom Khian (or Khiyaran, c. 1600 B.C.E.) was especially prominent. Since monuments of this ruler are attested at Bubastis as well as at Gebelein, south of Thebes, he must have been recognized as overlord in all of Egypt.

Objects bearing the name of Khian have also been found at Knossos on Crete, at Baghdad, and at the Hittite capital of Boğazköy; Hyksos finds extend as far as Spain and Carthage, but they could have reached those points by trade or been carried there at a later date, so they do not constitute proof of a Hyksos empire. Royal and private scarabs of the Hyksos Period are attested at most of the sites excavated in Syria-Palestine, testifying to close relationships between Egypt and western Asia at this time. In Nubia, trade relations extended as far as the new capital of Kerma, as they had during the Middle Kingdom, though their scope and importance were now much diminished. Meanwhile, an independent Nubian principality took form at the southern boundary of Egypt, one that recognized a loose overlordship of the Hyksos monarchs. As in the First Intermediate Period, Nubians were prized as soldiers in the service of Thebes, and their shallow burials, known as Pan Graves, have been found as far north as the region of Asyut.

The Hyksos kings took over the worship of Seth from the northwest Semitic immigrants, but their throne names were compounded, according to pharaonic custom, with the name of the sun god, Re. Their administration, documented by innumerable stamp seals, was headed by a treasurer; no vizier has yet been attested. In other ways, like so many conquerors who would follow, they appropriated the traditional forms of Egyptian culture. What they themselves contributed was little, but it was technologically and politically important: the battle chariot drawn by horses, the more powerful composite bow, and a number of other improvements in weapons technology. The new cavalry revolutionized the conduct of war, making armies more mobile, and it thus would become an important instrument in the imperial policy of the New Kingdom. In the longer run, what was more important still was the close connection between Egypt and western Asia that was initiated in the Hyksos Period; it broke through the spiritual isolation of the Nile floodplain, which had endured since the time of Menes notwithstanding all trade relations, and created more possibilities for influence in both directions. The Egyptians proved to be more open-minded than their conquerors, whom they had previously regarded as despised Bedouin tribes that embodied Asia and its culture. Increasing familiarity with the religion, art, literature, music, and lifestyle of western Asia, especially Syria, quickly led to the adoption of foreign forms and concepts and stimulated creative imaginations, thus preparing the way for the flowering of the New Kingdom.

Around 1573 B.C.E., Apophis ascended the Hyksos throne at Avaris, perhaps as the third successor of Khian; for nearly four decades he was recognized as overlord by all the land. As late as his year 33, a Theban scribe made a copy of the mathematical Papyrus Rhind without making note of the local "king," who was, to the Hyksos, merely the "prince of the southern city." After the end of Dynasty 13, which was finally recognized only in the south, a Theban family assumed the royal titulary, thus founding Dynasty 17. Most of the several kings of this dynasty ruled only for brief periods and were undistinguished, having only local importance, though their vassal kingdom extended at least as far north as Abydos, where they appear as architects. In their choice of personal names, they in part followed Dynasty 13 (Sebekemzaf, Figure 24), to which they might have been related, and in part Dynasty 11 (Inyotef, Mentuhotpe), which served as their political model. The quality of life was poor in this Second Intermediate Period, and art once again sank back to a provincial level. Theban scribes therefore zealously preserved the great literary, religious, and scientific works of the earlier heyday; many texts have come down to us only as copies made in this period, such as the previously mentioned mathematical Papyrus Rhind, the surgical Papyrus Edwin Smith, and (probably somewhat earlier) Papyrus Prisse, which contains the Maxims of Ptahhotpe and the Instruction for Kagemni.

About 1550 B.C.E., the Theban king Seqenenre Tao, whose mother, Tetisheri, was the first of the series of great female figures of the New

24. Relief depicting Sebekemzaf I or II and the god Montu. Photo by U. Schweitzer.

Kingdom, felt strong enough to revolt against the elderly Hyksos king, Apophis; we know nothing about the course or the outcome of the early fighting, but the wounds on his mummy show that he met his death in battle. His son Kamose took over a kingdom that already stretched from the First Cataract to Cusae, north of Asyut, and he energetically pursued the struggle against the Hyksos. In the temple of Amun at Karnak, the king had his treasurer, Neshi, erect two stelae whose texts contain a lively, detailed account of his northern campaign. One of these stelae came to light in 1954, in undamaged condition, inside the foundation of a statue of Ramesses II, while fragments of the complementary stela, along with a schoolboy's copy, both preserving the beginning of its text, had already been known for some time.

We can thus now follow in detail the course of this important Theban campaign. At the beginning of the depiction, the king sits on his throne holding court; this is described according to the already standard formulae of the Königsnovelle. Against the advice of his officials, the king ceremoniously declares that he will no longer remain a mere "prince" next to the Hyksos monarch, who "shares the land with me" and who is designated as "ruler." The struggle is thus preceded by a formal termination of the previously recognized overlordship of the Hyksos. Kamose then advances north at the head of a flotilla of ships; with the conquest of Neferusi, he penetrates the strong Hyksos position in the nome of Hermopolis. Single-mindedly, without troubling himself with Memphis and the Faiyum, the Theban leader advances to the very walls of Avaris, but the strong fortifications of the Hyksos Residence and the superior chariot troops of the opponent compel him to change strategy. Since Kamose does not yet have a chariot force of his own, he does not involve himself in a major battle on land but rather remains on the river, engaging in operations in which the Nubian soldiers who are emphasized in the text prove especially reliable. While the Thebans are fighting in the north, far from their capital, Apophis attempts to involve them in a war on two fronts by means of an alliance with the ruler of Kush. His messenger is captured on the oasis road, however, and the Kushites remain neutral. The fact that the sacrosanct Hyksos messenger is released afterward shows that fixed conventions for international relations already existed, even in time of war.

The indications of an expedition to Nubia by Kamose are highly uncertain, and it was probably Ahmose who first regained for Egypt the fortress of Buhen, which had been so important in the Middle Kingdom. When Kamose died after a brief reign in about 1539 B.C.E., leaving his throne to Ahmose, possibly his brother, the Hyksos had in fact not yet been expelled from Egypt, though they had been driven back to the latitude of the Faiyum. It was left to the new king, who probably came to the throne quite young, to eliminate the foreign rule over the north. Ahmose thus became the third king, after Menes and Mentuhotpe I, to unite all Egypt. With his reign, we begin Dynasty 18 and the last of the three great periods of the flowering of ancient Egyptian culture.

THE NEW KINGDOM

When he assumed the throne, Ahmose (1539–1514 B.C.E.) found an international situation that was favorable to him. Apophis, the elderly Hyksos king, died in that year; following him, yet another ruler, Khamudi, occupied the throne of Avaris for a short time, while the Indo-Germanic Hittites, under their kings Khattushili I and Murshili I, made powerful thrusts from Anatolia against the rulers of northern Syria, who were perhaps dependents of the Hyksos. After fierce battles Aleppo was conquered by Murshili, leaving the Hyksos in no position to deploy all their power against Ahmose, who in the meantime had improved the strike power of his army by means of a chariot force. Memphis was stormed by the Thebans, while well-fortified Avaris seems to have held out for a while. After the fall of the capital, what remained of the Hyksos sphere of influence fell apart within a few years, around 1540 B.C.E. Ahmose took possession of the entire delta, and he advanced into southern Palestine to secure the Sinai region, with its important copper mines. He was perhaps recognized as the new overlord by the previous vassals of the Hyksos kings as far away as Syria. A few years later (1531 B.C.E.), the vacuum in power politics that had taken shape in the northern Euphrates area enabled the Hittite king Murshili I to make a raid on Babylon; shortly thereafter, the Kassites, who were originally mountain people, founded a new dynasty there. The political map of the contemporary world was thus fundamentally altered within a few decades. In this connection, the Minoan frescoes discovered in Ahmose's palace at Avaris also serve to emphasize Egypt's strong ties to Crete.

In the south, Ahmose at the very least restored Egyptian sovereignty over Wawat (Lower Nubia); monuments bearing his name have been found as far south as the island of Sai, between the Second and Third Cataracts. This expansion put an end to the hitherto independent principality of Kush. The newly won Nubian territory, which would prove indispensable to the economic strength of the New Kingdom because of its quarries and gold mines, was secured by strong fortresses as in the Middle Kingdom; it also received a tight Egyptian administration, which from this time until early Dynasty 21 was headed by a viceroy with the titles of King's Son (of Kush) and Overseer of the Southern Foreign Countries. Ahmose Zatayt, upon whom King Ahmose conferred this office, presumably stemmed from the ruling dynasty. Ahmose Zatayt's son Turi, who later succeeded him in office, was first commandant of the fortress of Buhen at the Second Cataract. There, King Ahmose and his successors erected a huge fortified complex, with the smaller restored fort of Dynasty 12 serving as its citadel; the new fortress wall, which was strengthened by exterior bastions, was constructed of bricks to a height of thirty-six feet and made secure by a wide moat.

After successfully uniting the land and initiating a foreign policy in the areas of Palestine and Nubia, Ahmose devoted himself to putting together a new central administration. In doing so, he relied more on the tight organization of the state in Dynasty 12 than on the looser structure of the Hyksos realm, though the design of the civil administration became simpler than it had been in the Middle Kingdom. The inheritability of office, which had always served as an ideal principle in Egypt, was now even more important. On the other hand, a nomarchy like that which had caused so much trouble for the kings of Dynasty 12 was unable to develop again, though there was tangible internal opposition to the king in the form of a rebellion led by the otherwise obscure Tetian. Only the colonial region of Nubia had an administrative center of its own, with the viceroy residing at Aniba. Even after the conquest of the north, Thebes at first remained the administrative center and seat of the vizier, while as the chief cult center of Amun, king of the gods, the city was also the religious capital of the land. In addition Ahmose displayed a special predilection for Abydos, where he had extensive tomb and mortuary complexes erected for himself and members of his family. Here stood the last royal pyramids, and his memory therefore remained alive for a considerable time in this center of Osiris worship; in the Ramesside Period, he was revered as a deity who gave oracles.

Though Ahmose had forged the political framework of the state anew after eliminating foreign sovereignty and had contributed an important stimulus to religion and culture, it was the reign of his son Amenophis I (1514–1493 B.C.E.) that laid the foundations for a new flowering of culture. This king was able to assemble a creative elite the likes of which Egypt had not seen since the age of the pyramids and the days of Senwosret I. Only by accident do we know the names of some of the theologians, poets, architects, artists, and scientists who were gathered around the king, such as the astronomer Amenemhet, who boasts in his tomb of having constructed a water-clock, or the architect Inene, who transformed a lonely valley in the Theban mountains into the royal burial place, inaugurating the legendary Valley of the Kings. The hidden rock-cut tomb of Amenophis I anticipated the new type of royal tomb, though it was located in the vicinity of the tombs of Dynasty 17, which were surmounted by small brick pyramids, at Dra Abu el-Naga. The few private tombs of this reign also lie in this northern portion of the extensive Theban necropolis. It is not known where most of the high officials of early Dynasty 18 were buried, but it seems that Amenophis I was regarded as the founder of this great new national cemetery, and he was venerated, along with his mother, Ahmes-Nefertari, as the tutelary deity of the Theban necropolis.

A calendar on the verso of Papyrus Ebers is dated to the ninth year of the king's reign (1506 B.C.E.), preserving for us the calendrical date of the heliacal rising of Sothis (the rising of the star Sirius just before sunrise) in that year and thus providing a solid basis for the exact chronology of the New Kingdom Actually, this has been disputed; but fortunately, the chronology can also be established independently of the Ebers date, which remains the subject of debate. The papyrus itself continues the already time-honored tradition of Egyptian medicine. Of even greater importance was the religious literature of the period, which not only carried on old traditions but also exerted a continuing influence on the future with its host of new concepts and forms of expression. Amenophis I's theologians imparted to a whole series of rituals the form they would maintain for centuries to come. One of these religious thinkers, who was also a writer of the highest rank, composed a work that would serve as the model for the new genre of guides to the hereafter for Amenophis I or for Tuthmosis I, from whose tomb we have the earliest preserved copy. The richly illustrated work bears the title Book of the Hidden Chamber but is known by its later abbreviated name, Amduat. It takes up old concepts regarding the topography of the hereafter, lending them a new and systematic form. The main connecting thread of the work is its depiction of the sun god's journey through the netherworld during the twelve hours of the night; in word and picture, the Amduat describes the regions of the mortuary realm, with its blessed dead and its damned who are separated by the Judgment of the Dead; the damned are tortured with a rich catalogue of infernal punishments. Antedating Dante by three whole millennia, the Amduat is the earliest depiction of Hell and the grim concept of eternal damnation. Also stemming from this fertile period of religious writing around 1500 B.C.E. is the Litany of Re, which identifies the king with the sun god during his journey through all the regions of the cosmos so as to effect his daily resurrection as the solar disc. Since the theologians of the New Kingdom regarded Osiris as a netherworldly, nocturnal manifestation of the sun god, persons turned in unprecedented numbers to this all-encompassing deity. Hymns to the rising and setting sun were composed, employing new turns of expression, and the god was inserted into great religious works or depicted alone at the entrances to private tombs and on stelae. Alongside concepts regarding creation, beliefs concerning the afterlife now also fell into the domain of the sun god. It might be only somewhat of an exaggeration to say that the course leading to Akhenaten's religious revolution, that is, his solar monotheism later in the dynasty, had already been set by the theologians and religious writers at the court of Amenophis I and his successor.

The rich store of spells regarding death, burial, and fate in the afterlife recorded in the Pyramid Texts of the Old Kingdom and the Coffin Texts of the Middle Kingdom were now supplied to the deceased in varying collections on papyrus. Magic and its varied practices continued to thrive in this Book of the Dead, which bears all the hallmarks of an age-old folk tradition, while the new mortuary texts intended principally for the king remained free of this magic. At court, the scribes were interested not in magical spells but rather in enigmatic (also called cryptographic) writing, a mysterious script in which obscure meanings underlay known hieroglyphs, making the script comprehensible only to the initiated, who took delight in variety and ambiguity and not in the simplification that at just that very time was producing the earliest alphabetic writing systems in Syria-Palestine.

As an architect, Amenophis I was especially prominent at Karnak, where the monarchs of the New Kingdom were to outdo one another in honoring Amun-Re by adding to his great temple until the complex became a veritable labyrinth of pylons, courtyards, halls, and chambers. The spiritual and artistic achievement of Amenophis I's reign was not disrupted by any demands from foreign policy. In western Asia, Hittites and Hurrians were struggling over supremacy in northern Syria, while in Nubia, the new viceroy, Turi, was keeping affairs in order and extending the triangle of fortresses located south of the Second Cataract—Semna, Kumma, and Uronarti—which are already familiar from the Middle Kingdom.

Tuthmosis I (1493–1482 B.C.E.) seems to have come from a collateral line of the royal house, so that dynastically, he must be regarded as the actual founder of Dynasty 18. Though the composition of the court and its intellectual aura scarcely changed, a new era in foreign policy began with Tuthmosis I. He accepted the challenge presented by the new power center in Syria, the kingdom of Mitanni, and he was the first monarch to plant the Egyptian flag on the banks of the Euphrates, thus becoming the founder of the Egyptian empire. Technologically, this considerable expansion beyond Egypt's previous isolation was stimulated by the horse and chariot, but it also corresponded to a change in attitude. For the first time, a sort of belief in progress had developed, and attempts were made to surpass previous accomplishments.

In the second year of his reign, the king ventured far beyond the well-secured fortresses south of the Second Cataract, leaving inscriptions in the area of the Third Cataract and evidently even reaching the Fourth Cataract. Upper Nubia (Kush) was thus incorporated into the Egyptian empire as a new province, and it was likewise secured by means of fortresses in the period that followed. Its administration, like that of Lower Nubia (Wawat), was placed in the hands of Turi, the dependable viceroy. Now that his African imperium stretched more than 900 miles due south from the Mediterranean coast, the king turned to western Asia. We know only the end of this Asiatic campaign, not what happened during its course, but Tuthmosis seems to have penetrated through all of Palestine and Syria to the upper Euphrates without any resistance worthy of mention. There, in the kingdom of Mitanni, he was first countered by this new world power center, which had in the meantime consolidated itself militarily against the Hittites and was to be Egypt's chief opponent in the century that followed. The king thus contented himself with marking the new border of his realm by means of stelae set up on the bank of the Euphrates, in the region of Karkamish, and with hunting Asiatic elephants in northeastern Syria, after which he returned to his Residence.

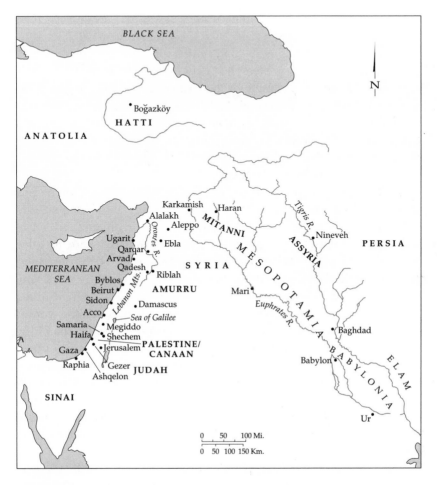

BLACK SEA

N

• Boğazköy

HATTI

ANATOLIA

Karkamish   Haran

Alalakh   • Aleppo

Ugarit •   **MITANNI**

Qarqar •   • Ebla

Arvad •

MEDITERRANEAN   Qadesh

SEA   Byblos   • Riblah

Beirut

Sidon   **AMURRU**

Acco   • Damascus

Samaria   • Megiddo   *Sea of Galilee*

Haifa   • Shechem

Gaza   • Jerusalem   **PALESTINE/**

Raphia   **CANAAN**

Ashqelon   Gezer   **JUDAH**

SINAI

Orontes R.

Lebanon Mts.

SYRIA

M
E
S
O
P
O
T
A
M
I
A

Tigris R.

ASSYRIA   • Nineveh

PERSIA

Mari •

Euphrates R.

• Baghdad

B
A
B
Y
L
O
N
I
A

Babylon •

E
L
A
M

Ur •

0   50   100 Mi.

0   50 100 150 Km.

Western Asia

Notwithstanding his great military successes in Asia and Africa, Tuthmosis I was by no means a hero only in battle. His court at Thebes remained the center of intellectual and spiritual life, while a military headquarters was established at Memphis, a more strategically suitable location because of its proximity to the Asiatic theater of war. From then on, the crown prince, designated generalissimo, would receive a military upbringing and training there. With Memphis the "chief headquarters," Egypt's foreign policy would remain oriented toward Asia for centuries. No special danger threatened from the south, and the borders established there by Tuthmosis I would prove to be lasting.

The chief artisan and architect Inene, whose career was crowned by the office of mayor of the capital city, was in charge of the king's extensive building activity at Karnak, the temple of Amun on the east bank of Thebes. There, within a few years, two pylons with a colonnade between them were erected in front of the sanctuary. For a century, the outermost of these, which we today count as the fourth pylon, would seal the temple off from the outside world; in front of it, the king had a pair of red granite obelisks erected. On the west bank, Inene supervised the work at the hidden location of the rock-cut royal tomb in the Valley of the Kings, which became the necropolis of the New Kingdom monarchs under Tuthmosis I. Along with the pyramid form, Amenophis I had already given up a close physical relationship between the tomb and its associated cult place; the royal mortuary temples were now located far from the tombs, on the edge of the cultivation. They were also dedicated to Amun, whose divine support had been sought by the kingship since Dynasty 17.

Since Amenmesse, the actual crown prince and generalissimo, predeceased his father, Tuthmosis I was succeeded by another of his sons, Tuthmosis II (1482–1479 B.C.E.). The new king elevated his half-sister Hatshepsut, who was descended from the founder of the New Kingdom through her mother, Ahmes, to the position of chief royal wife. The brief reign of Tuthmosis II was filled by demonstrations of military might in Nubia and Palestine as well as by lively building activity at the temple of Karnak. When he died in the spring of 1479 B.C.E., his marriage to Hatshepsut had produced only a daughter, Nefrure. The throne thus fell to the son of a lesser wife, Isis, who was still a minor; like both his predecessors, he bore the personal name Tuthmosis (Thoth is born). Under his throne name, Menkheperre, this third Tuthmosis (1479–1426 B.C.E.) would become, for his subjects as well as for neighboring peoples, an enduring and fearsome symbol of the grandeur of Egypt.

The young king's stepmother, Hatshepsut, acted as regent on his behalf. There had already been such female regencies in Egypt, but it was soon apparent that this energetic queen would not remain content with this status, nor did she intend to lay down the regency when the king reached his majority within a few short years. As early as February 1477 B.C.E., on the occasion of a procession of the barque of Amun, she had herself proclaimed king by will of the god and crowned with all due ceremony. And so the unheard-of happened: a woman assumed the purely masculine role of a pharaoh, conforming to it while stamping it with feminine characteristics. These events show the extent to which the Egyptian kingship's capacity for change could yield to the personalities of its respective bearers. In the Old and Middle Kingdoms, we find a clear-cut concept of kingship, while the personal idiosyncrasies of the rulers remain obscure. In the New Kingdom, beginning with Hatshepsut, we find that the ruling figures are clearly and uniquely delineated, while the contours of the institution of kingship are blurred. The weaker the experience of the institution's formal power, the more freely personalities could blossom—but also, the closer their bond to the will of the divine. Even Tuthmosis III based his legitimacy on an oracular decision on the part of Amun, which allows us to think that the priesthood of this god had now won political influence.

In her role as pharaoh, Hatshepsut had to assume warlike epithets ill suited to a woman and to the peaceful character of her reign, while royal ideology compelled her to have herself represented as a male or as a male sphinx. Yet within the conceptual restrictions imposed by the royal titulary and the traditional representations of monarchs, she often succeeded in expressing her feminine individuality: for instance, by having female bodily forms represented beneath the royal adornments, by designating herself "female Horus" or "daughter of Re" instead of the corresponding masculine titles, and by avoiding the usual title "Mighty Bull" in her Horus name.

For two decades (1477–1458 B.C.E.), the ruling power lay entirely in the hands of the queen and the ministers she appointed. After her coup d'état, she exercised the rulership no longer as a regent but rather as monarch of Egypt by virtue of divine command. Such unheard-of presumptuousness was mitigated by her coregency with a masculine partner (Figure 25). His stepmother's coup robbed Tuthmosis III of any prospect of exercising political power, to be sure, but he continued to reign nominally alongside her. Hatshepsut counted her own regnal years from Tuthmosis III's assumption of the throne, and she allowed

25. Relief depicting Hatshepsut and Tuthmosis III (far right) before the barque of Amun-Re. Red Chapel at Karnak. Photo by E. Staehelin.

her coregent to be mentioned in official inscriptions. Her only daughter, Nefrure, who had assumed Hatshepsut's title God's Wife (of Amun) and was intended to be the legitimate continuation of the dynastic line, died young; the aging queen was therefore obliged to resign herself to the idea of handing over the succession to her coregent.

Among the queen's leading statesmen were the spiritual and temporal heads of the temple of Karnak: the high priest of Amun, Hapuseneb, and the steward of this richest of all temples, Senenmut (Figure 26), who had also been entrusted with the upbringing of the crown princess, Nefrure. Both men, who shared in overseeing the queen's great building activities, were of humble origin; along with such native rising stars, Hatshepsut was also the first to appoint Asiatics to influential positions. In 1475 B.C.E., the vizierate passed from Ahmose Ametju to his son Useramun, though the latter was an insignificant figure compared to the two powerful favorites of the queen. In conjunction with this indubitably outstanding official elite, the queen imposed a new style on her monuments, her foreign policy undertakings, and the attitudes of her time, a style whose effects would prove to be long lasting. While her predecessors had even continued traditions of the Hyksos Period, her own reign rejected them as godless and was oriented instead to the classical model

26. Statuette of Senenmut.
Brooklyn Museum of Art,
Charles Edwin Wilbour Fund.
67.68. Photo courtesy of The
Brooklyn Museum.

of the Middle Kingdom; with that, she encountered already existing nationalistic trends that expressed themselves, inter alia, in the first condemnation of the god Seth, whom the Hyksos had preferred. Instead of
the imperialistic and militaristic policies of Tuthmosis I, there were
friendly relations with neighboring states; for Hatshepsut, economic
and cultural exchanges were paramount. Thus, while Egypt remained
passive and the Hittite realm was weakened by internecine warfare, the
Hurrian kingdom of Mitanni, which was headed by a ruling class of
Indo-Aryans, developed into a serious threat to the position achieved by
Egypt in Syria. But notwithstanding her predilection for peace, the
queen does not seem to have neglected the Egyptian army, and it has
been demonstrated that several campaigns were undertaken during her

reign; she must thus be given some credit for the swift military successes of her coregent.

Hatshepsut once again initiated, after a rather long interval, the traditional trading voyages to Punt on the Somali coast, where the Egyptians exchanged their own products (weapons, wares, jewelry) for incense as well as for ebony, ivory, gold, gum, valuable animal skins, and live animals. In 1471 B.C.E. the queen dispatched a noteworthy expedition there, under the supreme command of her treasurer, Nehesy; the events and the successful conclusion of the journey are commemorated in the Punt Reliefs of her mortuary temple. In building this temple (Figure 27), which was dedicated not only to the queen but also to the sun god, Re-Harakhty; the mortuary god, Anubis; Hathor; and especially Amun, she wanted to create a Punt in Egypt for the king of the gods. Like the myrrh terraces of that legendary land, the temple rises in three terraces from the first court, which was planted with myrrh trees, to the divine chapels hewed into the steep rear wall of the cliff-bound inlet of Deir el-Bahri. The harmonious insertion of the building into the rocky landscape testifies to the same love of nature that inspired the art of this period, especially the wall reliefs in the tombs at Thebes. Refinement of material culture and a taste for lyric poetry were on the rise from the time of Hatshepsut to the Amarna Period. In such fertile soil, delightful love lyrics took root and flourished, as well as solar hymns that vied with one another in poetic imagery to depict the god's care for all his creatures. On Crete, a lucrative goal for the queen's trading fleets, Egyptians encountered a related lyric tone in late Minoan art, one that continued to resonate in the palace art of late Dynasty 18 even after the fall of Knossos.

Amun, whose beloved daughter she felt herself to be, was Hatshepsut's most favored deity. She enlarged his earthly dwelling, the temple of Karnak, and on the occasion of her *sed* festival she adorned the temple with two granite obelisks that soared to a height of nearly 100 feet. Harkening back to earlier models, she had her divine origin and birth represented in the Divine Birth reliefs of her temple at Deir el-Bahri: Amun, lord of the gods, impregnates the queen with the child Hatshepsut, who is to be the legitimate heir to the throne, and it is promised that she will rule the world. But Hatshepsut also took care to display special piety regarding the memory of her earthly father, Tuthmosis I; his mummy was reburied in her own tomb, and the conduct of his mortuary cult was entrusted to the oldest son of the high priest Hapuseneb. The queen removed the damage wrought by the "godless" Hyksos at many sites in Egypt and Nubia, erecting new temples.

27. Mortuary temple of Hatshepsut at Deir el-Bahri. Photo © 1992 by Al Berens, Sure-design Graphics.

As a reigning monarch, Hatshepsut had to lay a claim to a tomb in the Valley of the Kings; Hapuseneb had the intended final resting place of the great queen excavated in the rock at the eastern end of a subsidiary valley separated by only a barrier of rock from her mortuary temple at Deir el-Bahri. Senenmut, her closest confidant, who as "greatest of the great ones in all the land" had an all-powerful influence on the affairs of state, was allowed to construct a new tomb for himself below the fore-court of the temple at Deir el-Bahri, whose construction he oversaw; though it took the form of a royal tomb, he had to eschew the royal Books of the Afterlife, the Amduat and the Litany of Re, and content himself with spells from the Book of the Dead and the Pyramid Texts, along with astronomical representations. The vizier, Useramun, on the other hand, had these royal texts included in his narrow burial chamber, where he is represented among the gods in the solar barque. No other monarchs of the New Kingdom permitted so great an assumption of royal privileges on the part of their officials. Senenmut was even al-lowed to have himself represented in the queen's mortuary temple, and a quartzite sarcophagus was executed for him, as though for a king. The high priest Hapuseneb evidently had a tomb in the Valley of the Kings; during the New Kingdom, high officials could be buried there by special grace of the king, but they had to be satisfied with undecorated shaft tombs.

Hapuseneb, Senenmut, and the treasurer, Nehesy, disappeared from official life at about the same time, circa 1462 B.C.E.; it was once thought that the queen's prominent ministers experienced a fall, but that now seems doubtful. Of her highest officials, only the vizier, Useramun, is attested later. He assumed the office of steward of the temple of Amun, which Senenmut had held, and he also maintained his offices after the queen's death; he thus had the trust of Tuthmosis III. After the early death of the crown princess, Nefrure, the approaching sole rule of Tuthmosis III loomed ever larger until it became a reality with the death of the queen in the winter of 1458–1457 B.C.E. Whether Hatshepsut came to a violent end we do not know. Not until some time after her death did an iconoclasm set in, one such as Egypt had not known before: statues of the queen were smashed to pieces, representations of her were hacked out of reliefs, her obelisks were walled in, and her name was erased from nearly every accessible monument. The later king lists omit her illegitimate reign. Of her high officials, evidently only the viceroy of Nubia fell victim to the change of regime; the new sole ruler accepted the rest, first and foremost the vizier, Useramun, who was succeeded in office a few years later by his nephew Rekhmire.

Tuthmosis III began his sole rule (1458–1426 B.C.E.) at a critical moment. Unchecked by the pacifist policy of his stepmother, a dangerous coalition of native princes in Syria had rallied around the prince of the city of Qadesh and sided with the rising great power of Mitanni. All Syria and a large part of Palestine were already lost to Egypt; the combined armed forces of the enemy were now on the move, threatening the last Egyptian bases on Asiatic soil. The new king immediately took steps to counter the danger. In the spring of 1457 B.C.E., he moved into Palestine with his army and attacked the coalition, which was prepared for battle, near Megiddo. The enemy force was defeated and its camp plundered, but this plunder hindered the immediate taking of the fortified city of Megiddo; the prolonged siege that followed ended after seven months with the besieged allowed to withdraw in freedom, though they were obliged to abandon their weapons, their horses, and more than nine hundred war chariots to the Egyptians. Smaller Egyptian divisions, advancing from the coast, had in the meantime harassed the hinterland of the enemy and recaptured the region around the Sea of Galilee. This first campaign thus did not restore the former extent of the Egyptian sphere of influence, but immediate danger was averted with the suppression of the enemy coalition, thus preparing the way for the recovery of the remaining territory.

Sixteen further campaigns were needed to win back and secure the Egyptian bases in Syria. Strategically, Tuthmosis III followed the plan of first acquiring a chain of bases along the Mediterranean coast as far as the Lebanon, so as to gain a secure basis for the push into the enemy's heartland in the north of Syria. A strong fleet assured the provisioning of the Egyptian garrisons in the port cities. In the north, the chain of bases reached at least as far as Byblos, where Tuthmosis III built a temple to Hathor, and perhaps farther still, to Ugarit. From this foothold, the king was finally able, on his eighth campaign (1447 B.C.E.), to penetrate as far as the Euphrates and thus to the interior of the kingdom of Mitanni. After battles near Aleppo, he crossed the river, which flowed from north to south and thus from the Egyptian point of view flowed upside down, near Karkamish and had new boundary stelae set up, after which he made a march of several days downstream. Since the king of Mitanni was avoiding battle, Tuthmosis III had to content himself with plundering the cities of the plain. The march home took him to the Orontes, where, following the example of his grandfather, he hunted elephants and crowned his most successful campaign with the taking of Qadesh. Knowledge of the Egyptian crossing of the Euphrates left a deep impression on the world of his day: the Hittites, the Babylonians, and the Assyrians sent embassies, and Egypt was once again the leading power in the territory of Syria. But a threat still existed from the kingdom of Mitanni, which had yet to be defeated, and in the following years repeated battles ensued, especially in the region of Aleppo. The extracts from the military daybooks that Tuthmosis III had inscribed in the temple of Karnak break off with the year 1438 B.C.E., with the result that the events in Syria during the last decade of his sole reign remain unknown. As seldom found in Egyptian historical writing, these so-called Annals evince an interest in depicting the course of history as something more than the enactment of timeless ritual, going so far as to include unique events and even failures.

Unlike his predecessors, Tuthmosis III was not satisfied with the simple recognition of his overlordship on the part of the princes of Syria and Palestine. Instead he imposed a rather tight administration on his Asiatic territory, as had long proved effective in Nubia. At its head was the general Djehuty, who had distinguished himself as a military leader on the first campaign; later the Asiatic sphere of influence would be divided into several provinces. Those princes who had submitted themselves to Egyptian sovereignty kept their territories; their sons were brought up at the royal court and many of their daughters found themselves in the royal harem. Egyptian garrisons secured the most important bases, while Egyptian chanceries concerned themselves with the administration of the area.

At the south of his empire, Tuthmosis III also reached beyond the previous borders. The region of Napata at Gebel Barkal, where he had a stela set up in 1433 B.C.E., was included in the province of Kush, and the Fourth Cataract would remain the southern boundary of Egypt for a long time to come. Here, the Egyptians came into contact with black Africans, who were henceforth to appear in representations in tombs along with other foreigners. A veritable river of gold flowed into Egypt from the gold mines of Nubia; in the reign of Tuthmosis III, it amounted to about 660 pounds per year, a huge amount for the economy of that time and one that made Egypt the much-courted dispenser of this sought-after precious metal for neighboring peoples.

In Tuthmosis III, military talent combined with greatness in statesmanship. In his own time, and for posterity, he was the great conqueror whose campaigns would live on among the people in many a tale of adventure. But at the same time, as a capable organizer he understood how to lend permanence to his conquests. He made sure that the crown prince, Amenophis, was familiar with the "work of (the war god) Montu" at an early age; the young prince grew up at Memphis, where the king certainly also stayed more often than at Thebes, the actual capital. Here the king was surrounded by a new class of military leaders, who soon also acquired political influence. But alongside this royal conqueror's many wars and the prominence of the military that they brought about, his nonmilitary achievements must not be overlooked. In addition to maintaining trade relations and consolidating the administration, he devoted himself in grand style to building activity in honor of the gods and goddesses. From Byblos to Gebel Barkal, temples were enlarged or newly built. In the Ptolemaic Period, the temples of Esna, Dendara, and Kom Ombo still referred to Tuthmosis III as the king who founded them anew. The temple of Amun at Karnak, however, stood far in the forefront, receiving the lion's share of the king's booty and foreign tribute. At the very beginning of his sole reign, at the east end of the temple, the king erected a festival court of stone with a clerestory for his mortuary cult and his festivals of renewal in the afterlife; in its form, the court resembled a basilica with three naves. The king had a pair of obelisks, which are today in London and New York, erected in front of the temple of the sun god at Heliopolis, and another pair erected at Karnak. And it cannot be regarded as surprising that in addition to the national triad of Amun, Re, and Ptah, the warrior god Montu and his sanctuaries at Madamud and Tod also received the special attention of the king.

When the great architect of the Egyptian empire died in March 1426 B.C.E., his son Amenophis II (1426–1400 B.C.E.) had already been lending support to the aging king as coregent for a short time. He had his father buried in the rock-cut tomb that had been prepared for him at the southernmost end of the Valley of the Kings and then endeavored with success, for a quarter of a century, to hold together the empire his predecessors had won. Even more so than his father, Amenophis II considered himself to be a warrior (Figure 28), and in his inscriptions, special emphasis is placed on his personal, superhuman accomplishments in war

28. Relief depicting Amenophis II smiting foreign prisoners. From the temple of Amun at Karnak. Photo by Sara E. Orel.

and sports, which would become an obligatory model for his weaker successors. The brutality that accompanied this attitude, though, seems to have been a personal trait of this king; he conducted his wars with a cruelty that was foreign to his father, and he had the bodies of slain princes hung from the bow of the royal ship. The adoption of warlike Asiatic deities was well suited to this new atmosphere. The royal court was dominated by men who had enjoyed a military upbringing alongside the king or who had proved their worth on his campaigns. The large extended family of the aged vizier, Rekhmire, who had held the highest office in the land for more than sixty years, had to cede its influence to the new king's comrades from childhood and war; the camaraderie he displayed in his communications with his closest followers is shown by the familiar tone of a personal letter from the king to his viceroy of Nubia, Usersatet, which has been preserved thanks to its "publication" on a stela.

In the first spring of his sole reign (1425 B.C.E.), Amenophis II set out for Syria to counter the advances made by the Mitannian king, Shaushtatar. By means of several campaigns in which a role was played for the first time by Ugarit, a port city occupied by an Egyptian garrison, the king was able to maintain his position on the Orontes, though he could not advance as far as the Euphrates. Mitanni was even able to carry the struggle into Palestine by instigating rebellions there. Toward the end of the reign of Amenophis II, however, a change in the balance of power becomes apparent. The Hittites once again became active in northern Syria, thereby threatening the expansion of the Mitannian realm at its flank. Even before the death of the king, the new situation perhaps led to overtures of friendship between Egypt and Mitanni, which would be successfully concluded under Tuthmosis IV.

Amenophis II was not his father's equal as an architect, but the warlike spirit of his reign was unable to inhibit the flourishing of all branches of art. The sarcophagus chamber of the king, decorated with scenes of deities and the Amduat with its visions of the netherworld, is a masterwork in the balance of its proportions, colors, and lines, and even today it captivates visitors.

His son Tuthmosis IV (1400–1390 B.C.E.; Figure 29) was not appointed to be successor from the very beginning. On a stela he had set up between the forepaws of the Great Sphinx at Giza, the new king related how in a dream, the sun god promised him the kingship if he would clear the sand away from his mighty lion form. The first great deed of his reign was to keep this promise.

29. Tuthmosis IV depicted four times in his tomb before various deities. Photo by A. Brod-beck.

With his reign, the age of an offensive policy in Asia was over, though Hittite penetration into northern Syria preoccupied the mighty forces of the kingdom of Mitanni. The location of Egypt's border on the Orontes was in the meantime pushed back to Qadesh, though the Syrian ports were retained, thanks to Egyptian supremacy at sea. The conclusion of a peace treaty with the kingdom of Mitanni brought a temporary relaxation of tensions; after lengthy negotiations, the treaty was followed by a dynastic marriage, and a daughter of the Mitannian king, Artatama, entered into the harem of Tuthmosis IV. Though he had a military upbringing in Memphis, the new king was not motivated by the warlike and brutal inclinations of his father. During his brief reign, he launched considerable building activity, gilding what was in his day the portal of the temple of Karnak at the fourth pylon and erecting in front of it a court with pillars inscribed with the king's wishes for a *sed* festival. He also had the obelisk now in the Lateran set up. Tuthmosis III had already prepared this obelisk, which was transported to Rome in the fourth century of our own era, but he had not erected it because its intended counterpart was not yet ready. Notwithstanding the architectural efforts he bestowed upon the temple of Amun, Tuthmosis IV endeavored to limit its economic and political power. The mortuary temple and the rock-cut tomb of the king, both intended to be substantially larger than the earlier constructions of Dynasty 18, remained uncompleted because of his early death, but they testify to a growing tendency toward the colossal, which would increase from the time of his son Amenophis III to its apogee in the Ramesside Period. This tendency was both complemented and mitigated by the delight in detail that permeates the art in the tombs from this reign. Standing between the peace that had reigned and the troubles yet to come, the lively grace that distinguishes the tombs of the astronomer Nakht, the grain scribe Menena, and other officials of Tuthmosis IV constitutes the high point of Egyptian painting.

In the early years of his reign, Amenophis III (1390–1353 B.C.E.; Figure 30) remained under the influence of his mother, Mutemwia. Against all tradition, he elevated Teye, the daughter of an official from the provincial city of Akhmim, to the position of Great Royal Wife; this sagacious and energetic woman grew into one of the most important female figures of the New Kingdom. Commemorative scarabs were issued on the occasion of their wedding, and the king also enjoyed issuing such bulletins regarding other events of his early reign, such as his hunts of lions and other wild animals and the construction of an artificial lake for Queen Teye near her native city of Akhmim.

Amenophis III's first decade, with its Nubian campaign and the king's great ritual hunts, was a last echo of the warlike tradition of the Tuthmosid era; in the three decades that followed, the king would remain enveloped in the oriental sumptuousness of his court, scarcely to emerge again. Queen Teye seems to have been the actual regent, and she was able to rely on a series of capable officials. Foreign policy thus took on feminine traits, as it had in the days of Hatshepsut. The king never set foot in the Asiatic provinces of his realm, thus declining to make Pharaoh's divinity and the irresistible power of his epiphany into a historical force. Instead, he—or rather Teye—conducted a practical policy of dynastic alliances through diplomatic marriages and rich gifts from Egypt's surplus of gold. He thus bought years of peace, but in the longer run, he bargained away his kingdom's position as a world power. With his gifts, he merely awakened the greed of his vassals and neighbors, while the political effect of his alliances sealed by diplomatic marriages remained slight. Far more weighty was the fact that Pharaoh, the earthly

30. Amenophis III wearing the Khepresh crown. Egypt, Dynasty 18, c. 1391–1353 B.C. Granodiorite, 39.1 × 30.25 cm. © The Cleveland Museum of Art, 1998, Gift of the Hanna Fund (1952.513). Photo courtesy of The Cleveland Museum of Art.

representative of the sun god to his Asiatic vassals, remained invisible, with the result that they turned to other luminaries beginning to shine in Syria, among them the Hittite king, who was also designated Sun.

In 1382 B.C.E., after protracted negotiations, the king was able to receive Gilukhepa, a daughter of the Mitannian king, Shuttarna, into his harem along with 317 ladies-in-waiting; this event was also celebrated by a commemorative scarab. There followed marriages to the daughters of lesser dynasts, to a Babylonian princess, and, toward the end of his reign, to Tadu-Khepa, another Mitannian princess; she was the daughter of the new king, Tushratta, who cultivated especially close relations with the Egyptian court. Politically, Tushratta had every reason to do so: around 1365, he had been able to repulse a direct attack by the new Hittite king, Shuppiluliuma, and send a share of the booty to his future son-in-law; but in the period that followed, an increasing number of the vassal princes sided with the Hittites, triggering a political upheaval that would finally bury the weakened kingdom of Mitanni before the Egyptians could rouse themselves to action. We are quite well informed about the events in Syria during the last years of Amenophis III and the reign of his son, thanks to the discovery and study of the archive of diplomatic correspondence at el-Amarna; further light is shed by the archive at the north Syrian coastal city of Ugarit, which at first remained under Egyptian influence. The ringleader of the insurgent movement was Abdi-Ashirta of Amurru, who ruled over the area between Ugarit and Byblos; officially, he behaved like a loyal Egyptian vassal so as inconspicuously to extend his base of power at the cost of other vassals. Prominent among the loyal vassals was Ribhaddi of Byblos, who in innumerable letters requested Egyptian intervention. After a long delay, a small armed force was dispatched, and it proved able to stabilize the situation temporarily during the king's last years.

Amenophis III's Nubian provinces delivered gold in quantities "like sand" for his gift-giving policy, and in return the king embellished Nubia with magnificent temples. Already during their lifetimes, statues of the royal couple were worshiped as divine, along with Amun, in the two temples of Soleb and Sedeinga north of the Third Cataract. The king would be surpassed only by Ramesses II in the number and colossal scale of his buildings. The temple of Amun at Karnak received a new pylon, and it was connected to the Nile by an avenue of sphinxes. On the west bank, the king's mortuary temple was to overshadow all those built to date in its size and magnificence, but time has preserved only modest remains of it, including the two colossal statues of sandstone known as the Colossi of Memnon (Figure 31); sixty-five feet high and weighing 720 tons apiece, they dominate the Theban plain to this very day. A colossal yet perfect harmony of proportions distinguishes the temple of Luxor, the most beautiful of the preserved buildings of Amenophis III, whose purpose was the ongoing renewal of his divinity.

As his architect, the king preferred his namesake, Amenhotpe son of

31. Colossi of Memnon (Amenophis III) at the site of the mortuary temple of Amenophis III. Photo © 1996 by Joseph Garcia, Suredesign Graphics.

Hapu. At the end of his rapid rise, which took him from scribe of recruits to steward of Queen Sitamun, this official received the royal privilege of a mortuary temple of his own. He lived on as a sage in popular memory, and in the Ptolemaic Period he was worshiped, like the sage Imhotep, as a god of healing and son of the Apis bull. The enormous amount of royal favor accorded to him, which calls to mind the similar acts of Hatshepsut, put a strain on the ethos of an officialdom that, surrounded by the overrefined, splendor-loving, and secularized society of the cosmopolitan cities of Thebes and Memphis, was already menaced by a plenitude of temptations.

Amenophis III had nearly six hundred statues of the lion-headed goddess Sakhmet set up in the temple of Mut at Karnak and in his mortuary temple; today, the majority of them are scattered throughout the world's museums. Did the sick king wish thus to put the dangerous goddess, who both sent and healed diseases, in a lenient mood? If so, we cannot see in him, for all his secularization, an enlightened monarch. It seems that religious interests were very much alive in him, notwithstanding the worldly splendor of his court. Animal cults found support from the royal court, while the worship of divinized kings that began at this time, especially Amenophis I, reflects the same yearning on the part of wider circles for new means of mediation between the human and the divine realms. The encounter with the religious world of Asia, with its different nature, led to a freer and more critical attitude toward tradition and to thinking that extended beyond the boundaries of a national religion. Those keeping in step with the times had to think through the concept of the divine in a new, more universal manner, thus enabling them to adopt to the pansyncretism of the Litany of Re. One of these progressive thinkers was the officer Aya, who was perhaps a relative of Teye and whom the king appointed tutor to his son Amenophis. When the prospect of the throne opened itself to the young prince following the death of his older brother, Tuthmosis, his tutor (the Egyptian title was god's father) found himself in a key position that enabled this devious man to become the éminence grise of the Amarna Period.

The king's last years were clouded by illness that could not be exorcised, not even by the healing image of the goddess Ishtar that his son-in-law, Tushratta, sent to him. The *sed* festival and the two repetitions of it that the king celebrated in his Theban palace at el-Malqata were supposed to effect the ritual renewal of the power of the aging king, and the elevation of two of his daughters, Sitamun and Isis, to the position of royal wife was probably connected with the idea of renewal; Teye, however, remained his chief wife. Amenophis III died in the summer of 1353 B.C.E., and he was buried in a secluded valley that branches off from the actual Valley of the Kings.

It has often been maintained that Amenophis III had a long coregency with his son Amenophis IV (1353–1326 B.C.E.; Figure 32), but this assertion cannot withstand serious scrutiny. During the early years of his reign, it was rather his mother, Teye, who, relying on seasoned officials of Amenophis III, had a decisive influence on the affairs of state. Her person guaranteed continuity of Egyptian policy for the allies in Asia, especially Tushratta. The new king had himself represented making offerings to the national god, Amun, as was usual, but he also displayed a preference for a deity called Aten, whom he at first worshiped as a manifestation of the old sun god Re-Harakhty. Tuthmosis IV and Amenophis III had already accorded divine honors to this Aten as the sun disk, but in the person of the new king, a single-minded rigor soon made itself visible, one that tended to excess and turned existing concepts and artistic conventions into fuel for a comprehensive revolution.

The course of this revolution, which successively affected the areas of art, administration, and religion, reveals careful planning and shows that Amenophis IV was anything but a religious zealot. In the king's fourth

32. Colossal statue of
Amenophis IV/Akhenaten,
originally from Karnak. Cairo
Museum. Photo by Nancy J.
Corbin.

regnal year (1350 B.C.E.), the high priest of Amun, whose political power
had already been circumscribed under Tuthmosis IV, was dispatched into
the eastern desert at the head of a quarrying expedition and thus removed for a time from what was happening in the capital. Perhaps the
king used this period to realize his revolutionary concepts for the first
time in the decoration of the temple he had built for the Aten at Karnak.
With their expressionism, the statues and reliefs in this temple make
a mockery of traditional aesthetic sensibilities. Employing the logical
consistency that distinguished all his actions, the king had himself

represented as the "father and mother" of his subjects, which Pharaoh, as the earthly representative of the creator god, had always been, though no one had previously dared to portray the king as a fecundity figure with female traits. This artistic boldness would also distinguish the Amarna Period. Inspired by the notion that anything can be expressed pictorially, artists created a whole series of enduring symbols, one of which, the ouroboros—a snake biting its own tail—lives on to this day. The monumental excess that had stamped the reign of Amenophis III was temporarily replaced by a return to smaller, more human scales and forms.

Along with these political measures and the coining of a new artistic style, Amenophis IV changed the appearance and the designation of the sun god he worshiped. In the place of the falcon-headed Re-Harakhty-Aten, there appeared the sun disk with rays. The king thus actualized an image that had long been expressed in literature: the rays of the sun protectively embracing all creatures and endowing them with life. In the colossal statues at Karnak, the god is interpreted and represented as the creator of all, while as the sun disk with rays he is the maintainer of his creation. As ruler of all creation, the god celebrated *sed* festivals of his own, and he received an ingenious titulary, which was enclosed in two royal cartouches. No trace exists of a persecution of other deities at first, but the sun disk with rays took Amun's place as the new national god.

This new style became law in the workshops of the palace. Soon the officials also had to comply with it in their tombs, especially the vizier, Ramose, who was still in office but who was relieved of his post a little later, along with other high officials whom Amenophis IV had inherited from his father. The king surrounded himself with a new group of civil officials, who were in large part from the lower classes or foreigners; along with Ramose, there was a northern vizier, Aper-El, an Asiatic, whose tomb is at Saqqara. These new subordinates were "nobodies" whom the king promoted ("built," to translate the ancient Egyptian term literally) to influential positions and who remained most obsequiously devoted to him; never had Egyptian officials bent their backs so deeply before their lord as in the representations of the Amarna Period. With this step, Amenophis IV had in his hands the political power to effect, against any opposition, his carefully planned reorganization of the state and its religion. Above all, this included the founding of a new Residence on virgin soil "belonging to no god and no goddess" and a change in the king's personal name. Both measures were unprecedented in Egyptian history and must have filled with consternation anyone committed to venerable tradition.

The king sought a location for his new capital in Middle Egypt, nearly halfway between Memphis and Thebes; today, the site is usually called el-Amarna, after the name of a modern Bedouin tribe. There, in his sixth regnal year, the area of the city was marked out by boundary stelae, though the court might well not have moved there until the end of the following year (1346 B.C.E.), after the first palaces, temples, and living quarters had been made ready. A short time earlier, the king had changed his personal name, Amenophis (Amun is gracious), to Akhenaten (pleasing to Aten) and celebrated his general renewal with an early *sed* festival. It appears that the Horizon of Aten, as el-Amarna was called in Egyptian, served as the cult place of the god Aten but as home only to the closer court circle around the king, while a larger part of the country's administration remained at Memphis and Thebes.

As soon as the royal court was settled in the new Residence, Akhenaten began to eradicate the traces of the past with a rigor that had already proved reliable. Gangs of iconoclasts swarmed throughout the land and as far away as distant Soleb in Upper Nubia, and wherever they encountered the name of Amun, they applied their chisels, even on the tips of obelisks, underneath the gilding of columns, and in archived letters written in cuneiform. The names of other deities were erased, especially those that were animal in form, though less systematically; sometimes even the hieroglyph for god fell victim to their wrath. We do not know the fate of the old temples, their priesthoods, or their considerable property; their cultic function was supposed to be assumed by sanctuaries of the new god, which were begun at Memphis and in Nubia, among other places. With the king's ninth year (1345–1344 B.C.E.), his religious revolution was complete. At that time, the god Aten received a new titulary, from which the old divine names Harakhty and Shu were removed; in the future, Re and Aten would be the only valid names of the god. Akhenaten had thus effected a monotheism as rigorous as Islam. At the same time, he had transformed himself from the high priest of Re-Harakhty, as he had styled himself at the beginning of his reign, into the promulgator of a new teaching and the sole intermediary between the god and humankind. His followers prayed before household altars depicting the royal family under the sun disk with its rays, and in their tomb inscriptions, they emphasize their personal instruction by the king, the only one who knew the essence of the god. Amarna religion can thus be characterized by the brief formula, "There is no god but Aten, and Akhenaten is his prophet."

The intimate representations of the royal family in public cannot deceive us regarding the deepened cleft between the royal prophet and his subjects. They derive from the emotional attitude of the period and were supposed to make it clear that the love and affection these people had for one another was a work of Aten and pleasing to him; they thus served as propaganda for the new teaching. Aten was supposed to embody light, life, and love; the nightside of reality was an empty place in Akhenaten's religious conception of the world, and the concerns of the Amduat and related compositions are absent from Amarna. The king's gaze, directed only at the goodness of the god, overlooked his fearsomeness. With its devotion to the bright and cheerful aspects of existence, the Amarna Period gives the impression of an idyll—which it doubtless was not. Despite the stress on the devotion of his officials, Akhenaten's police troops, made up of foreign soldiers, must have intervened often enough, and while the thoughts of the king lovingly contemplated the universal nature of his god, the Egyptian empire was being shaken to its very foundations.

When the capital was later abandoned, the Asian office of Akhenaten's "state department" left behind a portion of its documents. Thanks to the rescue of this archive, though it was not entirely successful, we have a lively picture of the events in Syria-Palestine between 1360 and 1340 B.C.E., though the cuneiform letters and drafts bear no dates, making it difficult to reconstruct the exact sequence of events. It is clear that when Akhenaten ascended the throne, Egypt's fronts in Syria were again thrown into agitation, and that once again the troublemaker was Amurru, under its prince, Abdi-ashirta. The cries for help from the few city-states whose princes remained loyal went unheard, and a newer, more dangerous adversary arose in the person of Aitakkama of Qadesh, who aligned himself with the Hittites. While Amenophis III had lent a personal touch to his diplomatic correspondence with Asia, his son left foreign affairs to his officials. The unrest soon spread from Syria to Palestine, though there, the troubles were more a matter of the machinations of individual princes and incursions by predatory bands of people known as the Khabiru. Worse was the loss of the northern harbors, which robbed the Egyptians of their supply bases; Ugarit sided with the Hittites, while Byblos, after the expulsion of the loyal Ribhaddi, went over to Aziru, the new king of Ammuru. The latter was constrained to come to terms with the superior Hittites. With the conquest of Aleppo and Alalakh and his sovereignty over Aziru and Aitakkama, the Hittite king, Shuppiluliuma, was lord of Syria, with only Damascus remaining on the side of the Egyptians. The kingdom of Mitanni, Egypt's most important ally, was thus isolated, and after the assassination of Tushratta, it was finished as a great power. Except for summoning Aziru to the royal court, Akhenaten beheld these dangerous developments without taking action.

A victory stela of year 12 (1342 B.C.E.) relates a campaign in Nubia, though it was modest in scale, with only 145 prisoners taken. There are no further official documents from the years that followed, but in connection with a visit by Aziru to the royal court, there was lively foreign policy activity aimed at saving the situation in western Asia. In these late years, the king's second wife, Kiya, seems to have played an important role at the royal court, along with Nefertiti and the latter's oldest daughter, Meritaten, but even she brought no solution to the problem of succession to the throne, which was now acute.

Since his chief wife, Nefertiti (Figure 33), had thus far borne him six daughters but no son, Akhenaten decided to make his young relation Smenkhkare his son-in-law and perhaps also his coregent, thus safeguarding the transition on the throne. At about the same time, Nefertiti died or perhaps fell into disgrace, since her name was replaced on some monuments by that of the crown princess, Meritaten. Additionally, following the example of his father, Akhenaten elevated two of his daughters to the queenship. Toward the end of his reign, the king must have sensed the failure of his revolution, which was to outlive him only briefly. Smenkhkare had a mortuary temple, which was also dedicated to Amun, built at Thebes, thus beginning a transition period of about five years during which Amun and Aten were worshiped next to each other at Thebes and el-Amarna. Radical persecution had not been able to exterminate the old deities of the land, and their worship had been kept up even by Akhenaten's officials; now, one could once again pray to Amun and Osiris without fear of the royal spies.

Shortly thereafter, at the beginning of 1336 B.C.E., Akhenaten died, and Smenkhkare also passed away after a brief reign. Their successor was Tutankhaten (1333–1323 B.C.E.; Figure 34), who was perhaps a brother of the coregent and also a son-in-law of Akhenaten. The "god's father" Aya acted as regent for the new king, who was still a boy; after already having been the most influential counselor during the reign of Akhenaten, this man now set the policy for the following decade, which amounted to a general though nonviolent restoration. The Residence remained at el-Amarna for another two years and was finally moved to Memphis in 1331. Amun's city of Thebes would never again be the capital of Egypt, and the restoration work of Aya and the latter's successor, Haremhab,

33. Fragment of a relief depicting Nefertiti. The Brooklyn Museum of Art, Gift of Christos G. Bastis (78.39). Ph
courtesy of The Brooklyn Museum.

can thus scarcely be interpreted as the reaction of the priesthood of
Amun. From Memphis, the young king, who was now called Tutankhamun, issued his Restoration Decree, definitively ending the brief but
eventful episode of Amarna. Aten was no longer invoked, but neither
was he persecuted; his memory just faded away.

The Amarna interlude had a lasting effect in a number of areas. Late
Egyptian, the colloquial language of the New Kingdom, was employed
as a written language from the reign of Akhenaten on, and in the Ramesside Period it produced a rich narrative literature; the older Middle
Egyptian remained in use for religious texts, however, until the end of
Egyptian culture. Aten's character as a universal god who, according to
Akhenaten's conviction, had even created the other races of humankind
and given them their distinctive languages and natures passed to other
deities; in the Book of Gates, composed at about this time as a new royal
guide to the hereafter, Re and Horus care for Egyptians and foreigners
alike as their "small cattle." Even stronger was the continued influence
of the art of the Amarna Period. Freed of its original excesses in the later
years of Akhenaten and of its dogmatic prescriptions under his successors, it attained its richest expression with its free rendering of motion

34. Solid gold funerary mask of Tutankhamun. Cairo Museum. Photo by Nancy J. Corbin.

and emotion. Famous reliefs of this late Amarna Period have been found in the tombs of the highest officials of Tutankhamun at Saqqara, the old cemetery of Memphis.

Generalissimo Haremhab, who was the most powerful man in the state next to Aya, also had a tomb prepared there. He proved able to lead Egypt's foreign policy out of its passive stance; in Syria, he led a thrust against Qadesh, and in Nubia a smaller campaign. At first nothing more could be accomplished than the securing of the remaining bases. Meanwhile, the young king endeavored to revive the cults of the old gods and goddesses throughout the land. At Thebes, he decorated the unfinished colonnade of the Temple of Luxor with festival scenes, and he had the tribute of the Nubian provinces presented to him there on the occasion of an official visit, but the importance of the proud metropolis continued to wane. Aside from the viceroy Huy, only priests such as Parennefer, the new high priest of Amun, and lesser officials continued to have themselves buried in the hills of the cemetery on the west bank. The representations in their tombs no longer displayed the cheerful this-worldliness of Dynasty 18, turning once again to the afterlife with an earnest and simple piety. But Thebes remained the burial place for the kings reigning in the distant north for another 250 years.

When Tutankhamun, who was barely an adult, died in the winter of 1323–1322 B.C.E., the actual regent, Aya, made a claim to the throne. This led the widowed Ankhesenamun, a daughter of Akhenaten, to decide on a bold step; she made an offer to the most dangerous opponent of her land, the Hittite king, Shuppiluliuma, to make one of his sons her husband and thus to install him as ruler of Egypt. The cautious monarch first made inquiries, and such a personal union of the two great kingdoms proved possible: Prince Zananza was dispatched to Egypt, but he was assassinated en route. In the meantime Aya, with the support of the military commander-in-chief, Haremhab, was able to eliminate the opposition to his claim to the throne. He appropriated the royal tomb that had been prepared, along with its associated mortuary temple, and he had the mummy of Tutankhamun buried in a tomb that had probably been intended for the use of someone else and could barely contain the quantities of goods customary in a royal burial. Accident preserved this improvised burial almost intact to an astounded posterity. Since Aya (1323–1319 B.C.E.), who was already well on in years, had no male heir, he designated the capable generalissimo Haremhab as his successor, with the title "deputy of the king". While Aya was still king, the latter had to repel a retaliatory military campaign on the part of the Hittites;

shortly thereafter, the death of the great Shuppiluliuma freed Egypt of its most dangerous adversary.

In the opinion of the Ramesside Period that was to follow, Haremhab (1319–1292 B.C.E.) was the first legitimate king since Amenophis III; like Hatshepsut, the Amarna kings fell victim to proscription, and this posthumous correction of history led modern researchers astray for many years. Haremhab himself in no way contemplated an obliteration of the Amarna Period but rather attempted to combine tradition with revolution and thus initiate a new and practicable course of action. Though he tore down temples of the Amarna Period and reused them in constructions of his own, he was only following a precedent set by earlier kings. He incorporated the reign of Aya into his own year count, and his reforms were directed against abuses in the administration and the economy of the land and corruption and high-handedness on the part of officials, problems that would prove to be typical in the Ramesside Period. The king visited Amun's city of Thebes only once yearly, on the occasion of the Opet festival, but he provided for the long-neglected temple of Amun at Karnak with new, large-scale building projects. In the course of his reign he erected or completed three new pylons there, and he began the construction of the great hypostyle hall between the Second and Third Pylons; the columns of the middle nave, at least, with their height of nearly sixty-nine feet, seem to go back to him.

In Syria, fresh battles arose with the Hittites, on whose side we once again find the old Aziru. Peace then ensued for a time, for the opponents of Egypt were weakened by a lengthy plague and their own constant fighting. After the provisional solutions that had been devised for Tutankhamun and Aya, Haremhab returned to the traditional form of the rock-cut royal tomb, though in his sarcophagus chamber, he replaced the Amduat with a new Book of the Netherworld, the Book of Gates. Haremhab appointed the seasoned front-line officer Paramessu to be his successor, and he provided him, as "deputy of his majesty in Upper and Lower Egypt," with power like that he himself had been accorded by Tutankhamun and Aya. Paramessu ascended the throne in 1292 B.C.E., and as Ramesses I (1292–1290 B.C.E.), he was the founder of Dynasty 19. Only now, in the two decades that followed, was an effort made to obliterate the traces of the Amarna Period, restoring the divine names that had been hacked out in the temples and persecuting the memory of the "heretic kings" by omitting them from the official king lists.

Ramesses I's reign was too short to leave behind substantial traces. As king, he continued the construction work on the hypostyle hall at Karnak, the oversight of which had been entrusted to him as vizier. When he died it was once again possible, for the first time in sixty years, for the crown to pass in a direct line of succession from father to son. Sethos I (1290–1279 B.C.E.; Figure 35), who was already the real regent of the land before ascending the throne, considered himself the founder of a new era, a "repeating of creation," with the establishment of a new order after the chaos of the Amarna Period.

As shown by preserved accounts from the early years of Sethos I, the royal court resided principally in Memphis; occasionally it was also in Heliopolis or Thebes, or traveling in the eastern delta. The latter area, which was perhaps the home of Dynasty 19, was to be the new center of the realm. In the vicinity of the Hyksos city of Avaris, near modern Qantir, the king erected a palace complex and revived the worship of Seth, who had been venerated by the Hyksos and later condemned. Like his grandfather, Sethos I was named after this god, and as crown prince he had borne the title of high priest of Seth. Seth thus joined ranks with Amun, Re, and Ptah, the deities venerated as a trinity in Papyrus Leiden

35. Relief at Abydos depicting Sethos I. Photo by Sara E. Orel.

I 350; at this time, the divisions of the Egyptian army came to be named after these four gods.

The king set out on his first campaign to Asia at the head of these divisions shortly after he came to the throne. His initial goal was the pacification of Palestine, but the campaign continued as far as the Lebanon, thereby securing the entire hinterland in preparation for a new clash with the Hittites. The regaining of Syria began during a subsequent campaign of Sethos I with a successful attack on Qadesh and Amurru, and it would later be continued by his son. The king was also militarily active in Nubia, and he had to repel an attack by the Libyans on the western edge of the delta: here, triggered by a migration of Berber tribes, loomed a new and serious danger to Egypt. Along with family and religious reasons, the threat posed to Memphis by Libyan tribes created perhaps a political reason for moving the royal Residence.

At Abydos and Karnak, major monuments indicating the king's indefatigable building activity have survived the ages. In the city holy to Osiris, god of the dead, Sethos I erected a cenotaph (false tomb, Figure 36) that was a reproduction of the mythic tomb of Osiris, and in front of it stood a temple for his own mortuary cult and for the cults of six deities; in its sharply delineated, well-proportioned reliefs we see no hint of the impending decline in artistic quality. At Karnak, the hypostyle hall, with its 134 columns, was now completed; Sethos I began to embellish it with reliefs and painted ornamentation that mitigated the oppressive force of this primeval marsh made of stone. The painted reliefs of the long corridor and the innumerable chambers of his rock-cut tomb in the Valley of the Kings contain a collection of all the important religious texts of this period, including the eschatological Book of the Heavenly Cow with its account of the intended destruction and fortunate salvation of the human race. Sethos I's mother, Sitre, received a tomb in another remote desert valley; this Valley of the Queens would be the resting place of the queens and princes of the Ramesside Period.

During his reign of sixty-six years, which was exceeded in length only by that of Pepy II, Ramesses II (1279–1213 B.C.E.; Figure 37) developed into a record setting pharaoh. His building projects were without precedent in number and in their colossal size. He was not the match of Tuthmosis III as a military leader, but he had to contend with more difficulties and opposition than did the earlier monarch. His long reign was a continuation and a fulfillment of what had preceded it, but it was lacking in creative originality. Even the city so closely connected with his name, the House of Ramesses (Pi-Riamsese, biblical Piramses) near Qan-

36. Cenotaph of Sethos I at Abydos. Photo by U. Schweitzer.

tir in the eastern delta, so often the subject of song in this period, was something he expanded out of the palace and dwelling quarters of his father. With the help of the children of Israel (according to biblical tradition; Egyptian sources are lacking), he had a series of splendid temples built there, and he adorned them with sphinxes, obelisks, and statues, most of them not newly created but rather conveyed there from all parts of the realm. Around 1260 B.C.E., the top levels of the administration, whose official ranks had been heavily infiltrated by foreigners, followed the royal court from Memphis to Ramesses's new city.

A first Asiatic campaign by the young king led to the annexation of Amurru under its king, Benteshina, with the result that the Egyptian sphere of influence once again extended as far as Ugarit. The Hittite king, Muwattalli, then threw his entire military might onto the scale in an effort to win back Amurru. In May 1274 B.C.E., Muwattalli awaited the Egyptian advance from the south near Qadesh, the strategically located city on the Orontes, along with his allies and 3,500 battle chariots.

37. Statue head of Ramesses II at the temple of Luxor. Photo © 1992 by Al Berens, Sure-design Graphics.

He succeeded in tricking Ramesses II, and by means of a sudden attack by his chariotry, he scattered half the Egyptian forces while the other half was still on the march. Though Ramesses was able to prevent a total defeat, he had to break off his advance and leave Amurru to the Hittites. Further battles in Syria and Palestine, which had once again become restive, dragged on until 1270 B.C.E. But the two great powers proved willing to turn from confrontation to a peaceful settlement, and after protracted negotiations, a treaty of friendship and alliance was solemnly concluded in November 1259 B.C.E. The treaty, written on silver tablets and preserved to us in Akkadian and Egyptian copies, put an end to the bellicose contendings of the two great powers, obligated them to mutual military assistance in the event of rebellion or enemy attack, and arranged for the return of political fugitives. The Hittite king, hitherto called the "enemy of Khatti" in Egypt, was now recognized as the "great king of the land of Khatti," though he later felt obliged to complain that Ramesses II was treating him "like a subject." The establishment of a boundary proceeded on the basis of the status quo, so that a portion of Amurru was retained by Egypt, while Qadesh remained Hittite.

This earliest preserved international treaty between two great powers, evidently concluded according to Hittite law, was scrupulously adhered to by both parties and afforded them the opportunity to turn to other opponents. The relationship between the two treaty partners, which remained rather cool at first, was to be improved through personal relationships and ties. On the Egyptian side, a state visit by Khattushili to Ramesses's capital was contemplated, on which occasion Ramesses intended to go to Canaan to meet his high-ranking guest. Such a state visit, which would have been unprecedented in ancient history, was perhaps prevented only by a (diplomatic?) illness on the part of the Hittite king. There ensued prolonged and vacillating negotiations regarding a dynastic marriage, like those conducted about a century earlier by Amenophis III with Babylon and Mitanni, though on this occasion there was a double correspondence, between the kings on the one hand and the queens on the other. Khattushili, who was suffering from an eye ailment, requested Egyptian physicians and medicines, both held in high esteem in those times, for himself and for his sterile sister. A daughter of the Hittite king was at last agreed on for the dynastic marriage, and she was conducted to Egypt with all due pomp in the winter of 1246–1245 B.C.E. The official account celebrating this "miraculous" event was inscribed in a number of temples throughout the land, and it laid special emphasis on how Egyptians and Hittites fraternized at joint banquets: the religious conviction that the sun god shone over all peoples became for a time a political reality, overcoming age-old nationalistic prejudices against "wretched Asiatics."

Later, Ramesses II received yet another Hittite princess into his harem, which was probably as international an assemblage as his officialdom. Additionally, his chief wives, Nofretari and Isisnofret, rank among the foremost of ancient Egyptian queens; Ramesses married them at the same time, though Egyptian kings usually had only one chief wife. Nofretari received lasting monuments in the form of her tomb, the most beautiful in the Valley of the Queens, and her rock-cut temple at Abu Simbel, while Isisnofret perhaps was given an undecorated tomb in the Valley of the Kings. But Ramesses II designated the sons of Isisnofret for the succession; his daughter Bentanta, whom he made his wife, as Amenophis III and Akhenaten had done, was also borne to him by this preferred queen. His unusually large number of children led to the unique solution of a collective tomb in the Valley of the Kings, across from the king's own final resting place. We know only the names of most of the more than fifty sons and daughters of the king; aside from his successor, Merneptah, Khaemwese in particular achieved historical importance, and he lived on in popular memory as a fabled sage and magician. This prince served for many years at Memphis as high priest of Ptah, and he carried out restoration work on many monuments of the Old Kingdom, which even then had aroused the historical and esthetic interest of sightseers. One of the colossal statues of the king that Khaemwese set up in front of the temple of Ptah now lies in the palm grove of Mit Rahina amid the few scattered ruins of this former cosmopolitan city.

The treaty with the Hittites procured decades of peace for Ramesses II. The Libyans were held in check by a chain of fortresses along the Mediterranean coast, while Egyptian rule in Nubia would long remain secure. The economic resources of this rich land could thus be devoted to Ramesses II's unprecedented zeal for construction work. In Egypt and Nubia alike, there is scarcely an excavation site where monuments of this king have not come to light. Among the most impressive preserved examples are the two rock-cut temples at Abu Simbel (Figure 38) and his constructions at Thebes; he completed the relief decoration of the hypostyle hall at Karnak, and he embellished Amenophis III's Temple of Luxor with a new court fronted by a pylon, while on the west bank, the Ramesseum was erected to serve as his mortuary temple. His early monuments still displayed the mature, elegant style of his father, but with the increase in quantity and the move into the colossal dimension, a coarseness set in. A development from elegant slenderness to awkward bulk can be clearly seen in Ramesside columns, while in relief sculpture, there was an ever-increasing preference for the technique of sunken relief, which was easier to produce and which could achieve a more powerful plastic effect. Temple walls facing the outside world were covered with monumental representations of battles; victory over enemies, which in fact was becoming increasingly difficult to achieve, thus attained a cultic permanence. At the same time these representations, along with literary accounts of battles, testify to the fact that the king bowed to divine will and guidance even in his historical deeds.

Merneptah (1213–1203 B.C.E.), the thirteenth son of Ramesses II, was named to succeed his father, who was nearly ninety years of age; presumably, he was already conducting the affairs of state before the latter's death. As king, Merneptah favored Memphis over the new, swamp-encircled delta Residence, and he erected an important palace

38. Temple of Ramesses II at Abu Simbel. Photo by Nancy J. Corbin.

complex near the temple of Ptah. This old capital city, which rose to renewed splendor with his aid, held him in thankful memory; in the Ptolemaic Period, two statues of the king were still venerated there. A mortuary temple, and presumably a cenotaph, were also erected in Memphis
for Merneptah. But the royal tomb itself (Figure 39) was still located at
Thebes, where in every future reign it would be enlarged to include new
elements, for the ongoing "extension of the existing" was also a part of
Pharaoh's role.

Egypt continued to maintain friendly relations with its former opponents in Asia, Khatti, Ugarit, and Amurru; at the beginning of his reign,
Merneptah aided the kingdom of Khatti, which was afflicted by a
famine, with deliveries of grain. But a little later, a new danger loomed,
one that would sweep away the allies in Asia and threaten the existence
of Egypt itself. The Sherden people, who later gave their name to Sar-
dinia, had arrived at the eastern coast of the Mediterranean as early as
the Amarna Period, making their appearance as soldiers in Egyptian
service. Later, a further wave of Sea Peoples came from the region of the

39. Scene from the entrance to the tomb of Merneptah depicting the king and the god Re-Harakhty. Photo by A. Brodbeck.

Black Sea, among them the Shekelesh (later in Sicily), the Luka (Lycians), and the Tursha (possibly Etruscans). In the spring of 1208 B.C.E., these warlike northerners united with tribes of Libyans, who were on the move with their wives and children, in a joint attack on Egypt. Merneptah's generals met them in the western delta and were able to beat them back near Buto in a bloody battle that purportedly cost the enemy more than eight thousand dead. On the Israel Stela, which celebrates this victory, a people Israel appears for the first time in a list of the places and peoples ruled by Egypt, along with Canaan, Ashqelon, and Gezer. However, the idea that Merneptah was the biblical pharaoh of the later Exodus tradition has been abandoned by many scholars.

Like his father, Merneptah distinguished himself as a usurper of older monuments, since his major battles with the Libyans and the Sea Peoples left little means for quarrying expeditions. The mighty mortuary temple of Amenophis III behind the Colossi of Memnon was the most seriously affected, for it was obliged to yield its blocks to Merneptah's mortuary temple.

The Nubian viceroy, Messui, himself a member of the royal house, rebelled against Merneptah's son and successor, Sethos II. After lengthy struggles, he managed to assume control of Upper Egypt. He exercised a fleeting rule under the name Amenmesse (Figure 40) but was defeated while attempting to advance further to the north; Sethos II had the inscriptions carefully erased from the tomb the usurper had made for himself in the Valley of the Kings. Egypt was thus weakened by internal turmoil during the critical years around 1200 B.C.E., when the Sea Peoples overran the Hittite kingdom, Ugarit, Amurru, and Cyprus, and was unable to afford any assistance to its Asiatic treaty partners. The Asiatic coast was ravaged by the Sea Peoples as far as Haifa and Acco; the old Egyptian base of Byblos was evidently not affected, though, and southern Palestine also remained under Egyptian control for a time.

At this time, the actual power lay in the hands of a woman, Twosre. She began at the side of her husband, Sethos II, and then ruled on behalf of Siptah, who was still a child and probably a son of Sethos II. Like Hatshepsut, Twosre eventually assumed a royal titulary, though in her own case she continued the year count of Sethos II, ignoring the regnal years of Siptah. Finally, she ruled alone for about two years (1190–1188 B.C.E.) after the early death of the young Siptah. As a reigning pharaoh, she had a rock-cut tomb prepared in the Valley of the Kings; in a peculiar manner, it combines elements of a royal tomb and a queen's tomb, clearly re-

40. Statue head of Amenmesse.
The Metropolitan Museum of
Art, Rogers Fund, 1934 (34.2.2).
Photo courtesy of The
Metropolitan Museum of Art.

flecting the three stages of her career: queen, regent, and pharaoh. A
small tomb was prepared next to hers for her favorite, the chancellor
Bay. The latter was a foreigner, probably of Syrian origin, and he is cred-
ibly described in inscriptions as a kingmaker and the real wielder of
power at this time. This fits the mention of a Syrian usurper in the Great
Papyrus Harris, though the depiction of anarchy in this text stems from
a need to draw a picture of these historical developments as a chaos that
reigned before the establishment of the new Dynasty 20, with its recapit-
ulation of the moment of creation. In political reality, though, most royal
officials outlasted the change in dynasty, thus guaranteeing administrative continuity.

The origin of Sethnakhte (1188–1186 B.C.E.), the founder of the new dynasty, is unknown. All his successors had the personal name Ramesses, and culturally, the Ramesside Period continued until the end of Dynasty 20. Sethnakhte's son Ramesses III (1186–1155 B.C.E.; Figure 41) was the last important ruling figure of the New Kingdom, though he saw himself as a successor of Ramesses II and modeled himself on that king, copying his throne name and even his mortuary temple. In his own temple, he went so far as to have a copy made of the representations of the battle fought by Ramesses II at Qadesh against the now defunct Hittite realm, though in fact he surpassed his predecessor as a military leader. During his reign, a double wave of migrating Libyans and Sea Peoples surged against the borders of Egypt yet one more time. Ramesses III's historic achievement was that he was able to master this danger, thus sparing his land from foreign rule for more than another two centuries. Fortunately, the attacks of these two powerful groups occurred separately. The Libyans, who advanced from the west in 1182 and again in 1176 B.C.E., were utterly destroyed. The land-hungry host of Sea Peoples, augmented meanwhile by Philistines, Teucrians, and other new groups, was annihilated at the mouths of the delta branches

41. Statue of Ramesses III. Cairo Museum. Photo by Sara E. Orel.

of the Nile in 1179, and it proved possible to block a simultaneous Sea Peoples attack in Syria or northern Palestine. The innumerable prisoners of war from these three battles were either welcomed into the Egyptian army as soldiers or settled en masse in endangered parts of the realm. Thus, the Philistines received new homes around Gaza and Ashqelon to defend the Egyptian supply routes in Palestine against attack. The Libyans were settled in military colonies in Lower and Middle Egypt and were quickly integrated into Egyptian culture, which served to unify the colorful mixture of peoples in the land.

Things seem to have remained quiet on Egypt's borders in the later years of Ramesses III. The king's enthusiasm for construction work left traces from the delta to Soleb, and on Theban soil his three temples are well preserved: a barque station at Karnak; the temple of Khons, which would be completed by his successors, to the south of Karnak; and on the west bank, the mighty mortuary temple of Medinet Habu, which was elaborated into a fortress and was adjoined by the palace where the king stayed while in Thebes. After the successful battles against the Libyans and the Sea Peoples, Ramesses III and his successors had to contend increasingly with internal difficulties. In the written sources from this period we read frequent complaints regarding the high-handedness of officials, wages in arrears, and economic problems; prices more than quintupled within a short period. An especially deep insight into the daily vicissitudes and growing problems of the upper working class from the reign of Ramesses II on is afforded by the papyri and ostraca (inscribed potsherds and pieces of stone) from the workmen's village of Deir el-Medina. In this settlement, isolated from the outside world, lived the artists and craftsmen who worked on the construction and decoration of the royal and private tombs on the west bank of Thebes, along with their families. Like that of the contemporary Instruction of Amenemope, their religious attitude was characterized by a humble piety resigned to the unfathomable will of the divine and trusting in its capacity for deliverance. Economically, however, they were dependent on provisioning by the state for which they worked; their situation began to deteriorate under Ramesses III, and it was a source of constant concern for the vizier, To, under whose jurisdiction they fell. In November 1156 B.C.E., when their in-kind payments were already two months in arrears, the workers went on strike and staged a protest march on the administrative center located in the Ramesseum. Unrest of this sort would often break out among the workers in the period that followed, when incompetence and corruption constantly threatened their economic maintenance, while the officials attempted with success to exempt portions of their own wealth from taxation by means of private donations for the benefit of the king.

There was also opposition and unrest at court and in the administration. Just before the workmen's strike, the king removed one of his two viziers from office, but shortly thereafter, he fell victim to a conspiracy. In the spring of 1155 B.C.E., queen Teye made common cause with a number of higher officials, among them several Asiatics, to bring her son Pentaweret to the throne. The conspirators succeeded in doing away with the king during a stay at Medinet Habu, but as in the case of the assassination of Amenemhet I, the legitimate successor prevailed and ascended the throne as Ramesses IV (1155–1148 B.C.E.). In a legal proceeding whose official record is preserved to us, the conspirators were condemned by a specially appointed tribunal; the most prominent among them were permitted to commit suicide, while their minions were sentenced to have their noses and ears cut off. When he assumed the throne, the new king issued a manifesto, which is preserved on the Great Papyrus Harris. In this document, he confirms the donations made by his father to the temples throughout the land, and especially to those at Thebes, amounting to one-tenth of all the cultivable land. Since Ramesses III also had to remunerate his soldiers with landholdings, the economic means of the kingship were becoming increasingly modest. Nevertheless, Ramesses IV attempted great building projects, and he sent an expedition of more than eight thousand men to the stone quarries of the Wadi Hammamat. His early death left his ambitious plans unfulfilled, and beginning with his tomb (Figure 42), there was a departure from the earlier tendency to expand each royal tomb by adding new elements.

Ramesses IV was succeeded by Ramesses V (1148–1143 B.C.E.), who died young of smallpox, and by the aging Ramesses VI (1143–1135 B.C.E.), who was probably another son of Ramesses III. Both worked on an extended rock-cut tomb in the Valley of the Kings (Figure 43), whose wall decorations once again included all the Books of the Netherworld and a number of other religious texts; the artistic decline since the reign of Sethos I can be clearly read in its coarse sunken reliefs. The still considerable extent of the empire is indicated by a statue base of Ramesses VI found at Megiddo and by cartouches of the king in the Temple of Kawa south of the Third Cataract. Since the Near East had in the meantime entered the Iron Age, the copper mines now lost their importance as a destination for expeditions; the last Egyptian bases in the south of

42. View into the tomb of Ramesses IV. Photo by F. Teichmann.

43. Burial chamber of the tomb of Ramesses VI. Photo by A. Brodbeck.

Palestine thus lost their strategic value and could be abandoned in the decades that followed. Egyptian activity in the Sinai ended with Ramesses VI.

The long reign of Ramesses IX (1127–1108 B.C.E.) was filled with economic and political difficulties. Symptomatic were the tomb robberies in the Theban necropolis, which for a long time were quietly tolerated; when a judicial investigation finally occurred, it uncovered an overwhelming amount of corruption and neglect extending to the very top of the administration. It is no wonder that in the late Ramesside Period, the satire always loved by Egyptians was transformed into a bitter scorn and derision that spared neither kingship nor the divine. The artisans of

Deir el-Medina were now transferred to the fortified Medinet Habu, which had become the new administrative center.

Under Ramesses X (1108–1104 B.C.E.), the outraged necropolis workers once again laid down their tools; the journal of the cemetery notes their complaint ("We are weak and hungry, for we are not receiving the rations Pharaoh gives us") along with an exclamation smacking of class warfare on the part of one of the workers: "Let the vizier carry the planks himself!" But their strike achieved little, for the vizier and his king now held limited power, while the high priest of Amun and the viceroy of Kush were becoming increasingly independent, to the point of securing the inheritance of their offices through several generations. The southern portion of the realm, which had led a shadowy political existence for quite some time, was thus coming to the forefront once again and developing into a state within a state. Energetic political and military leadership were especially necessary in this, for Libyan penetration of the Nile valley had now extended as far as Thebes.

Despite fresh efforts, the last Ramesside, Ramesses XI (1104–1075 B.C.E.), was unable to halt the internal collapse of his kingdom. Thefts were now discovered even at Karnak, and corruption was becoming more widespread. The hopeless economic situation and the famine that resulted were aggravated by battles between the high priest Amenhotpe and the viceroy of Kush, Panehsy, who even made an armed intervention in Middle Egypt and drove Amenhotpe from Thebes. The greater part of Egypt thus fell under the rule of a military dictatorship able to rely on its seasoned Nubian soldiers. But in 1087 B.C.E., Panehsy was obliged to leave Thebes and withdraw, as an avowed enemy of the state, to his former area of jurisdiction, where he died soon thereafter. The new lord of Upper Egypt was the general and high priest Piankh; he was soon succeeded by his son-in-law (?) Herihor, who also bore the titles of viceroy of Kush and generalissimo of Upper and Lower Egypt. In the nineteenth year of his reign (1086 B.C.E.) Ramesses XI inaugurated a Renaissance era, attempting to address the deplorable state of affairs in the Thebaid through a series of judicial proceedings. During his new era, the king faded more and more into the background; at the time of his death, Herihor held the actual power and bore both priestly and royal titles.

Toward the end of his reign, Ramesses XI was also obliged to place the real power in the north of his realm into the hands of others. In his adventure-filled report on his travels, the Theban official Wenamun, who was charged with bringing wood from the Lebanon for the processional barque of Amun, mentions that by 1082 B.C.E., Smendes and his queen, Tentamun, were the real regents in Lower Egypt. His report further shows that Byblos had been independent of Egypt for at least a generation. Byblos had turned to a new world power and was now tributary, along with Sidon and Arvad, to the Assyrian king, Tiglath-pileser I (1115–1076 B.C.E.), who had advanced as far as the Lebanon. Egypt's imperial era was finished.

THE LATE PERIOD

With the death of the last of the Ramessides, the kingship of the pharaohs passed with no evident difficulty to Smendes (1075–1044 B.C.E.), who founded Dynasty 21. His origins are obscure, but it is certain that he was related by marriage to the royal family. Thus began a transitional period between the New Kingdom and the actual Late Period, one that is now usually called the Third Intermediate Period. It brought Egypt a fresh isolation; the Asiatic regions were lost, and Nubia and its eastern desert, with their gold mines, soon slipped from Egyptian authority. With Herihor, the title viceroy of Kush became extinct. In contrast to the earlier intermediate periods, however, national unity was formally maintained. The Tanite kings were recognized in Upper Egypt, and even if some high priests occasionally bore royal titles and perhaps assumed year datings of their own, they apparently did so with the approval of the legitimate rulers in the north; there can be no question of an actual double monarchy at this time, and the leading families in Tanis and Thebes were related to one another.

In practice, the Thebaid was a military dictatorship ruled by the high priest, but in theory it was a theocracy in which the all-powerful divine ruler Amun guided all that happened, down to the solving of crimes and the appointment of officials, through his oracular decisions. "Amun is king" was the new dogma even at Tanis, for the formulation was the name of one of the kings, Amenemnesu. The institution of kingship thus ceded responsibility for the course of events to the divine, culminating a development that can be traced through the Amarna Period and the Ramesside era.

The new dynasty was careful to continue the traditions of the Ramesside Period. Tanis (Figure 44), the city that served as the royal Residence, was conceived as a new city of Amun, patterned on Thebes, and it also lay in the immediate vicinity of the House of Ramesses; for the monarchs of this dynasty, Ramesses became an honorary title like the later Caesar. The Theban dictators, on the other hand, oriented themselves to Dynasty 18, which had turned Thebes into a world capital. The relationships between the two centers of the land remained close and friendly; King Psusennes I (c. 1040–990 B.C.E.) might have been a son of the high priest Pinudjem I (c. 1070–1055 B.C.E.; Figure 45) and a Ramesside princess, and the divine triad of Thebes also dominated the royal court in the north.

The royal tombs of this period were located no longer in the Theban desert but in the temple precinct of the new Residence of Tanis. In the plundered Valley of the Kings, the high priests reinterred the royal

44. Tanis: remains of the gateway of Shoshenq III (left), with colossus of Ramesses II in the background. Photo by Geoffrey Graham.

45. Statue of Pinudjem I. Though
he bears the titles of a high
priest in the inscriptions, he is
depicted wearing the royal
nemes headdress. Cairo Museum.
Photo © by Aidan Dodson.

mummies that were still preserved in two caches, which survived into
the modern era. The available remains of their burial equipment were
treated with less piety: Psusennes I had himself buried in a coffin that
had belonged to Merneptah and Pinudjem I in a coffin of Tuthmosis I,
while all that remained of their burial treasures was evidently incorporated into the state treasury. The building activity of Dynasty 21 was
also essentially confined to the appropriation of older monuments,
though at Karnak the decoration of the temple of Khonsu was continued. The low standard of living of the high priests at Thebes stood in
strange opposition to the former vastness of the temple's property,
which had evidently suffered badly in the turmoil at the end of Dynasty
20. The priests endowed their male and female relatives with prebends
to give them a basic income. The fortifications of the Tanite and Theban

potentates show how unsafe the times were. When Pinudjem's son and successor, Masaharta, died (1017 B.C.E.), serious unrest again developed at Thebes; as would also happen in the Christian and modern periods, political opponents were exiled to the oases of the western desert.

Under Siamun (978–960 B.C.E.), the ruling house at Tanis felt strong enough to conduct an active foreign policy once again. A successful campaign led to the conquest of the Philistine city of Gezer and posed a threat to the new Israelite monarchy. Further conflict was avoided by means of a marriage alliance, and an Egyptian princess entered the harem of King Solomon (963–931 B.C.E.), who at the same time received the disputed city of Gezer as a dowry. In the south, the Thebaid underwent a considerable decline in importance after the death of the high priest Pinudjem II (987–970 B.C.E.), and while Dynasty 21 had at first represented a high point in the decoration of coffins and papyri, which replaced the Theban tomb painting of the New Kingdom, artistic creativity also declined at this time. Above all else, iconography had undergone a development in this period, and many new motifs were invented.

The influence of the Libyan tribal chieftains, who were indispensable to the Tanite kings as military leaders, increased under Psusennes II (960–945 B.C.E.) to the point where the king lost his power. Nimrut, the Great Chief of the Meshwesh, and his son Shoshenq were the real lords of Lower Egypt. Early on, their family acquired influence in the city of Bubastis in the delta and at Herakleopolis, and it then allied itself through marriage with the lineage of the high priests of Memphis. Supported by a strong power base, Shoshenq I (945–924 B.C.E.), the founder of Dynasty 22, was able to assume the throne after the death of the last of the Tanites and to marry his son Osorkon to a princess of the old royal family. Egypt thus came under the foreign rule of Libyan chieftains; but since it had been assimilating to Egyptian culture and customs for several generations, the new royal house of the Bubastids did not seem essentially different, at least in the north with its colorful ethnic mix. A certain reserve was unmistakable in the south, however, and only with hesitation did the priestly ruling class recognize the new Dynasty 22, whose kings did not deny their foreign origin in their choice of names.

But there was soon a reconciliation with ancient traditions. Around 936 B.C.E., Shoshenq I sent his son Iuput to Thebes to be high priest of Amun, and there he married into the priesthood of Amun and administered the divine state as the king's governor. At the same time, a collateral branch of the Libyan royal house was established at Herakleopolis,

which was placed under the rule of Prince Nimrut. The political character of Egypt would thus be determined for centuries by a feudalism
based on the organization of the Libyan tribes. Under such conditions,
neither a strict centralism nor a vigorous foreign policy could be developed. The campaign to Jerusalem that Shoshenq I undertook in 926
B.C.E. was little more than a fleeting raid, though it did bring back rich
booty. Palestine was weakened by the division of the Solomonic state,
but Egypt was unable to secure a permanent foothold there. Even Byblos, with which Shoshenq I resumed the old relations, remained an independent city state. But the rich booty from his campaign to Palestine enabled the king to make ambitious building plans, especially in the
temple of Karnak, where his son Iuput directed the work. New sandstone quarries were opened at Gebel el-Silsila, but the death of the king
left most of his plans unfulfilled.

Osorkon I (924–889 B.C.E.) was able to afford donations of great quantities of gold, silver, and lapis lazuli to the more important temples, and
a statue of him was sent to Byblos. He installed his son Shoshenq as high
priest at Thebes, thus maintaining the custom of entrusting the governorship of Upper Egypt to a royal son. Later, as his father's coregent,
this high priest was buried in the royal tomb at Tanis. A short time later,
Shoshenq's son Harsiese was able to acquire his father's office and
achieve a largely independent status vis-à-vis the kingship, sharing the
military command over Upper Egypt with the ruler of Herakleopolis. To
date, the sources have yielded very little information regarding Osorkon's successor, Takelot I.

Osorkon II (874–850 B.C.E.; Figure 46), the most important ruler of this
dynasty, was able to reassert the authority of the kingship one last time
before a steady decline set in. At Memphis, he replaced the influential
family of high priests, itself related to the royal house, with his son, the
crown prince, Shoshenq, whose descendants were to hold the office
until the end of the dynasty. Another prince, Harnakhte, served as high
priest of Amun at Tanis. Finally Nimrut, a son of the king and prince of
Herakleopolis, was installed as governor at Thebes as the successor of
Harsiese, who had gone so far as to assume a royal titulary of his own.
The tomb of the king and its rich burial equipment were found at Tanis,
which was the official capital as it had been in Dynasty 21. After Tanis,
Bubastis remained the preferred Residence of the kings; Osorkon II
adorned the city with temple constructions, in particular a festival gateway whose representations commemorated the *sed* festival he celebrated
in his twenty-second regnal year. Two years later, the aging king ap-

46. Bronze statuette of
Osorkon II(?). Private collection.
Photo by S. Hertig.

pointed his son Takelot II (850–825 B.C.E.) as coregent. A new reconstruction of the late Libyan Period, however, takes Takelot II to be the first king of Dynasty 23, and thus the predecessor of Pedubaste, while making Shoshenq III the successor of Osorkon II at Tanis.

Steady trade relations continued with the former Egyptian territories in western Asia; alabaster vessels of Osorkon II have been found at the city of Samaria in Palestine and—as Phoenician trade goods—as far away as Spain. In addition to trade, political interests were at stake, and Egyptian troops assisted the princes of Syria-Palestine against the great power Assyria in the battle of Qarqar in 853 B.C.E.

Takelot II was at first generally recognized as king after the death of his father, thanks to his coregency. But fresh unrest soon broke out in Thebes, this "world capital that had gone to rack and ruin, and even had difficulty maintaining its food supply," as the Egyptologist Hermann Kees once described it. In 846 B.C.E., the crown prince Osorkon went to Thebes from his headquarters in the fortress at el-Hiba in Middle Egypt, and as the new high priest he restored order; his political enemies met with a fearful punishment. His brother Bakenptah was installed in the princedom of Herakleopolis, and his sisters married high officials in the Thebaid, with the result that at times all four of the highest positions in the priesthood of Amun at Karnak were occupied by members or relatives of the royal house.

This policy had no lasting effect; only four years later, new and long-lasting unrest broke out, in the course of which Osorkon acquired an "antipope" in the person of his relative Harsiese II. When Takelot II died, it was not the crown prince Osorkon who was recognized as king, but rather a Shoshenq III (825–773 B.C.E.), whose origin is unknown. He was recognized in Upper Egypt only at the beginning of his lengthy reign; starting around 818 B.C.E., double datings were being made at Thebes, according to the regnal years of Shoshenq III and those of a further king, Pedubaste, whom Manetho considers the founder of Dynasty 23. The royal house of the Bubastids thus split into two branches, and its royal authority was soon to become still further splintered.

Osorkon III (787–759 B.C.E.; Figure 47) was the only prominent successor of Pedubaste; he appointed his son Takelot as both high priest of Amun at Thebes and high priest of Harsaphes at Herakleopolis, with the result that he had command of all Upper Egypt. The last kings of Dynasty 22 now exercised a limited rule in the eastern delta, while Great Chieftains of the Libu seized power in the western delta. After the death of Osorkon III, the general disintegration quickly continued. His son was recognized at Thebes as Takelot III, but the hereditary rulers at Herakleopolis and at Hermopolis now assumed royal titles and their own year datings. Upper Egypt was thus split into several small, powerless kingdoms, while a corresponding development proceeded in the north. At Memphis, chieftains of the Libu served as high priests of Ptah, while Tefnakhte of Sais, another Libyan chieftain, was able to make himself lord of the entire western delta (725–718 B.C.E.). With this capable ruler began a new struggle to unite the fragmented land, a feat that would eventually be accomplished by Psammetichus I.

Beginning in the middle of the eighth century B.C.E., a new political power appeared in the extreme south. The "Ethiopian" king, Kashta,

47. Statuette depicting Osorkon III launching a boat. Cairo Museum. Photo © Aidan Dodson.

was recognized as ruler at Elephantine, and the troops of his son Piye (Piankhy) occupied the Thebaid soon after the death of Osorkon III. The two rulers stemmed from a Nubian house that for some generations had been building up an important kingdom from their center at Napata at the Fourth Cataract. Like the Libyan tribal chiefs, these Nubian kings, whom Greek writers called Ethiopian, felt themselves to be Egyptian in culture and religion. They adopted the Egyptian writing system, the forms of the Egyptian institution of kingship, and the worship of Amun; the temple of Amun built at Napata in Dynasty 18 played the role of the temple of Karnak in their realm. On Egyptian soil, they subscribed to an archaism that would in the future determine the cultural picture of the Late Period. Age-old titles whose use had already died out in the New Kingdom were revived, monuments of earlier dynasties were restored, and old texts were copied "from worm-eaten papyri." Their worship of Amun was rigidly orthodox, and they placed special value on correct outward forms, such as ritual purity. The pyramid form was revived in their tombs, which lie near Napata. The Ethiopian Period would bring new momentum to Egyptian sculpture, emphasizing a greater realism in portraiture.

Piye allowed the formal continuation of the Theban theocracy of Amun. His sister Amenirdis was adopted by the Divine Adoratrice Shepenwepet, a daughter of Osorkon III, and she was thus accepted as her successor. The high priests, who had all too often temporally abused their spiritual office and ruled as military dictators, continued in office, but Amun's worldly governorship was placed in the hands of the reigning Divine Adoratrice. These women were always of royal origin, and since they had no worldly husbands, they transmitted their office through adoption; they celebrated *sed* festivals and enclosed their names in cartouches, thus laying claim to kingly rights, even in the form of their tombs. The real power was probably exercised by their chief officials, who had large tombs made for themselves in the old cemetery on the west bank.

A few years after the occupation of Thebes by the Ethiopians, a struggle began between the Egyptianized Libyan and Nubian rulers over the future ownership of their culturally common home. Tefnakhte of Sais was able to extend his sphere of influence far beyond Memphis to the fortress of el-Hiba, compelling "King" Nimrut of Hermopolis to join him and laying siege to "King" Peftjauawybast of Herakleopolis, who opposed him, in his Residence. This situation, which menaced the Thebaid, led Piye to dispatch an army to the north; after he had observed his cultic duties in Thebes, he personally assumed its high command. His victory stela is an important source for our understanding of the structure of power in Egypt in his time; it relates how Nimrut of Hermopolis was conquered, Herakleopolis relieved, Tefnakhte beaten, and Memphis conquered. After the fall of the ancient Residence, most of the Libyan chieftains in the delta paid homage to the conqueror. As Piye continued his advance into the delta, the now isolated Tefnakhte also decided to pay homage, though he avoided a personal submission. Piye contented himself with the formal recognition of his sovereignty by the many petty kings in the delta, where anarchic disunity was to continue unchanged until Psammetichus I, and then he withdrew to his distant capital of Napata. When the kingdom of Israel became Assyrian with the fall of Samaria (722 B.C.E.) and a new threat thus arose on the eastern frontier of Egypt, the Ethiopians remained inactive; it was the petty kings of the delta who mustered the Egyptian troops that unsuccessfully opposed Sargon II on the side of Hanno of Gaza in the battle of Raphia in

720 B.C.E. Tefnakhte was at this time confined to his hereditary seat in the western delta, but his son Bocchoris (718–712 B.C.E.) once again strove for greater power. Manetho counts him as the founder and only king of Dynasty 24, while Diodorus describes him as an important law-giver. When he succeeded in bringing Memphis under his control, Piye's brother and successor, Shabaka (712–698 B.C.E.; Figure 48), decided on a reprisal, which brought an end to the dynasty of Sais. Beginning with 712 B.C.E., year datings were made to the regnal years of the Ethiopian kings of Dynasty 25 throughout the delta, as had long been the case in Upper Egypt. Peaceful relations with Assyria prevailed under Shabaka, and he went so far as to hand over the exiled prince of Ashdod.

With the support of the rich gold deposits of Nubia, the Ethiopians endowed the impoverished land with a new economic ascendancy and with monumental constructions such as had not been built since Dynasty 20. Taharqa (690–664 B.C.E.) emulated the great kings of the Middle and New Kingdoms as an architect, lavishing special attention on Amun's cities of Napata and Thebes; at Karnak, he built several colonnades with colossal but well-proportioned columns. At this time, the political lord of the Thebaid and the king's actual governor in Upper Egypt was Mentuemhet (Figure 49), a priest of Amun and the mayor of Thebes, whom the Ethiopian royal house even allied with themselves through marriage. Aside from the office of Divine Adoratrice, the two highest priestly offices of the Theban Amun remained occupied by relatives of the dynasty. Of the events that occurred in the peaceful early years of Taharqa, the greatest impression was left by the Nile inundation of his sixth regnal year (685 B.C.E.); at a height of more than twenty-one cubits (over thirty-six feet), it was the largest inundation known to antiquity, and after nothing comparable was found in the "annals of the fore-bears," it was commemorated on stelae in temples from Napata to Tanis. This inundation undoubtedly caused great devastation, yet the Egyptians saw in it above all else an overflowing of divine grace, so that in this instance a natural disaster was recorded. This was exceptional; such events were otherwise not mentioned, because they did not belong to the "right" order of the world.

Also not mentioned in the Egyptian texts are the far worse disasters that overtook Egypt in the later years of Taharqa's reign. The Assyrian king, Esarhaddon (681–669 B.C.E.), turned against the land that had so often supported the small states in Palestine against the new world power. A first attack on the part of the Assyrians ended in defeat in the spring of 673 B.C.E., but in 671 B.C.E., Esarhaddon was able to advance as

48. Stela depicting Shabaka presenting the hieroglyph for "field(s)" to the god Horus and the goddess Wadjit. The Metropolitan Museum of Art, Rogers Fund, 1955 (55.144.6). Photo courtesy of The Metropolitan Museum of Art.

49. Mentuemhet (right) and Shepetenmut, one of his three wives. Seattle Art Museum 53.80. Purchased from Bequest of Archibald Stewart and Emma Collins Downey. Photo by Paul Macapia. Photo courtesy of the Seattle Art Museum.

far as Memphis, conquer the ancient capital, and compel Taharqa to flee southward. The Assyrian king permitted the continued existence of the small states in the delta. They were natural allies, for they had adhered to the Ethiopians only with reluctance. Among their Libyan rulers, Necho I (672–664 B.C.E.) of Sais played a leading role at this time. Since Taharqa subsequently proved able to regain his strength, Esarhaddon was obliged to conduct another campaign to Egypt, during which he died, as early as 669 B.C.E. His successor, Assurbanipal, was at first occupied with other problems and had to defer an Egyptian campaign. Taharqa was thus able to win back Memphis and to induce some of the delta rulers, among them Necho, to break with the Assyrians. Assurbanipal did not appear in Egypt until the winter of 667–666 B.C.E. to wreak his overdue vengeance. The disloyal Libyan rulers were deported to

Nineveh, but the nimble Necho succeeded not only in obtaining a pardon, but also in being installed as "king" of Sais and Memphis; his son Psammetichus received the princedom of Athribis as the traditional property of a crown prince. But Assurbanipal hoped in vain that the rulers of Sais, to whom he had assigned such preeminence, would defend the Assyrian claim to sovereignty against the Ethiopians. Situated between the two foreign power blocs, this Saite Dynasty 26 conducted a nationalistic policy of its own, securing for Egypt a renewed independence, a position of political power, and a flowering of culture.

In 664 B.C.E., Taharqa died in far-off Napata without having won back Lower Egypt. Immediately upon assuming the throne, his successor, Tantamani, marched northward and advanced without meeting a fight as far as Memphis, where he encountered the fierce resistance of the delta rulers. At their head once again was Necho I, who apparently fell in the fighting; his son Psammetichus fled to the Assyrians. After the withdrawal of Tantamani, an Assyrian army once again pitched camp, installed Psammetichus I (664–610 B.C.E.) in the enlarged inheritance of his father, and this time also pursued the Ethiopian to Upper Egypt; on this occasion, Thebes was thoroughly sacked and suffered severe damage from which it never entirely recovered. But the Assyrians contented themselves with their demonstration of power and turned over all of Upper Egypt, from Hermopolis to Elephantine, to the Ethiopian governor, Mentuemhet; in Thebes, datings were made according to the regnal years of Tantamani, and construction work was carried out under his commission until 656 B.C.E.

Trusted by the Assyrians and undisturbed by the Ethiopians, Psammetichus I was able to put an end to the fragmentation in the delta in the years that followed. He was aided in this by the Ionian and Carian soldiers of King Gyges of Lydia, who was interested in having a new ally against the Assyrians, now at the apogee of their power. A Great Chieftain of the Libyans was mentioned for the last time in 657 B.C.E., and at about the same time, Psammetichus set about incorporating Upper Egypt into his realm. The arrangements were made by the Master of Shipping, Sematawytefnakhte, who had oversight of navigation and harbors from Memphis to Elephantine and who occupied a largely independent position in Middle Egypt, with his official seat at Herakleopolis. In March 656 B.C.E., at the commission of Psammetichus (and surely with a military escort), he accompanied the king's daughter Nitokris to Thebes, where she was solemnly received by Mentuemhet and adopted by the incumbent Divine Adoratrice, Shepenwepet II. With that, the sov-

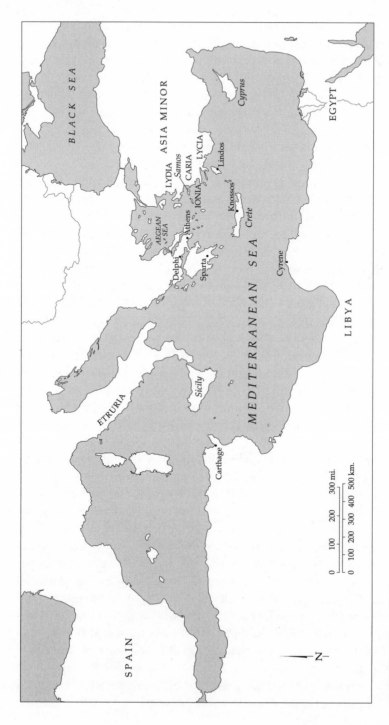

The Mediterranean world

ereignty of Dynasty 26 over all Egypt was realized. The peaceful nature of this reuniting of the land shows that Psammetichus I was a patient and deliberate statesman. He avoided a rupture with the Ethiopian dynasty at Napata by recognizing Shepenwepet II as regent of the Thebaid until her death, while high Ethiopian officials such as Mentuemhet and the high priest Harakhbit, a grandson of Shabaka, remained in office for at least another five years. Replacement by officials of the Saite court occurred gradually and quite carefully, but it brought the Thebaid under the firm control of the king during the ensuing decades. Under the rulership of a Divine Adoratrice from the reigning royal house, its form of government remained unchanged, but it had played out its political role and would in the future stand on the sidelines of events. In Egyptian religion, Amun of Thebes would become less important than the deities of the Osirian circle, who would eventually receive worldwide veneration in the cults of Isis and Serapis during the Roman era. It would seem that at this time, cultic forms and religious beliefs were finally congealing into the patterns that would later be encountered by ancient Greek travelers and writers.

During these years, the Assyrian empire was too preoccupied by growing internal tensions, which culminated in the great civil war of 651–648 B.C.E., and by the struggles that ensued with Elam, to deploy its might yet again to counter its renegade vassals in Egypt; even the state of Judah, under Josiah, slipped away from Assyrian sovereignty. The motley assembly of Psammetichus's "foreign legion" thus did not need to prove itself against external enemies; under the command of Libyan generals stood Ionian, Carian, Nubian, and Libyan mercenaries who would soon be supplemented by Phoenician and Jewish soldiers. Strong tensions reigned among these various groups, especially between the Libyans and the Greeks, which occasionally exploded into mutiny. Rivalry between Egyptian and foreign merchants aggravated the tensions, though the Saite monarchs always succeeded in evening them out. Strong foreign influences notwithstanding, the Saite Period sought to maintain the great heritage of the Egyptian past, and it was especially oriented to the monuments and the rigidly hierarchical structure of the Old Kingdom. Ancient texts and works of art were carefully copied, and even the mortuary cults of the ancient kings of the age of the pyramids were revived in the region of Memphis. Extremely careful copies of old mortuary texts were included in the richly decorated tombs of officials. With such an emphasis on outward form, this era proved itself to be a genuinely "late" period.

Toward the end of his long and peaceful reign, Psammetichus I was drawn into the maelstrom of a realignment in world politics. In the hope of maintaining the balance of power in western Asia, he supported Assyria in its final struggle against Nabopolassar of Babylon; during the battles of the summer of 616 B.C.E., an Egyptian relief force appeared in Mesopotamia. There were initial successes, but the intervention of the Medes on the side of Babylon led to the swift demise of the Assyrian empire. When the capital of Nineveh fell in 612 B.C.E., an Assyrian prince continued the struggle from Haran, under the name Assur-uballit II, with Egyptian assistance. Psammetichus I died while Babylonian troops were advancing on this city, and after the fall of Haran, his son Necho II (610–595 B.C.E.) was obliged to leave the area east of the Euphrates to the victorious Babylonians and Medes. In the first spring season of his reign (609 B.C.E.), the new king marched to Asia with a strong force. Josiah of Judah, who encountered him near Megiddo, was defeated and killed; his land was made tributary, and the cities of the Phoenician coast came under Egyptian sovereignty. Necho set up headquarters at Riblah on the Orontes, where the exiled Assur-uballit evidently also made an appearance. Thus, for the first time since Ramesses II, Syria experienced a personal appearance by Pharaoh, and the heyday of the New Kingdom seemed to have returned. But the tables were soon turned. An Egyptian advance across the Euphrates failed, and the following years saw inconclusive battles west of the river. In 605 B.C.E., Necho was decisively defeated near Karkamish and forced back to Egypt by the Babylonian crown prince Nebuchadnezzar. There, he was able to repel a Babylonian advance against the Nile valley (601 B.C.E.), thus lending encouragement to the small states of Palestine one more time, but in 597 B.C.E. he was obliged to observe passively the first conquest of Jerusalem by Nebuchadnezzar and the installation of Zedekiah, a representative of the anti-Egyptian party, as king.

Necho was more successful at sea. He created a fleet of triremes after the Greek model, and—so reports Herodotus—Phoenician sailors under his commission conducted the first circumnavigation of Africa. A canal through the Wadi Tumilat connecting the Red Sea to the Nile was begun by him, but it was first put into operation by Darius I. The foreign policy of his son Psammetichus II (595–589 B.C.E.) was directed toward the south. Perhaps he feared that the important contemporary Ethiopian king, Aspelta (c. 593–568 B.C.E.), would take advantage of Egypt's difficulties in Asia to attempt to win back the land. In 593 B.C.E., his generals Amasis and Potasimto, commanders of the Egyptian troops and the foreign soldiers, respectively, ventured south beyond the Third Cataract and threatened the capital of Napata. Greek inscriptions on one of the colossal statues of Ramesses at Abu Simbel recall this campaign, which removed a possible threat to Egypt and at the same time triggered profound changes in the Ethiopian kingdom: the center of the realm was shifted further south, from Napata to Meroe above the mouth of the Atbara, where Aspelta was the first king to build in grand style, though the royal pyramid tombs would long continue to lie in the region of Napata. The kingdom of Meroe later became a part of the Hellenistic world, and not until ca. 300 C.E. did it fall victim to the onslaught of the Nobataeans, who were followed fifty years later by the great royal conqueror Aezanes of Axum. With this campaign of Psammetichus II, there began in Egypt a condemnation of the Ethiopian kings and a persecution of their memory, which the previous Saite monarchs had respected. Psammetichus II erected the earliest known building on the island of Philae, which in the Ptolemaic and Roman Periods would become a religious center whose influence extended deep into Nubia.

The king maintained peace with the great power of Babylon and evidently avoided interfering in the affairs of Palestine. Immediately after taking the throne, however, his young son Apries (589–570 B.C.E.), the Hophra of the Old Testament, supported the Jewish king, Zedekiah, and the Phoenician cities in their break with Nebuchadnezzar. But the desired weakening of Babylon's power failed to materialize; Nebuchadnezzar surrounded Jerusalem and repelled a relief attempt by Apries. In midsummer 586 B.C.E., Nebuchadnezzar's troops stormed the city and led large portions of the Jewish population into the Babylonian Captivity. Many other Jews, among them the prophet Jeremiah, sought refuge in Egypt; in the period that followed, many served as soldiers in the Egyptian army. On the island of Elephantine at the First Cataract, where the Greek garrison mutinied under Apries, a Jewish military colony appeared with its own temple to Yahweh; with the aid of papyri written in Aramaic, we can follow the changing destiny of this community down to the end of the fifth century. Although the last buffer state between the Babylonian empire and Egypt fell with the kingdom of Judah, Nebuchadnezzar displayed no inclination to repeat the Assyrian conquest of the land of the Nile. The remainder of Apries's reign thus proceeded peacefully. In 586 B.C.E., Ankhnesneferibre, a sister of the king, was inducted into the office of Divine Adoratrice of Amun at Thebes. Surrounded by capable officials from the royal court, she administered the divine state of the Thebaid for more than sixty years, until the Persian conquest.

Around 570 B.C.E., Apries answered a call for help from Libyan tribes seeking support from Egypt against the rising power of the Greek colony of Cyrene, and in doing so he added fresh fuel to the internal feuding of the Libyans and Greeks in Egypt. After the Greeks of Cyrene annihilated an Egyptian expedition at the Well of Thestis, Apries's troops mutinied and elevated the general Amasis (570–526 B.C.E.; Figure 50) to the throne. Notwithstanding help from Babylon, Apries was defeated, though he was able to reassert himself several times until he was finally killed after a series of indecisive battles. It fell to the new king to master the divisiveness at home and effect at least the appearance of a reconciliation of Egyptians, Libyans, and Greeks. He gave his predecessor an honorable burial and recognized his sister as regent of the Thebaid. Amasis concluded a treaty of friendship with Cyrene and sealed it with a dynastic marriage. In Siwa Oasis, he built a temple of Amun where oracles were given and to which Croesus, and later Alexander the Great, made pilgrimages.

Amasis ceded the Milesian settlement of Naukratis in the western delta to the Greeks as a trading colony; here arose the first polis on Egyptian soil, adorned with Greek temples. With his philhellenic policy, which was recalled with gratitude from Herodotus down to the Roman authors, Amasis established political and cultural ties as far away as the Greek mainland. He made a generous contribution to the restoration of the temple of Apollo at Delphi after it was destroyed, and he sent lavish dedicatory offerings to Lindos and Samos; the German author Schiller memorialized his friendship with the tyrant Polycrates of Samos. In the face of the growing hatred of foreigners in the land, which was buttressed by the religious puritanism of the Late Period and vented especially against Jews and Greeks, the latter were grateful for these friendly gestures on the part of the king. But Amasis earned the devotion of the Egyptians as well through zealous attention to the temples of the land and through important reforms that allayed grievances with the courts and the administration. In Dynasty 26, Demotic became the accepted form of cursive script in the royal chanceries. The official ranks seem to have been less rife with foreigners than in the Ramesside Period, though the bureaucracy did occasion the following outburst in the contemporary Instruction of Ankhshoshenq: "If Re is wroth with a land, he sets scribes to be its rulers." In the Saite Period, only some superficial forms remained of the divine kingship of the pharaohs; renowned as a drunk-

50. Relief from Karnak depicting Amasis. Photo © Aidan Dodson.

ard, Amasis seemed especially like a commoner in his relationships with his subjects.

The rise of the Persian empire led Amasis to abandon the policy of nonintervention he had previously maintained with regard to Babylon and Cyrene. As reported by Herodotus (*Histories*, book I, chapter 77),

Egypt even took part in a defensive alliance against the Persians with Babylon, Lydia, and Sparta but did not engage in any fighting, and in 546 B.C.E., the Lydian king, Croesus, lost his kingdom to Cyrus. The Persian entry into Babylon on October 12, 539 B.C.E., was followed by the defeat of the Phoenician cities, and Egypt had to reckon that it would be the next goal of the great conqueror Cyrus. The attack was delayed, however, until the reign of his son Cambyses (530–522 B.C.E.). Amasis died at the beginning of the winter of 526–525 B.C.E., while Cambyses was preparing his campaign against Egypt. Amasis's son Psammetichus III (Figure 51) must have encountered the Persian king at Pelusium in May 525 B.C.E. He was defeated, and when Memphis was lost after a brief siege, he fell prisoner to the Persians; according to Herodotus, he was later put to death because of an attempted uprising. Within a short time, Cambyses occupied the remainder of the land, and without a battle, the Libyans, the Cyreneans, and the Barcids submitted to the new overlord. But his campaign against the Ethiopians and his expedition to Siwa Oasis ended in failure and the loss of many lives.

Egypt thus became a satrapy of the Persian empire. The rulers of this world empire, who for the first time united the entire Orient in a single grasp, made their appearance in Egypt bearing the regalia and titles of pharaohs, but they met with more resentment than the Libyan and Ethiopian rulers who preceded them: the very word Mede became an insult. This hatred, which the later Greek writers could understand and enjoyed embellishing, was concentrated on the person of the conqueror Cambyses, and the most fearful atrocities were ascribed to him. After the emphatically pious demeanor of the recent native kings, the priesthood and the faithful masses must have felt especially pained by the Persian king's scant interest in the temples of the land.

His successor, Darius I (522–486 B.C.E.), displayed greater consideration for their religious sensibilities and thus was able to strengthen the reputation of the new regime; at Saqqara, he enlarged the Serapeum, the burial place of the Apis bulls, and he erected the temple of Hibis for Amun in el-Kharga Oasis, which was located on an important caravan route. At his order, Egyptian law was codified, and the old laws were also recorded in Aramaic, the official language of the Persians. Since few Persian officials were active in Egypt aside from the satrap and his staff, the new official language could not have attained the importance of Greek under the Ptolemies. The Persian provincial governors had to rely on a proven Egyptian administration that was prepared for loyal collaboration; in the eyes of these officials, Darius proved himself through his

51. Relief at Karnak depicting Psammetichus III (left) and the god Amun. Photo © Aidan Dodson.

deeds to be a legitimate pharaoh, though his Residence lay in a far-off land, as had been the case under the Ethiopian kings. The revolts that broke out after the news of the Greek defeat of the Persians in the first half of the fifth century B.C.E. were initiated by the Libyans of the western delta and remained confined to Lower Egypt. When Greek military assistance ended with the Peace of Callias in 449 B.C.E., quiet was restored in the land. At the beginning of this period of peace, which lasted for nearly half a century, Herodotus visited Egypt, like many a Greek traveler before and after him. With these travelers began an era of fruitful interaction between the two cultures—the younger, western one with its open attitude and the self-contained eastern one that bore the burden of thousands of years of history and had answers from primeval times at hand for all questions. Like many writers in the twentieth century, the Greeks allowed themselves to be creatively stimulated by the alterity of the culture of this "most pious of all peoples," as Herodotus calls them, and interpreted it after their own fashion.

At the death of Darius II (404 B.C.E.), Egypt was finally able to shake off Persian rule. Once again it was a Libyan, Amyrtaios of Sais, who led the uprising and was also able, some years later, to drive the Persians out of Upper Egypt, where Artaxerxes continued to be recognized until 401 B.C.E. Manetho counts him as the single king of Dynasty 28 (404–399 B.C.E.). The hands of the Persians were tied by the civil war involving the younger Cyrus and by the ensuing war with Sparta. Nepherites I, the founder of Dynasty 29, was thus able to devote himself to peaceful reconstruction, and a modest building activity blossomed; he constructed his tomb in Mendes. Of his successors, only Hakoris was of importance; he was able to repulse a Persian attempt to win back Egypt in a war that lasted from 385 to 383 B.C.E. Nepherites had the first Egyptian coins, copies of Athenian tetradrachms, minted for his army, which was led by the Athenian Chabrias. After the death of Hakoris, his son was compelled to yield to the usurper Nectanebo I of Sebennytos.

With him began Dynasty 30 (380–343 B.C.E.), the last native dynasty. It brought a worthy conclusion to the history of ancient Egypt; from Tanis to Elephantine and Philae, its capable monarchs left monuments and enlarged the possessions of the temples through new donations of land. They conducted successful battles to repel the Persian empire, which continued to view Egypt as an apostate satrapy, and they even went on the offensive; with a campaign to Syria in 360 B.C.E., Teos imitated the brilliant tradition of Dynasty 18, which also served as the model for the art of this period. In the autumn of 343 B.C.E., however, the Persians, under Artaxerxes III, succeeded in regaining the land; the last pharaoh, Nectanebo II, fled to Nubia. But the situation remained unstable, and parallel to the sovereignty of the Persian ruler Arses (338–336 B.C.E.), an apparently Lower Nubian prince, Khababash, succeeded in bringing Egypt under his control. For the ensuing two millennia, one foreign rule would be followed by another.

With the conquest by Alexander the Great in 332 B.C.E. Egypt entered a new period of radical change, and under the Ptolemaic successors of this conqueror of the world, it made its contribution to the cultural mix of Hellenism. As has occurred so often in the history of the land, the essence of this new period is most purely expressed in a tomb that was supposed to preserve beyond death the sum of an earthly life and in so doing served as a mirror of cultural attitudes. At the beginning of the Ptolemaic Period, Petosiris, a high priest of the god Thoth, had a tomb built in the cemetery of Hermopolis, one whose relief decoration is clearly divided into secular and cultic portions. The representations of daily life, which are illuminated by daylight from the outside, employ elements of Greek style strangely mixed with Egyptian forms, while in the darkness of the inner chamber, the cultic representations and texts preserve an age-old body of religious thought in traditional form. This juxtaposition of old and new was to determine the character of Egypt during the five centuries that ensued. Alongside the mixed Hellenistic culture of Alexandria appeared temples in purely Egyptian style, especially in Upper Egypt; many of them, like the charming temple of Hathor at Dendara, would be completed only under the Roman emperors. Roman legionaries would carry the worship of Egyptian deities to the furthest provinces of the empire, while the mummified remains of Egypt's once flowering culture, now hardened into bizarre forms, continued to lure throngs of Greek and Roman tourists to the land. Their written accounts, as well as the tradition of other ancient authors, determined the western picture of Egypt until Champollion and continue to have an effect to this day. With the decipherment of the hieroglyphs and the inception of systematic excavations in the Nile valley, the path to earlier and purer sources was cleared; since then, the periods of cultural flowering and decline in ancient Egypt have taken on ever clearer shape. For all their alterity, the Egyptians succeeded in creating a "pure, constrained / human, narrow strip of land between river and rock" (Rainer Maria Rilke, second Duino Elegy), and thus in erecting milestones on the spiritual road of humanity.

GLOSSARY

Amduat   An illustrated work that served as a guide to the twelve regions of the netherworld; first attested in tombs of the New Kingdom.

Amun   God worshiped principally at Thebes; eventually the chief god of Egypt.

Apis bull   Sacred bull worshiped in the Memphite area.

Aten   Designation of the sun disk and name of the god worshiped by King Akhenaten.

Ba   A sort of soul or manifestation of a deity or human being.

Block statue   Cube-shaped, stylized depiction of a person in a squatting position.

Capstone   Pyramid-shaped block of stone at the apex of a pyramid. *See also* **pyramidion.**

Cartouche   An oval sign, representing a loop of rope, used to enclose certain names, principally the throne name and the personal name of a monarch (*see* Royal titulary).

Cataract   A section of the Nile where the riverbed is shallow and rocky, making navigation difficult.

Cenotaph   A false tomb, constructed at a distance from one's actual tomb.

Colossal statue   A statue larger than life-size, usually considerably so.

Coptic   The last stage of the ancient Egyptian language, written with the Greek alphabet plus a few extra signs to indicate sounds not in the Greek language; first attested in the second century C.E.

Coregency   The practice in which two kings, usually father and son, shared the throne by mutual consent.

Determinative   A hieroglyph that was not read aloud but was placed at the end of a word to indicate the word's basic category of meaning, such as a seated woman after a woman's name, or three ripples of water after a word indicating a kind of liquid.

Ennead   A Greek word meaning a group of nine; principally used in reference to the nine deities of a creation myth that originated in the city of Heliopolis.

Epagomenal days   Five extra days added to the months of the solar calendar; there were 12 months of 30 days plus the epagomenal days, making a year of 365 days.

Execration texts   Texts listing potential foreign and domestic enemies of Egypt, and hostile forces more generally. They were written on pots and statuettes of bound captives, which were ritually smashed in an attempt to avert these inimical forces by means of magic.

Geb   Earth god and member of the Ennead of Heliopolis.

God's father   The title of a type of priest whose specific duties remain unclear.

Harmachis   A sun god whose name means "Horus in the horizon."

Harsaphes   Ram-headed god worshiped principally at Herakleopolis.

Heb-sed   See "Sed festival."

Heliacal rising   The rising of the star Sirius on the eastern horizon just before sunrise.

Horus   Sky god and god of kingship, depicted as a falcon or a falcon-headed man.

Hypostyle hall   A temple hall with two central rows of columns taller than those on either side of it, creating a raised central roof area with windows to admit light.

Judgment of the Dead   A postmortem trial in which the heart of the deceased was weighed on a scale against a feather representing Maat (q.v.); Osiris and his court presided over the trial.

Ka   Vital essence, or life force, of a human or a deity.

Königsnovelle   A text genre in which the king is depicted consulting with his advisers and making a bold decision, often against their advice.

Khentamentiu   A god of the dead at Abydos, identified with Osiris (q.v.) by the time of the Middle Kingdom.

Kush   The ancient name of Upper Nubia (q.v.).

Litany of Re   A religious composition, first attested in royal tombs of the New Kingdom, dealing with the forms of the sun god Re.

Lower Egypt   The Nile delta.

Lower Nubia   The Nile valley between the First and Second Cataracts.

Maat   The order of the created cosmos, personified as a goddess.

Mastaba   An Arabic word meaning bench, used to describe Old Kingdom tomb superstructures that are benchlike in form.

Middle Egypt   The northern portion of Upper Egypt. Unlike Upper Egypt and Lower Egypt, Middle Egypt does not correspond to an ancient designation of a portion of the country.

Montu   Warrior god, worshiped at Karnak as the son of the god Amun and Mut; also worshiped at Madamud and Tod.

Mut   Consort of Amun at the temple of Karnak.

Neith   Goddess worshiped primarily at Sais.

NN   Stands for the name of a person. *See* **Osiris NN.**

Nomarch   Administrator who governed a nome.

Nome   One of the administrative/geographical districts, or provinces, into which Egypt was divided.

Nubia   The Nile valley south of the First Cataract.

Osirid   Carved in the form of Osiris, as an Osirid statue.

Osiris   God of the dead and ruler of the netherworld; his resurrection after he was murdered by his brother Seth reflected the yearly revival of plant life.

Osiris NN   The name of Osiris, used as an epithet, followed by the name of an individual.

Ostracon   (plural **ostraca**) Inscribed potsherd or piece of stone.

Palermo Stone   Fragment, now in Palermo, of a slab of stone originally carved with the annals of the first five dynasties of ancient Egyptian kings.

Primeval Mound   Mound of earth upon which the creator god was believed to have emerged from the waters of chaos.

Pyramidion   The pyramid-shaped stone at the apex of a pyramid. *See also* **capstone.**

Re   Sun god, worshiped principally at Heliopolis, and also in the sun temples built by the kings of Dynasty 5 in the Memphite cemetery area.

Re-Harakhty   Sun god whose name combines that of Re with that of another sun god, Harakhty, which means "Horus of the horizon."

Regnal year   Year of a king's reign, as in "year 1 under the majesty of." The ancient Egyptians recorded dates in this manner, rather than numbering years sequentially from the beginning of an era, as we do.

Residence   Translating an ancient Egyptian word, Residence refers to a city serving as a capital.

Rock-cut tomb   Tomb tunneled into the side of a hill or cliff; a facade was sometimes carved around the entrance.

Royal titulary   A sequence of five titles, each accompanied by a name of the king, developed during the Archaic Period and the Old Kingdom. The first title was Horus; the second associated him with the Two Ladies, Nekhbet and Wadjit, the patron goddesses of Upper and Lower Egypt, respectively; the third was Horus of Gold; the fourth was King of Upper and Lower Egypt; and the fifth was Son of Re. The name following the fourth title is today called the prenomen or the throne name. The name following the fifth title, today called the nomen or personal name, was the name the king had received at birth; he assumed the other four names upon ascending the throne.

Sakhmet   Lion-headed goddess believed to send and heal illnesses.

Sed **festival**   A festival celebrated to renew the magical, creative powers of the king; it was typically celebrated after thirty years of rule and every few years thereafter.

Serapeum   Burial place of the Apis bulls (q.v.), beginning with Dynasty 18; located at Saqqara.

Serdab   A walled-up chamber in a tomb, containing one or more statues of the owner of the tomb and family members; *serdab* is an Arabic word meaning cellar.

Seth   God of the desert; member of the Ennead of Heliopolis.

Shu   God of air and light; member of the Ennead of Heliopolis.

Sobek   Patron deity of the Faiyum; represented as a crocodile or a crocodile-headed man.

Sokar   Falcon-headed god of the dead at Memphis.

Sothic date   Date of the heliacal rising (q.v.) of Sothis (q.v.)

Sothis   The star Sirius.

Thebaid   The southern portion of Upper Egypt; in the Late Period, the Thebaid became a state within a state, ruled from Thebes.

Theophoric name   Personal name that includes the name of a deity, such as Amenophis, which means "Amun is satisfied."

Thoth   God worshiped principally at Hermopolis; represented as an ibis, an ibis-headed man, or a baboon.

Titulary   *See* **Royal titulary.**

Two Lands   An ancient Egyptian way of referring to Egypt, which was composed of Upper Egypt (q.v.) and Lower Egypt (q.v.).

Upper Egypt   The Nile valley north of the First Cataract.

Upper Nubia   The Nile valley south of the Second Cataract.

Verso   The back of a sheet of papyrus.

Vizier   The official who headed the royal administration; a sort of prime minister.

Wawat   The ancient name of Lower Nubia (q.v.).

BIBLIOGRAPHY

Abbreviations

AA	*Artibus Asiae*
ÄAT	Ägypten und Altes Testament
ACF	*Annuaire Collège de France*
ADAIK	Abhandlungen des Deutschen Archäologischen Instituts Kairo, Ägyptologische Reihe
ADAW	Abhandlungen der Deutschen Akademie der Wissenschaften zu Berlin, Philolosphisch-historische Klasse
ÄgAbh	Ägyptologische Abhandlungen
ÄgFo	Ägyptologische Forschungen
AH	Aegyptiaca Helvetica
AJA	*American Journal of Archaeology*
ÄL	*Ägypten und Levante*
AMAW	Akademie der Wissenschaften und der Literatur Mainz, Abhandlungen der Geistes- und sozialwissenschaftliche Klasse
AnOr	Analecta Orientalia
AO	*Acta Orientalia*
ASAE	*Annales du Service des Antiquités de l'Égypte*
ASAW	Abhandlungen der Sächsischen Akademie der Wissenschaften zu Leipzig
AUUB	Acta Universitatis Uppsaliensis, Boreas
AVDAIK	Archäologische Veröffentlichungen des Deutschen Archäologischen Instituts, Abteilung Kairo

AW	*Antike Welt*
BA	Bibliotheca Aegyptiaca
BÄ	Beiträge zur Ägyptologie
BÄBA	Beiträge zur altägyptische Bauforschung und Altertumskunde
BASOR	*Bulletin of the American Schools of Oriental Research*
BBB	Bonner Biblische Beiträge
BE	Bibliothèque d'Étude
BEHE	Bibliothèque de l'École des Hautes Études, IVe section, Sciences historiques et philologiques
BES	Brown Egyptological Studies
BES	*Bulletin of the Egyptological Seminar*
BG	Bibliothèque Générale
BIFAO	*Bulletin de l'Institut Français d'Archéologie Orientale*
BM	Bibliothèque du Muséon
BMFA	*Bulletin of the Museum of Fine Arts, Boston*
BO	*Bibliotheca Orientalis*
BOS	Bonner Orientalische Studien, NS
BS	Bollingen Series
BSEG	*Bulletin de la Société d'Égyptologie de Genève*
BSFE	*Bulletin de la Société Française d'Égyptologie*
BTAVO	Beihefte zum Tübinger Atlas des Vorderen Orients, Reihe B: Geisteswissenschaften
CE	*Chronique d'Égypte*
CRAIBL	*Comptes rendus de l'Académie des Inscriptions et Belles-Lettres*
DE	*Discussions in Egyptology*
DFIFAO	Documents des Fouilles de l'Institut Français d'Archéologie Orientale
ECEA	Étude (Connaissance de l'Égypte Ancienne)
FIFAO	Fouilles de l'Institut Français d'Archéologie Orientale
GB	*Grazer Beiträge*
GM	*Göttinger Miszellen*
GO	Göttinger Orientforschungen, IV. Reihe: Ägypten
HÄB	Hildesheimer ägyptologische Beiträge
HCPHA	*Hafnia: Copenhagen Papers in the History of Art*
HPBM	Hieratic Papyri in the British Museum
HPSMB	Hieratische Papyri aus den Staatlichen Museen zu Berlin–Preussischer Kulturbesitz
IEJ	*Israel Exploration Journal*
JA	*Journal Asiatique*
JAOS	*Journal of the American Oriental Society*
JARCE	*Journal of the American Research Center in Egypt*

JEA	*Journal of Egyptian Archaeology*
JEOL	*Jaarbericht Ex Oriente Lux*
JESHO	*Journal of the Economic and Social History of the Orient*
JNES	*Journal of Near Eastern Studies*
JS	*Journal des Savants*
KBS	*Kölner Beiträge zur Sportwissenschaft*
MAFS	Mission archéologique française au Soudan
MAIBL	Mémoires de l'Académie des Inscriptions et Belles-Lettres, Nouvelle Série
MÄS	Münchner Ägyptologische Studien
MDAIK	*Mitteilungen des Deutschen Archäologischen Instituts, Abteilung Kairo*
MDOG	*Mitteilungen der Deutschen Orientgesellschaft*
MEEF	Memoir of the Egypt Exploration Fund
MEES	Memoir of the Egypt Exploration Society
MF	*Mannheimer Forum*
MIFAO	Mémoires publiés par les membres de l'Institut Français d'Archéologie Orientale
MIO	*Mitteilungen des Instituts für Orientforschung*
MMJ	*Metropolitan Museum Journal*
MRE	Monographies Reine Élisabeth
MTAMM	Markaz Tasjīl al-Āthār al-Miṣrīyah, Mémoires
MV	Monographien zur Voelkerkunde
NAWG	Nachrichten der Akademie der Wissenschaften in Göttingen, Philosophisch-historische Klasse
OA	*Oriens Antiquus*
OBO	Orbis Biblicus et Orientalis
OIP	Oriental Institute Publications
OLA	Orientalia Lovaniensia Analecta
PÄ	Probleme der Ägyptologie
PBA	Proceedings of the British Academy
PMMAEE	Publications of the Metropolitan Museum of Art Egyptian Expedition
PS	*Palestinskii Sbornik*
PYEEP	Pennsylvania-Yale Expedition to Egypt 1961–1962 Publications
RAPH	Recherches d'archéologie, de philologie et d'histoire
RE	*Revue d'Égyptologie*
RIDA	*Revue international des droits de l'antiquité*
SABMD	*Scholae Adriani de Buck Memoriae Dedicatae*
SAGA	Studien zur Archäologie und Geschichte Altägyptens
SAK	*Studien zur altägyptischen Kultur*
SAOC	Studies in Ancient Oriental Civilization

SCF Second Cataract Forts
SCL The South Cemeteries of Lisht
SCO *Studi Classici e Orientali*
SDAIK Sonderschrift des Deutschen Archäologischen Instituts Abteilung Kairo
SEL *Studi Epigrafici e Linguistici sul Vicino Oriente antico*
SÖAW Sitzungsberichte der Österreichischen Akademie der Wissenschaften
SSAW Sitzungsberichte der Sächsischen Akademie der Wissenschaften, Philologisch-historische Klasse
SSEAP Society for the Study of Egyptian Antiquities Publication
SSL The South Cemeteries of Lisht
UCOIAS The University of Chicago Oriental Institute Architectural Survey
UCPNES University of California Publications Near Eastern Studies
UERTFL Université Égyptienne, receuil de travaux publiés par la Faculté des Lettres
UF *Ugarit-Forschungen*
ULBFPL Université Libre de Bruxelles, Faculté de Philosophie et Lettres
Urk. *Urkunden des ägyptischen Altertums*
VB Vorderasiatische Bibliothek
VT *Vetus Testamentum*
WM Wilbour Monographs
WVDOG Wissenschaftliche Veröffentlichung der Deutschen Orientgesellschaft
WZKM *Wiener Zeitschrift für die Kunde des Morgenlandes*
ZÄS *Zeitschrift für ägyptische Sprache und Altertumskunde*
ZAW *Zeitschrift Antike Welt*
ZDMG *Zeitschrift der Deutschen Morgenländischen Gesellschaft*
ZDPV *Zeitschrift des Deutschen Palästina-Vereins*

General Treatments (Selection)

Assmann, J. *Ägypten: Eine Sinngeschichte.* Munich, 1996.
The Cambridge Ancient History. 3d ed. Cambridge and New York, 1970.
Grimal, N. *Histoire de l'Égypte ancienne.* Paris, 1988. Published in English as *A History of Ancient Egypt,* trans. Ian Shaw. Oxford, 1992.
Helck, W. *Geschichte des alten Ägypten.* Handbuch der Orientalistik. Pt. 1, vol. 1. Leiden, 1968.
Kemp, B. J. *Ancient Egypt: Anatomy of a Civilization.* London and New York, 1989.
Trigger, B. G., B. Kemp, D. O'Connor, and A. B. Lloyd. *Ancient Egypt: A Social History.* Cambridge, 1983.
Vercoutter, J., and C. Vandersleyen. *L'Égypte et la vallée du Nil.* 2 vols. Paris, 1992–1995.
Wolf, W. *Das alte Ägypten.* Munich, 1971.

For a survey of the entire field of Egyptology, including history and cultural history, see E. Hornung, *Einführung in die Ägyptologie*, 4th ed. (Darmstadt, 1993). There are articles on individual monarchs and topics in W. Helck and E. Otto, eds., *Lexikon der Ägyptologie*, 6 vols. (Wiesbaden, 1975–1992); P. Vernus and J. Yoyotte, *Dictionnaire des Pharaons*, 2d ed. (Paris, 1996); Th. Schneider, *Lexikon der Pharaonen*, 2d ed. (Zurich, 1996). On the royal titulary, see J. von Beckerath, *Handbuch der ägyptischen Königsnamen*, MÄS 20 (Berlin, 1984).

The Archaic Period

For a general survey, see W. B. Emery, *Archaic Egypt* (Harmondsworth, 1961). On the inscriptions of the Archaic Period, see P. Kaplony, *Die Inschriften der ägyptischen Frühzeit*, ÄgAbh 8 (Wiesbaden, 1963), with supplements: ÄgAbh 9 (1964) and ÄgAbh 15 (1966). On the cultural background, see H. Junker, *Die Geisteshaltung der Ägypter in der Frühzeit*, SÖAW 237/1 (Vienna, 1961); W. Helck, *Untersuchungen zur Thinitenzeit*, ÄgAbh 45 (Wiesbaden, 1987).

On prehistory, see the basic survey by M. A. Hoffman, *Egypt before the Pharaohs*, 2d ed. (London, 1991), and also B. Midant-Reynes, *La préhistoire de l'Égypte* (Paris, 1992); and for complementary studies on Nubia, see F. Wendorf and N. M. Taos, *The Prehistory of Nubia* (Dallas, 1968) and I. Hofmann, *Die Kulturen des Niltals von Aswan bis Sennar*, MV 4 (Berlin, 1967); for the delta, see Th. von der Way, *Untersuchungen zur Spätvor- und Frühgeschichte Unterägyptens*, SAGA 8 (1994), and E. C. M. van den Brink, *The Nile Delta in Transition: 4th–3rd Millennium B.C.* (Tel Aviv, 1992). On early social differentiation as exemplified at Tarkhan, see St. J. Seidlmayer, *GM* 104 (1988): 25–51. For a survey of recent research, especially on climatic history, see M. Cornevin, *RE* 47 (1996): 183–203.

On the problems of the unification and the Palermo Stone, see W. Kaiser, *ZÄS* 91 (1964): 86–125, and W. Barta, *ZÄS* 108 (1981): 11–23. The king lists and annals are treated by D. B. Redford, *Pharaonic King-lists, Annals and Day-Books: A Contribution to the Study of the Egyptian Sense of History*, SSEAP 4 (Mississauga, 1986).

On King Menes and his achievements as a culture hero, see H. Brunner, *ZDMG* 103 (1953): 22–26; on the question of his historicity, see S. Morenz: *ZÄS* 99 (1972): X–XVI, and also *Skarabäen und andere Siegelamulette aus Basler Sammlungen* (Mainz, 1976), pp. 44–45; I. Foti, *Oikumene* 2 (1978): 113–126. On early kings and later recollections of them, see D. Wildung, *Die Rolle ägyptischer Königen im Bewusstsein ihrer Nachwelt*, pt. I, MÄS 17 (Berlin, 1969); J. Baines, "Origins of Egyptian Kingship," in *Ancient Egyptian Kingship*, ed. D. O'Connor and D. P. Silverman (Leiden and New York, 1995), pp. 95–156.

On the problem of the early Libyans, see G. Fecht, *ZDMG* 106 (1956): 37–60.

For treatments of the divinity of the king, see W. Barta, *Untersuchungen zur Göttlichkeit des regierenden Königs*, MÄS 32 (Berlin, 1975); M.-A. Bonhême and A. Forgeau, *Pharaon: Les secrets du pouvoir* (Paris, 1988); and from the earlier literature, especially H. Frankfort, *Kingship and the Gods: A Study of Ancient Near Eastern Religion as the Integration of Society and Religion* (Chicago, 1948). On the queen, see L. Troy, *Patterns of Queenship in Ancient Egyptian Myth and History*, AUUB 14 (Uppsala, 1986).

On the administration, see W. Helck, *Untersuchungen zu den Beamtentiteln des ägyptischen Alten Reiches*, ÄgFo 18 (Glückstadt, 1954); K. Baer, *Rank and Title in the Old Kingdom* (Chicago, 1960); and N. Strudwick, *The Administration of Egypt in the Old Kingdom* (London, 1985).

The finds from Dynasty 1 in Palestine have been studied by S. Yeivin, *OA* 2 (1963): 205–213; idem, *BO* 23 (1966): 20 with n. 14; idem, *JNES* 27 (1968): 37–39; and A. R. Schulman in *For His Ka: Essays Offered in Memory of Klaus Baer*, ed. D. P. Silverman, SAOC 55 (Chicago 1994), pp. 241–244.

The tomb of Aha at Saqqara was published by W. B. Emery, *Hor-Aha* (Cairo, 1939). On the question of whether the royal tomb was located at Saqqara or at Abydos in this period, see most recently the contradictory positions of B. J. Kemp, *JEA* 52 (1966): 13–22, and J.-Ph. Lauer, *MDAIK* 25 (1969): 79–84. On the annalistic tablets and early writing, see S. Schott, *Hieroglyphen: Untersuchungen zum Ursprung der Schrift*, AMAW, 1950/24.

On the inscription of Djer at the Second Cataract, see W. Helck, *MDAIK* 26 (1970): 85, and I. Hofmann, *BO* 28 (1971): 308–309. On Den, see G. Godron, *Études sur l'Horus Den* (Geneva, 1990).

On changes in concepts of the divine, see E. Hornung, *Der Eine und die Vielen: Ägyptische Gottesvorstellungen* (Darmstadt, 1973), published in English as *Conceptions of God in Ancient Egypt: The One and the Many*, trans. John Baines, 2d ed. (Ithaca, 1996).

On the *sed* festival and the problematic of its historical occurrences, see E. Hornung and E. Staehelin, *Studien zum Sedfest*, AH 1 (1974).

The statue of Ninetjer was published by W. K. Simpson, *JEA* 42 (1956): 45–49. On his tomb at Saqqara, see P. Munro, *SAK* 10 (1983): 278–282.

Old Kingdom

On the cultural background, see H. Junker, *Pyramidenzeit: Das Wesen der altägyptischen Religion* (Einsiedeln, 1949). For a more recent survey, see G. Andreu, *L'Égypte au temps des pyramides* (Paris, 1994), published in English as *Egypt in the Age of the Pyramids*, trans. D. Lorton (Ithaca, 1997). For a general survey of the pyramids, see I. E. S. Edwards, *The Pyramids of Egypt*, rev. ed. (London, 1991), and R. Stadelmann, *Die ägyptischen Pyramiden: Vom Ziegelbau zum Weltwunder*, 3d ed. (Mainz, 1997).

On the Djoser complex at Saqqara: publications by C. M. Firth and J. E. Quibell, *The Step Pyramid* (Cairo, 1935); J.-Ph. Lauer, *La Pyramide à degrés*, 5 vols. (Cairo, 1936–1959); and the interpretation by H. Ricke, *Bemerkungen zur ägyptischen Baukunst des Alten Reiches*, 2 vols., BÄBA 4–5 (Zurich, 1944/Cairo, 1950). For the epithet "who opened the stone," see S. Schott, *MDOG* 84 (1952): 6; on Imhotep, see D. Wildung, *Imhotep und Amenhotep: Gottwerdung im Alten Ägypten*, MÄS 36 (Berlin, 1977). For a general study of Dynasty 3, see N. Swelim, *Some Problems on the History of the Third Dynasty* (Alexandria, 1983), and idem, in *The Intellectual Heritage of Egypt*, ed. U. Luft (Budapest, 1992), pp. 541–554; J. Kahl, N. Kloth, and U. Zimmerman, *Die Inschriften der 3. Dynastie: Eine Bestandsaufnahme*, ÄgAbh 56 (Wiesbaden, 1995).

On the biography of Metjen, see H. Goedicke, *MDAIK* 21 (1966): 1–71, and K. B. Gödecken, *Eine Betrachtung der Inschriften des meten im Rahmen des Sozialen und rechtlichen Stellung von Privatleuten im ägyptischen alten Reich*, ÄgAbh 29 (Wiesbaden, 1976).

On the pyramid of Sekhemkhet, see Z. Goneim, *Excavations at Saqqara: Horus Sekhem-khet, the Unfinished Step Pyramid at Saqqara*, pt. 1 (Cairo, 1957), and idem, *The Lost Pyramid* (New York, 1956).

On Huni and his inscription at Elephantine, see H. Goedicke, *ZÄS* 81 (1956):

18–24. On the transition from Dynasty 3 to Dynasty 4, see A. M. Roth, *JARCE* 30 (1993): 33–55.

Snofru: On the length of his reign (30–31 years, as opposed to higher estimates), see R. Krauss, *JEA* 82 (1996): 43–50. On the valley temple of the Bent Pyramid, see A. Fakhry, *The Monuments of Sneferu at Dahshur*, 2 vols. (Cairo, 1959–1961). On trade, see R. Müller-Wollermann, *JESHO* 28 (1985): 121–168, and on administration, idem, *BES* 9 (1987–1988): 25–40.

On the nomes, see the survey by W. Helck, *Die altägyptischen Gaue*, BTAVO 5 (Tübingen, 1974).

On the tombs of Dynasty 4 at Thebes, see D. Arnold, *Gräber des Alten und Mittleren Reiches in El-Tarif*, AVDAIK 17 (Mainz 1976).

For Khufu's boats, see M. Zaki Nour et al., *The Cheops Boats*, pt. 1 (Cairo, 1960), and P. Lipke, *The Royal Ship of Cheops: A Retrospectival Account of the Discovery, Restoration, and Reconstruction* (Oxford, 1984). On Khufu, see also H. Brunner, *OLZ* 53 (1958): 293–301, and S. Morenz, *ZÄS* 97 (1971): 111–118. The statuette in Cairo has been dated to Dynasty 26 by Z. Hawass, in *Mélanges Gamal Eddin Mokhtar*, ed. P. Posener-Kriéger, vol. 1 (Cairo, 1985), pp. 379–394. The Egyptian name of the king is actually Khnum-khufu(i) ("Khnum, may he protect me").

Son of Re: On the earliest attestation under Radjedef, see H. W. Müller, *ZÄS* 91 (1964): 131. On the effect of the new solar beliefs on the plan of the Sphinx temple, see S. Schott, *BSFE* 53/54 (1969): 31–41. S. Morenz draws a general picture of the development of the relationship of the king to the divine in *Die Heraufkunft des transzendenten Gottes in Ägypten*, SSAW 109/2 (1964).

On Radjedef and Khephren, see I. E. S. Edwards in *The Unbroken Reed: Studies in the Culture and Heritage of Ancient Egypt in Honour of A. F. Shore* (London, 1994), pp. 97–105, and R. Stadelmann, *SAK* 11 (1984): 165–172. The pyramids of Abu Rawash have now been taken up again by M. Valloggia.

For the Sphinx temple of Khephren, see H. Ricke, *Der Harmachistempel des Chefren in Giseh*, BÄBA 10 (Wiesbaden, 1970). On the debated reading of the king's name (also read as Rakhaf), see most recently H. Brunner, *ZÄS* 102 (1975): 94–99.

On the stone quarry at Tushka, see R. Engelbach, *ASAE* 38 (1938): 369–371. On the royal seal impressions at Buhen, see W. B. Emery, *Kush* 11 (1963): 119.

On the pyramid of Zawyet el-Aryan, see J.-Ph. Lauer, *RE* 14 (1962): 21–36; idem, *Histoire monumentale des pyramides d'Égypte*, vol. 1: *Les pyramides à degrés* (IIIe dynastie), BE 39 (Cairo, 1962), pp. 206–211; V. Maragioglio and C. A. Rinaldi, *L'architettura delle piramidi Menfite*, vol. 2 (Turin, 1963), pp. 41–49; D. Wildung, *Die Rolle ägyptischer Könige im Bewusstsein ihrer Nachwelt*, vol. 1, MÄS 17 (Munich, 1969), pp. 211–213.

For the mastaba of Shepseskaf, see G. Jéquier, *Le Mastabat Faraoun* (Cairo, 1928).

Queen Khentkaus and the transition to Dynasty 5 have been studied by H. Altenmüller, *CE* 45 (1970): 223–235, and M. Verner, *SAK* 8 (1980): 243–268.

On the conception and representation of the divine birth of the king, see H. Brunner, *Die Geburt des Gottkönigs: Studien zum Überlieferung eines altägyptischen Mythos*, ÄgAbh 10, 2d ed. (Wiesbaden, 1986).

On the sun temples of Dynasty 5, see W. Kaiser, *MDAIK* 14 (1956): 104–116, and E. Winter, *WZKM* 54 (1957): 222–233. The temple of Userkaf has been published by H. Ricke, *Das Sonnenheiligtum des Königs Userkaf*, 2 vols., BÄBA 7–8 (1965–1969), and that of Neuserre by F. W. v. Bissing et al., *Das Re-Heiligtum des Königs Ne-woser-re (Rathures)*, 3 vols. (Berlin, 1905–1928).

Still older than the colossal statue of Userkaf, though it cannot be dated exactly, is a colossal granite head in the Brooklyn Museum; see *Ägyptische Kunst aus dem Brooklyn Museum* (Berlin, 1976), no. 12 (with citations of earlier literature).

On recent finds at the causeway leading to the mortuary temple of Sahure, see Z. Hawass and M. Verner, *MDAIK* 52 (1996): 177–186.

Relations with Asia Minor and the Aegean: The supposed finds by Dorak at Troy have not been confirmed; for bibliography, see J. Leclant, *Orientalia* 38 (1969): 298–299. From Asia Minor, there is the golden cylinder seal of an official bearing the names of the last two kings of Dynasty 5; see *BMFA* 70 (1972): 11. On relations with the Aegean world, see J. Vercoutter, *L'Égypte et le monde égéen préhellénique*, BE 22 (Cairo, 1956), and W. Helck, *Die Beziehungen Ägyptens und Vorderasiens zur Ägäis bis ins 7. Jahrh. v. Chr.*, 2d ed. (Darmstadt, 1995).

The papyrus archive at Abusir was published by P. Posener-Kriéger and J. L. de Cénival, *The Abu Sir Papyri*, HPBM, 5th ser. (London, 1968), and the commentary was published by P. Posener-Kriéger, *Les archives du temple funéraire de Néferirkarê-Kakaï (les papyrus d'Abousir)*, 2 vols., BE 65 (Cairo, 1976). On the more recent finds at Abusir, see M. Verner, *Ztracené pyramidy, zapomenutí faraoni* (Prague, 1994); published in English as *Forgotten Pharaohs, Lost Pyramids: Abusir* (Prague, 1994).

For the Weltkammer of Neuserre, see E. Edel, *Zu den Inschriften aus den Jahreszeitenreliefs der "Weltkammer" aus dem Sonnenheiligtum des Niuserre*, 2 vols., NAWG 1961/8 and 1963/4–5, and the publication by E. Edel and St. Wenig, *Die Jahreszeitenreliefs aus dem Sonnenheiligtum des Königs Ne-User-Re* (Berlin, 1974).

On the titles of officials: The citation is from W. Helck, *Untersuchungen zu den Beamtentiteln des ägyptischen Alten Reiches*, ÄgFo 18 (Glückstadt, 1954), p. 112; see also K. Baer, *Rank and Title in the Old Kingdom* (Chicago, 1960), and N. Kanawati, *Governmental Reforms in Old Kingdom Egypt* (Warminster, 1980).

The Pyramid Texts in the pyramid of Unas have been published by A. Piankoff, *The Pyramid of Unas*, BS 40/5 (New York, 1968). The basic edition remains that of K. Sethe, *Die altägyptischen Pyramidentexte nach den Papierabdrücken und Photographien des Berliner Museums neu herausgegeben und erläutert*, 4 vols. (Leipzig, 1908–1922; rpt. 1960). A complete translation and additional texts have been published by R. O. Faulkner, *The Ancient Egyptian Pyramid Texts*, 2 vols. (Oxford, 1969). On the famine scene from the causeway of the pyramid of Unas, see S. Schott, *RE* 17 (1965): 7–13, and on the parallels see above under Sahure.

All the relevant wisdom texts have been translated by H. Brunner, *Die Weisheitsbücher der Ägypter* (Zürich, 1991); see also M. Lichtheim, *Ancient Egyptian Literature: A Book of Readings*, vol. 1: *The Old and Middle Kingdoms* (Berkeley, 1973).

On Asiatic policy in the pharaonic period, see W. Helck, *Die Beziehungen Ägyptens zu Vorderasien im 3. und 2. Jahrtausend v. Chr.*, ÄgAbh 5, 2d ed. (Wiesbaden, 1971). On the expedition to Punt in the reign of Izezi, see K. Sethe, *Urkunden des Alten Reichs* (Leipzig, 1933), pp. 128–129.

On Teti, see J.-Ph. Lauer and J. Leclant, *Le temple haut du complexe funéraire du roi Téti: Mission archéologique de Saqqarah*, vol. 1, BE 51 (Cairo, 1972). His immediate successor was the ephemeral Userkare. On the founding of Dynasty 6, see H. Altenmüller, in *Festschrift Jürgen von Beckerath*, HÄB 30 (Hildesheim, 1990), pp. 1–20, and R. Stadelmann, in *Hommages à Jean Leclant*, BE 106 (Cairo, 1994), vol. 1, pp. 327–335. A very fragmentary annalistic text of early Dynasty 6 has been published by M. Baud and V. Dobrev, *BIFAO* 95 (1995): 23–63.

For the cylinder seal of Pepy I, see H. Goedicke, *MDAIK* 17 (1961): 69–90 (on

Montu, see pp. 80–81). His queens are treated by C. Berger, in *Hommages à Jean Leclant*, BE 106 (Cairo, 1994), vol. 1, pp. 73–80. On the debated beginning of the cult of Amun in this period, see F. Daumas, *BIFAO* 65 (1967): 213–214, and D. Wildung, *MDAIK* 25 (1969): 212–219. Tombs of Dynasty 6 have been found in el-Dakhla Oasis; see A. Fakhry, in *Textes et langages de l'Egypte pharaonique: cent cinquante années de recherches, 1922–1972, hommage à Jean-François Champollion*, vol. 2 (Cairo, 1974), pp. 220–221, and M. Valloggia, *Balat*, vol. 1: *Le mastaba de Medou-nefer*, FIFAO 31 (Cairo, 1986). On the inscription of Weni, see P. Piacentini, *L'autobiografia di Uni* (Pisa, 1990).

On the expeditions of Harkhuf and political and cultural change in Nubia, see E. Edel, *Orientalia* 36 (1967): 133–158; M. Bietak, *Studien zur Chronologie der nubischen C-Gruppe: Ein Beitrag zur Frühgeschichte Unternubiens* (Vienna, 1968); H. Goedicke, *JNES* 40 (1981): 1–20 . There is a translation of Harkhuf's account in M. Lichtheim, *Ancient Egyptian Literature: A Book of Readings*, vol. 1: *The Old and Middle Kingdoms* (Berkeley, 1973), pp. 23–27.

Pepy II: On a rather shorter reign of 64 years, see H. Goedicke, *SAK* 15 (1988): 111–121. For his mortuary temple and the finds there, see G. Jéquier, *Fouilles à Saqqarah: Le monument funéraire de Pépi II*, 3 vols. (Cairo, 1936–1940). On Heqaib, see L. Habachi, *Elephantine*, vol. 4: *The Sanctuary of Heqaib*, AVDAIK 33 (Mainz 1985), and D. Franke, *Das Heiligtum des Heqaib auf Elephantine: Geschichte eines Provinzheiligtums im Mittleren Reich*, SAGA 9 (Heidelberg, 1994).

For the folktale about Pepy II, "Neferkare and General Sisene," see G. Posener, *RE* 11 (1957): 119–137.

The royal decrees of the late Old Kingdom have been comprehensively treated by H. Goedicke, *Königliche Dokumente aus dem Alten Reich*, ÄgAbh 14 (Wiesbaden, 1967).

Coffin Texts: On the problem of dating, see W. Schenkel, *Frühmittelägyptische Studien*, BOS 13 (Bonn, 1962). Complete translations have been published by R. O. Faulkner, *The Ancient Egyptian Coffin Texts*, 3 vols. (Warminster, 1973–1978), and P. Barguet, *Les textes des sarcophages égyptiens du Moyen Empire*, (Paris, 1986).

On the democratization of the title Osiris, see H. G. Fischer, *ZÄS* 90 (1963): 35–38.

On the successors of Pepy II, see J. von Beckerath, *JNES* 21 (1962): 140–147, and on Queen Nitocris, see C. Coche-Zivie, *BIFAO* 72 (1972): 122–132 (taking her to be a historical personage). A climatic explanation of the emergent "Dark Age" as a period of drought was attempted by B. Bell, *AJA* 75 (1971): 1–26. The end of the Old Kingdom has been studied by R. Müller-Wollermann, *Krisenfaktoren im ägyptischen Staat des ausgehenden Alten Reiches* (Tübingen, 1986); and for the developments that ensued, see L. Gestermann, *Kontinuität und Wandel in Politik und Verwaltung des frühen Mittleren Reiches in Ägypten*, GO 18 (Wiesbaden, 1987).

On the Herakleopolitan Period (Dynasty 9/10): J. von Beckerath, *ZÄS* 93 (1966): 13–20; H. Goedicke, *MDAIK* 24 (1969): 136–143; J. Lopez, *RE* 25 (1973): 178–191; F. Gomaà: *Ägypten während der Ersten Zwischenzeit*, BTAVO 27 (Wiesbaden, 1980); D. Lorton, *DE* 8 (1987): 21–28; St. J. Seidlmayer, *GM* 157 (1997): 81–90. E. Brovarski has argued for a longer duration of the First Intermediate Period in *AJA* 89 (1983): 581–584. The textual sources for the period are collected by W. Schenkel, *Memphis—Herakleopolis—Theben: Die epigraphischen Zeugnisse der 7.–11. Dynastie Ägyptens*, ÄgAbh 12 (Wiesbaden, 1965); and see further H. G. Fischer, *Inscriptions from the Coptite Nome: Dynasties VI–XI*, AO 40 (Rome, 1964), and idem, *Dendera in the Third Millennium B. C. Down to the Theban Domination of Upper Egypt* (New York, 1968). A fundamental study of the archaeological sources has been made by St. J. Seidlmayer, *Gräberfelder aus dem Übergang vom Alten zum Mittleren Reich: Studien zur Archäologie der Ersten Zwischenzeit,* SAGA 1 (Heidelberg, 1990). On foreign relations, see W. A. Ward, *Egypt and the East Mediterranean World 2200–1900 B.C.* (Beirut, 1971).

On Ankhtifi of Moalla, see J. Vandier, *Mo'alla: La tombe d'Ankhtifi et la tombe de Sébekhotep,* BE 18 (Cairo, 1950), and H. Kees, *Orientalia* 21 (1952): 86–97.

On the Antefs of Dynasty 11: Their tombs were excavated by D. Arnold in the northern part of the Theban necropolis; preliminary reports were published in *MDAIK* 23 (1968), 29 (1973), and 30 (1974); his definitive publication is *Gräber des Alten und Mittleren Reiches in El-Tarif,* AVDAIK 17 (Mainz, 1976). On Dynasty 11, see O. D. Berlev, in *Studies presented to H. J. Polotsky,* ed. D. W. Young (East Gloucester, 1981), pp. 361–377.

On the Instruction for Merikare, see J. F. Quack, *Studien zur Lehre für Merikare,* GO 23 (Wiesbaden, 1992), with a treatment of the history of the period.

On the end of the Herakleopolitan Period, see H. G. Fischer, *AA* 22 (1959): 240–252 (on the prison overseer Inyotef and artistic influences on Dynasty 11), and H. Goedicke, *JSSEA* 12 (1982): 157–164. On the mass grave of Theban soldiers, see H. E. Winlock, *The Slain Soldiers of Neb-Hepet-Re* (New York, 1945).

Middle Kingdom

General: H. E. Winlock, *The Rise and Fall of the Middle Kingdom in Thebes* (New York, 1947); D. Wildung, *Sesostris und Amenemhet: Ägypten im Mittleren Reich,* (Munich, 1984); J. Bourriau and St. Quirke, *Pharaohs and Mortals: Egyptian Art in the Middle Kingdom* (Cambridge, 1988). On the intellectual foundations, see H. G. Evers, *Staat aus dem Stein: Denkmäler, Geschichte und Bedeutung der ägyptischen Plastik während des Mittleren Reichs,* 2 vols. (Munich, 1929). A prosopography has been compiled by D. Franke, *Personendaten aus dem Mittleren Reich,* ÄgAbh 41 (Wiesbaden, 1984). On administration, see L. Gestermann, *Kontinuität und Wandel in Politik und Verwaltung des Frühen Mittleren Reiches in Ägypten,* GO 18 (Wiesbaden, 1987); W. A. Ward, *Index of Egyptian Administrative and Religious Titles of the Middle Kingdom* (Beirut, 1982), to which must now be added H. G. Fischer, *Egyptian Titles of the Middle Kingdom,* rev. ed. (New York, 1997); and W. A. Ward, *Essays on Feminine Titles of the Middle Kingdom and Related Subjects* (Beirut, 1986). I follow here the chronology of D. Franke, *Orientalia* 57 (1988): 113–138, which is based on R. Krauss, *Sothis- und Monddaten: Studien zur astronomischen und technischen Chronologie Altägyptens,* HÄB 20 (Hildesheim, 1985), in particular the Illahun Date of 1830 B.C.E. The years 1955, 1963, and 1976 have also found support as the date of the beginning of Dynasty 12; see, e.g., J. von Beckerath, *Orientalia* 64 (1995): 445–449.

The tomb of Montuhotep at Deir el-Bahri has recently been studied and published by D. Arnold, *Der Tempel des Königs Mentuhotep von Deir el-Bahari,* 3 vols., AVDAIK 8, 11, and 23 (Mainz, 1974–1981), and idem, *The Temple of Mentuhotep at Deir el-Bahari* (New York, 1979). In the numbering of the Montuhotpes, which differs considerably in the literature, we follow D. Arnold, *MDAIK* 24 (1969): 38–42, where the "ancestral" Montuhotpe receives no number, though in more recent literature the Montuhotpe who reunited the land is almost always designated Montuhotpe II.

Meketre's models were published by H. E. Winlock, *Models of Daily Life in Ancient Egypt* (Cambridge, Mass., 1955). On their redating to the beginning of Dynasty 12, see Do. Arnold, *MMJ* 26 (1991): 5–48.

On the Heqanakhte letters, see T. G. H. James, *The Hekanakhte Papers and Other Early Middle Kingdom Documents* (New York, 1962). and H. Goedicke, *Studies in the Hekanakhte Papers* (Baltimore, 1984).

On the transition from Dynasty 11 to Dynasty 12, see L. Habachi, *ASAE* 55 (1958): 167–190, and J. von Beckerath, *ZÄS* 92 (1965): 4–10. On the new Residence and its name, see W. K. Simpson, *JARCE* 2 (1963): 53–59.

The beginning of Dynasty 12 has been treated by J. Omlin, "Amenemhet I. und Sesostris I" (Ph.D. diss., Heidelberg University, 1962); L. M. Berman, "Amenemhet I" (Ph.D. diss., Yale University, 1985); and C. Obsomer, *Sésostris Ier: Étude chronologique du règne*, ECEA 5 (Brussels, 1995). W. K. Simpson has published many important administrative documents from this period in *Papyrus Reisner I* (Boston, 1963), *Papyrus Reisner II* (Boston, 1965), *Papyrus Reisner III* (Boston, 1969), and *Papyrus Reisner IV* (Boston, 1986). On the new royal necropolis at Lisht, see D. Arnold, *The Pyramid of Senwosret I*, SSL 1 (New York, 1988), and idem, *The Pyramid Complex of Senwosret I*, PMMAEE 25 (New York, 1992).

On stelae from Abydos, see J. Spiegel, *Die Götter von Abydos: Studien zum ägyptischen Synkretismus*, GO 1 (Wiesbaden, 1973), W. K. Simpson, *The Terrace of the Great God at Abydos*, PYEEP 5 (New Haven and Philadelphia, 1974); and M. Lichtheim, *Ancient Egyptian Autobiographies Chiefly of the Middle Kingdom*, OBO 84 (Freiburg and Göttingen, 1988).

For the fortress of Buhen, see W. B. Emery, H. S. Smith, and A. Millard, *The Fortress of Buhen: The Archaeological Report*, MEES 49 (London, 1979).

On the background of the assassination of Amenemhet I, see E. Hornung and E. Staehelin, *Studien zum Sedfest*, AH 1 (1974), pp. 59–60. The assassination and the coregency with Sesostris I have been the subjects of recent controversy; here I follow E. Blumenthal, *ZÄS* 110 (1983): 104–121 and 111 (1984): 85–107. K. Jansen-Winkeln sees the (failed) assassination attempt as the stimulus for the appointment of Senwosret as coregent; see *SAK* 18 (1991): 241–264. On coregencies in general, see W. J. Murnane, *Ancient Egyptian Coregencies*, SAOC 40 (Chicago, 1977). On the building inscription at Tod, see D. B. Redford, *JSSEA* 17 (1987): 36–57. Ch. Barbotin and J. J. Clère have pointed to strong political opposition to Senwosret I; see *BIFAO* 91 (1991): 1–32.

The fundamental study of the political literature of the Middle Kingdom remains G. Posener, *Littérature et politique dans l'Égypte de la 12ᵉ dynastie*, BEHE 307 (Paris, 1956).

On the royal statuary of Dynasty 12, see H. G. Evers, *Staat aus dem Stein: Denkmäler, Geschichte und Bedeutung der ägyptischen Plastik während des Mittleren Reichs*, 2 vols. (Munich, 1929). On the institution of kingship, see also E. Blumenthal, *Untersuchungen zum ägyptischen Königtum des Mittleren Reiches*, vol. 1, *Die Phraseologie*, ASAW 61/1 (Berlin, 1970).

On the meaning of the *sed* festival ritual as preserved in the dramatic Ramesseum papyrus, see H. Altenmüller, *JEOL* 19 (1965–1966): 421–442. On the order of the individual scenes, see also W. Barta, *ZÄS* 98 (1970): 9–12.

On the contracts of Djefaihapy, see A. Théodoridès, *RIDA* 18 (1971): 109–252. The nomarch's larger-than-life-size statue, which is dealt with in the contracts, is now in the Louvre; see J. Vandier, *CRAIBL* (1971): 356–375.

A survey of the Execration Texts is given by G. Posener in *Lexikon der Ägyptologie*, ed. W. Helck and E. Otto, vol. 1 (1972), pp. 67–69; on the expeditions, see R. Gundlach and E. Blumenthal, *ibid.*, vol. 2 (1975), pp. 55–68.

Amenemhet II: B. Fay, *The Louvre Sphinx and Royal Sculpture from the Reign of Amenemhat II* (Mainz, 1996); on the annalistic inscription, see H. Altenmüller and A. M. Moussa, *SAK* 18 (1991): 1–48, and J. Malek and St. Quirke, *JEA* 78 (1992): 13–18. On the Tod treasure, see F. Bisson de la Roque, G. Contenau, and F. Chapouthier, *Le trésor de Tôd*, DFIFAO 11 (Cairo, 1953). On the Minoan pottery, see B. Kemp and R. Merrillees, *Minoan Pottery in Second Millennium Egypt* (Mainz, 1980).

There is a survey of the papyri from el-Lahun (Kahun Papyri) in U. Kaplony-Heckel, *Ägyptische Handschriften*, which is vol. 20, pt. 1 of *Verzeichnis der orientalistischen Handschriften in Deutschland*, ed. W. Voigt (1971); see also U. Luft, *Die chronologische Fixierung des ägyptischen Mittleren Reiches nach dem Tempelarchiv von Illahun*, SÖAW 598 (Vienna, 1992), and idem, *Das Archiv von Illahun: Briefe*, HPSMB 1 (Berlin, 1992). On the town site, see A. Badawy, *A History of Egyptian Architecture*, vol. 2 (Berkeley, 1966), pp. 22–27. On Qasr el-Sagha, see D. and Do. Arnold, *Der Tempel Qasr el-Sagha*, AVDAIK 27 (Mainz, 1979).

On the statuettes found at Megiddo, see J. A. Wilson, *AJSL* 58 (1941): 225–236. On a more recent find, see J. Leclant, *Orientalia* 35 (1966): 166, and on Middle Kingdom finds in western Asia generally, and especially at Byblos, see W. A. Ward, *Ugarit-Foschungen* 11 (1979): 799–806.

Block statues: On the origins and meaning of this statue type, see H. W. Müller and A. Eggebrecht in *Festgabe für Dr. Walter Will* (Cologne and Berlin, 1966), pp. 121–163. See also the assessment by R. Schulz, *Die Entwicklung und Bedeutung des kuboiden Statuentypus*, 2 vols., HÄB 33–34 (Hildesheim, 1992).

Senwosret III: R. D. Delia, *A Study of the Reign of Senwosret III* (Ph.D. diss., Yale University, 1980); L. Gestermann, in *Per aspera ad astra*, ed. L. Gestermann (Kassel, 1995), pp. 31–50. Doubts entertained by R. A. Parker regarding a reign of thirty-six years, on the basis of the lunar datings, are mentioned by W. K. Simpson, *CE* 47 (1972): 45–54. Dated monuments end with year 19, but cf. now the recent finds in his cenotaph at Abydos, on which see J. W. Wegner, *JNES* 55 (1996): 249–279.

Nomarchs: New material has been furnished in particular by the excavations conducted by E. Edel since 1960 in the cemetery at Aswan; the finds are in the process of publication, beginning with E. Edel, *Die Felsengräber der Qubbet el Hawa bei Assuan* (Wiesbaden, 1967). D. Franke has modified the previous picture of an "abolition" of the nomarchy; see St. Quirke, ed., *Middle Kingdom Studies* (New Malden, Eng., 1991), pp. 51–65.

Nubian fortresses: Of the more recent publications, see especially D. Dunham and J. Janssen, *Semna Kumma*, SCF 1 (Boston, 1960); D. Dunham, *Uronarti. Shalfak. Mirgissa*, SCF 2 (Boston, 1967); and J. Vercoutter, *Mirgissa*, vol. 1, MAFS 1 (Paris, 1970). On the problem of data regarding unusually high Nile flood levels and the possible construction of a dam at the Second Cataract, see J. Vercoutter, *Kush* 14 (1966): 125–164, and B. Bell, *AJA* 79 (1975): 223–269. On the extremely high Nile levels at the end of Dynasty 12, see also Th. De Putter, *SAK* 20 (1993): 255–288.

On Egyptian influence on Byblos during the Middle Kingdom, see W. S. Smith, *AJA* 73 (1969): 277–281.

The Semna Dispatches were published by P. C. Smither, *JEA* 31 (1945): 3–10.

On the Sinai expeditions, see A. H. Gardiner, T. E. Peet, and J. Černý, *The Inscriptions of Sinai*, pt. 2, MEES 45 (London, 1955). On Harwerre, see especially H. Goedicke, *MDAIK* 18 (1962): 14–25, and L. Pantalacci, *GM* 150 (1996): 87–91, and D. Kurth, ibid. 154 (1996): 57–63.

Amenemhet III: R. J. Leprohon, *The Reign of Amenemhat III* (Ph.D. diss., University of Toronto, 1980); I. Matzker: *Die letzten Könige der 12. Dyn.* (Frankfurt a.M., 1986). On the question of the Labyrinth at Hawara, see A. B. Lloyd, *JEA* 56 (1970): 81–100; D. Arnold, *MDAIK* 35 (1979): 1–9; and C. Obsomer, in *Amosiadès: Mélanges offerts au Professeur C. Vandersleyen par ses anciens étudiants,* ed. C. Obsomer (Louvain-la-Neuve, 1992), pp. 221–324.

The tomb of Princess Nefruptah was published by N. Farag and Z. Iskander, *The Discovery of Neferwptah* (Cairo, 1971). For a summary of the treasures of the other princesses of late Dynasty 12 discovered at el-Lahun and Dahshur, see W. Wolf, *Funde in Ägypten* (Göttingen, 1966), pp. 131–142. On the pyramid complex at Dahshur, see D. Arnold, *Der Pyramidenbezirk des Königs Amenemhet III. in Dahschur,* vol. 1: *Die Pyramide,* AVDAIK 53 (Mainz, 1987).

On Amenemhet IV, see M. Valloggia, *RE* 21 (1969): 107–133. On Queen Nefrusobek, see idem, *RE* 16 (1964): 45–53, and E. Staehelin, *BSEG* 13 (1989): 145–156; on her throne name, see S. Aufrère, *BIFAO* 89 (1989): 1–13.

Folk tales and related material have been translated by E. Brunner-Traut, *Altägyptische Märchen,* 8th ed. (Munich, 1963). On hymnic poetry, see J. Assmann, *Ägyptische Hymnen und Gebete* (Zurich and Munich, 1975). On the "Book of the Two Ways," see L. H. Lesko, *The Ancient Egyptian Book of Two Ways,* UCPNES 17 (Berkeley, 1972), and E. Hermsen, *Die zwei Wege des Jenseits,* OBO 112 (Freiburg and Göttingen, 1991).

The fundamental study of Dynasties 13 to 17 is J. von Beckerath, *Untersuchungen zur politischen Geschichte der zweiten Zwischenzeit in Ägypten,* ÄgFo 23 (Glückstadt, 1965); and on chronology, see D. Franke, *Orientalia* 57 (1988): 245–274. On the royal tombs of Dynasty 13, see A. Dodson, *ZÄS* 114 (1987): 36–45. On the indirect synchronism of Neferhotep with Zimrilim and Hammurabi, see the critical remarks by Ch. Eder, *Die ägyptische Motive in der Glyptik des östlichen Mittelmeerraumes* (Leuven, 1995), p. 13. D. B. Redford sees in Dynasty 14 a list of Hyksos "ancestors"; see *Pharaonic King-Lists, Annals and Day-Books: A Contribution to the Study of the Egyptian Sense of History,* SSEAP 4 (Mississauga, Ont., 1986), pp. 199–201; on Dynasty 14, see also J. Yoyotte, *BSFE* 114 (1989): 17–63.

For the papyrus in Brooklyn, see W. C. Hayes, *A Papyrus of the Late Middle Kingdom in the Brooklyn Museum [Papyrus Brooklyn 35.1446]* (Brooklyn, 1955); reprinted, with errata and additional bibliography, as WM 5. The accounts of the royal court were published by A. Scharff, *ZÄS* 57 (1922): 51–68.

On the Hyksos Period, in addition to the works cited above by von Beckerath *(Untersuchungen zur politischen Geschichte)* and Helck *(Beziehungen Ägyptens zu Vorderasien),* see J. van Seters, *The Hyksos: A New Investigation* (New Haven, 1966), and D. B. Redford, *Orientalia* 39 (1970): 1–51; here I follow the reconstruction by Th. Schneider, *Lexikon der Pharaonen* (1996), p. 495, and other individual articles. For recent results of the current Austrian excavations at Tell el-Daba in the eastern delta, see M. Bietak, *Avaris the Capital of the Hyksos: Recent Excavations at Tell el-Dab'a* (London, 1996). On the contemporary Kerma culture in Nubia, see J. Vercoutter in M.-L. Bernhard, ed., *Mélanges offerts à Kazimierz Michalowski* (Warsaw, 1966), pp. 205–226; Ch. Bonnet, *Kerma, Territoire et Métropole: Quatres leçons au Collège de France,* BG 9 (Cairo, 1986), and idem, *BSFE* 133 (1995): 6–16. On finds from this period in Israel, see R. Giveon, *CE* 49 (1974): 222–233.

The expulsion of the Hyksos: On the end of the Hyksos, see H. Goedicke, in *Egyptological Studies in Honor of R. A. Parker,* ed. L. H. Lesko (Hanover and London, 1986), pp. 37–47. The stela of Kamose was published by L. Habachi, *The Second Stela of Kamose and His Struggles against the Hyksos Ruler and His Capital,* ADAIK 8 (Glückstadt, 1972). On the investigation of the mummy of Seqenenre and other royal mummies, see J. Harris and K. Weeks, *X-raying the Pharaohs* (London, 1973). On the chronology of Dynasty 17, see A. Dodson, GM 120 (1991): 33–38.

New Kingdom

There has been no recent comprehensive treatment of the New Kingdom. On Dynasty 18, see C. Lalouette, *Thèbes ou la naissance d'un Empire* (Paris, 1986), and on Dynasty 19, idem, *L'Empire des Ramsès* (Paris, 1985). The most important historical sources from Dynasty 18 are collected in K. Sethe, *Urkunden der 18. Dynastie*, 2d ed. (Leipzig, 1906–9; rpt. Berlin, 1961), continued by W. Helck (Berlin, 1955–1958), with German translations by K. Sethe (1914) and W. Helck (Berlin, 1961, rpt. 1984) and an English translation by B. Cumming, *Egyptian Historical Records of the Late 18th Dynasty* (Warminster, 1982–1984). The historical records from Dynasties 19–20 are published by K. A. Kitchen, *Ramesside Inscriptions, Historical and Biographical* (Oxford, 1968–1989); volumes of *Translations* of those records have been appearing since 1993, as have *Notes and Comments*. On chronological questions, see E. Hornung, *Untersuchungen zur Chronologie und Geschichte des Neuen Reiches* (Wiesbaden, 1964), and J. von Beckerath, *Chronologie des ägyptischen Neuen Reiches*, HÄB 39 (Hildesheim, 1994). On relations with western Asia, see W. Helck, *Die Beziehungen Ägyptens zu Vorderasien im 3. und 2. Jahrtausend v. Chr.*, ÄgAbh 5, 2d ed. (Wiesbaden, 1971), as well as Th. Schneider, *Asiatische Personennamen in ägyptischen Quellen des Neuen Reiches*, OBO 114 (Freiburg and Göttingen, 1992). On Nubia, see T. Säve-Söderbergh, *Ägypten und Nubien* (Lund, 1941), and W. B. Emery, *Egypt in Nubia* (London, 1965), also published as *Lost Land Emerging* (New York, 1967). The economy has been treated by W. Helck, *Materialien zur Wirtschaftsgeschichte des Neuen Reiches*, (Wiesbaden, 1961–1970); Jac. J. Janssen, *SAK* 3 (1975): 127–185; and D. A. Warburton, *State and Economy in Ancient Egypt: Fiscal Vocabulary of the New Kingdom*, OBO 151 (Freiburg and Göttingen, 1997). On the administration, see W. Helck, *Zur Verwaltung des Mittleren und Neuen Reiches*, PÄ 3 (Leiden, 1958), with *Register* (Leiden, 1975). On the problematic of a Nubian campaign by Kamose, see R. Krauss, *Orientalia* 62 (1993): 17–29.

Ahmose and his reign are treated in detail by C. Vandersleyen, *Les guerres d'Amosis, fondateur de la XVIIIe dynastie*, MRE 1 (Brussels, 1971). See also idem, *RE* 19 (1967): 123–159 and 20 (1968): 127–134 on the Tempest Stela, which sheds light on Ahmose's activities at Thebes, and also H. Goedicke, *Studies about Kamose and Ahmose* (Baltimore, 1995). On internal politics (the rebellion of Tetian), see W. Helck, *SAK* 13 (1986): 125–133.

Conquest of Avaris: On the date, see Vandersleyen, *Guerres d'Amosis*, pp. 33–35, and W. Helck, *GM* 19 (1976): 3–34. On the Minoan frescoes at Avaris, see M. Bietak, *ÄL* 5 (1995): 50–7, and idem, *BSFE* 135 (1996): 5–29.

On the purchase of offices (the "Juridical Stela"), see H. Kees, *Orientalia* 23 (1954): 57–63, and I. Harari, *ASAE* 56 (1959): 139–201.

Amenophis I: F.-J. Schmitz, *Amenophis I.*, HÄB 6 (Hildesheim, 1978). The assignment of a tomb to the king by H. Carter, *JEA* 3 (1916): 147–154, has been debated, but attempts to localize it in the Valley of the Kings have not been carried through. On the Theban royal necropolis in the Middle and New Kingdoms, see E. Thomas, *The Royal Necropoleis of Thebes* (Princeton, 1966); E. Hornung, *Tal der Könige: Die Ruhestätte der Pharaonen*, 3d ed. (Zurich, 1985), published in English as *The Valley of the*

Kings: Horizon of Eternity, trans. D. Warburton (New York, 1990); and N. Reeves and R. H. Wilkinson, *The Complete Valley of the Kings*, (London, 1996). On the tombs of officials, see the fundamental study by F. Kampp, *Die Thebanische Nekropole: Zum Wandel des Grabgedankens von der XVIII. bis zur XX. Dynastie*, Theben 13 (Mainz, 1996).

Ahmose-Nofretari and the later veneration of her are treated by M. Gitton, *L'Épouse du dieu Ahmès Néfertary* (Paris, 1975).

On the Amduat, see E. Hornung, *Das Amduat: Die Schrift des Verborgenen Raumes*, 3 vols., ÄgAbh 7 and 13 (1963–1967), and idem, *Ägyptische Unterweltsbücher*, 2d ed. (Zurich, 1984), which also contains translations of the other Guides to the Hereafter.

On the Litany of Re, see A. Piankoff, *The Litany of Re*, BS 40/4 (New York, 1964), and E. Hornung and A. Brodbeck, *Das Buch der Anbetung des Re im Westen*, 2 vols., AH 2–3 (Geneva, 1975–1977).

There are complete translations of the Book of the Dead by P. Barguet, *Le Livre des Morts des anciens Égyptiens* (Paris, 1967); T. G. Allen, *The Book of the Dead; or, Going Forth by Day: Ideas of the Ancient Egyptians as Expressed in Their Own Terms*, SAOC 37 (Chicago, 1974); E. Hornung, *Das Totenbuch der Ägypter* (Zurich, 1979); and R. O. Faulkner, *The Ancient Egyptian Book of the Dead* (London, 1985).

The temple of Karnak has been treated by P. Barguet, *Le temple d'Amon-Rê à Karnak*, RAPH 21 (Cairo, 1962); C. Traunecker and J.-C. Golvin, *Karnak: Résurrection d'un site* (Freiburg, 1984) (on the modern history of Karnak); and J.-C. Golvin and J.-C. Goyon, *Les bâtisseurs de Karnak* (Paris, 1987).

On the significance of Memphis, see A. Badawi, *Memphis als zweite Landeshauptstadt im Neuen Reich* (Cairo, 1948); on its New Kingdom cemeteries, see G. T. Martin, *The Hidden Tombs of Memphis* (London, 1991), and A.-P. Zivie, *Memphis et ses nécropoles au Nouvel Empire* (Paris, 1988).

Tuthmosis I: On his Nubian policy, see H. Goedicke, *JNES* 55 (1996): 161–176; on his building activity at Karnak, see J. Jacquet and H. Jacquet-Gordon, *Le trésor de Thoutmosis Ier*, 2 vols., FIFAO 32 (Cairo, 1983–1988); on his sarcophagus and tomb, see P. Der Manuelian and Ch. E. Loeben, *JEA* 79 (1993): 121–155.

Tuthmosis II: On the controversy concerning the length of his reign, see L. Gabolde, *SAK* 14 (1987): 61–81; idem, *BIFAO* 89 (1989): 127–139; and J. von Beckerath, *SAK* 17 (1990): 65–74.

Hatshepsut and her reign are treated by S. Ratié, *La Reine Pharaon* (Paris, 1972), and idem, *La Reine Hatchepsout: Sources et problèmes* (Leiden, 1979). On her statues, which display a gradual "masculinization," see R. Tefnin, *La statuaire d'Hatshepsout: Portrait royal et politique sous la 18e dynastie* (Brussels, 1979). The exact date of her usurpation of the throne remains uncertain; see J. Yoyotte, *Kêmi* 18 (1968): 85–91, and R. Tefnin, CE 48 (1973): 232–242. A positive assessment of her coregency with Tuthmosis III is offered by J.-L. Chappaz in *Individu, société et spiritualité dans l'Égypte pharaonique et copte: Mélanges égyptologiques offerts au Prof. A. Théodoridès*, ed. Ch. Cannuyer and J.-M. Kruchten (Ath, 1993), pp. 87–110.

Senenmut is treated by C. Meyer, *Senenmut: Eine prosopographische Untersuchung* (Hamburg, 1982); P. F. Dorman, *The Monuments of Senenmut*, (London and New York, 1988); and idem, *The Tombs of Senenmut* (New York, 1991). On the vizier User-amun, see E. Dziobek, *Die Gräber des Vezirs User-Amun, Theben Nr. 61 und 131*, AVDAIK 84 (Mainz, 1994).

On the trading expedition to Punt, see Abdel Aziz Saleh, *Orientalia* 42 (1973): 370–382. The land has been located within Sudan by R. Herzog, *Punt*, ADAIK 6

(Glückstadt, 1968), but cf., inter alia, the critical observations by W. Vycichl, *CE* 45 (1970): 318–324, and K. A. Kitchen, *Orientalia* 40 (1971): 184–207; on the question, see also G. Posener, *ACF* 73 (1972–1973): 369–374.

The temple at Deir el-Bahri was published by E. Naville, *The Temple of Deir el Bahari*, 7 vols., MEEF 12 (London, 1894–1908), and H. E. Winlock, *Excavations at Deir el Bahri, 1911–31* (New York, 1942). For the divine birth legend, see H. Brunner, *Die Geburt des Gottkönigs: Studien zur Überlieferung eines altägyptischen Mythos*, ÄgAbh 10, 2d ed. (Wiesbaden, 1986). A neighboring temple of Tuthmosis III was discovered by a Polish expedition in 1961; see J. Lipińska, *The Temple of Tuthmosis III: Architecture* (Warsaw, 1977).

The persecution of the memory of Hatshepsut began either upon her death or only after a long time had passed; on the latter possibility, see Ch. Nims, *ZÄS* 93 (1966): 97–100, and C. Meyer in *Miscellanea Aegyptologica*, ed. H. Altenmüller and R. Germer (Hamburg, 1989), pp. 119–126.

On Tuthmosis III, see M. della Monica, *Thoutmosis III, le plus grand des pharaons* (Paris, 1991). The Battle of Megiddo has been treated by R. O. Faulkner, *JEA* 28 (1942): 2–15; see also H. Grapow, *Studien zu den Annalen Thutmosis des Dritten*, ADAW 1947/2 (Berlin, 1947), and the aforementioned volume by Helck, *Die Beziehungen Ägyptens mit Vorderasien*. On General Djehuti, see J. Yoyotte, *BSFE* 91 (1981): 33–51. On the colonial administration of western Asia, see E. D. Oren, *JSSEA* 14 (1984): 37–56.

On obtaining gold from Nubia, see J. Vercoutter, *Kush* 7 (1959): 120–153.

For another interpretation of Tuthmosis III's festival hall at Karnak, see G. Haeny, *Basilikale Anlagen in der ägyptischen Baukunst des Neuen Reiches*, BÄBA 9 (Wiesbaden, 1970).

Amenophis II: P. Der Manuelian, *Studies in the Reign of Amenophis II*, HÄB 26 (Hildesheim, 1987); on his coregency with Tuthmosis III, see, inter alia, W. Helck, *MDAIK* 17 (1961): 106–108; D. B. Redford, *JEA* 51 (1965): 107–122; and R. A. Parker, in *Studies in Honor of John A. Wilson, September 12, 1969*, SAOC 35 (Chicago, 1969), pp. 75–82.

On the sporting activities of Egyptian kings, see the fundamental study by W. Decker, *Die physische Leistung Pharaos: Untersuchungen zu Heldentum, Jagd und Leibesübungen der ägyptischen Könige* (Cologne, 1971).

The letter to the viceroy Usersatet has been published by W. Helck, *JNES* 14 (1955): 22–31. See also S. N. Morschauser, *SAK* 24 (1997): 203–222.

On the military campaigns of Amenophis II, see E. Edel, *ZDPV* 69 (1953): 97–176, and Sh. Yeivin, *JARCE* 6 (1967): 119–128.

On Tuthmosis IV, see B. M. Bryan, *The Reign of Thutmose IV* (Baltimore, 1991); on Tuthmosis IV and Asia, see R. Giveon, *JNES* 28 (1969): 54–59.

The reign of Amenophis III is treated by E. Riefstahl, *Thebes in the Time of Amunhotep III* (Norman, Okla., 1964), and also in the catalog by A. P. Kozloff and B. M. Bryan, *Egypt's Dazzling Sun: Amenhotep III and His World* (Cleveland, 1992); see also M. Müller, *Die Kunst Amenophis' III. und Echnatons* (Basel, 1988), and M. Schade-Busch, *Zur Königsideologie Amenophis' III.: Analyse der Phraseologie historischer Texte der Voramarnazeit*, HÄB 35 (Hildesheim, 1992). The commemorative scarabs are to be found in C. Blankenberg–van Delden, *The Large Commemorative Scarabs of Amenhotep III* (Leiden, 1969). An important source for foreign relations has been published by E. Edel, *Die Ortsnamenlisten aus dem Totentempel Amenophis III.*, BBB 25 (Bonn, 1966). On developments in western Asia, see W. J. Murnane, *The*

Road to Kadesh: Historical Interpretation of the Battle Reliefs of King Sety I at Karnak, SAOC 42, 2d ed. (Chicago, 1990).
The fall of Tushratta occurred in year 6 to year 8 of Akhenaten, according to D. B. Redford, *History and Chronology of the Eighteenth Dynasty of Egypt: Seven Studies* (Toronto, 1967), pp. 216–218.
Temples of Soleb and Sedeinga: The excavations of the Mission M. Schiff Giorgini, starting in 1957, were published by M. Schiff Giorgini et al., *Soleb,* 2 vols. (Florence, 1965–1971). On the ritual purpose of the temple of Luxor, see L. Bell, *JNES* 44 (1985): 251–294.
Amenhotpe son of Hapu is treated in the posthumously published work by A. Varille, *Inscriptions concernant l'architecte Amenhotep, fils de Hapou,* BE 45 (Cairo, 1968). On the posthumous veneration of Amenhotpe, see D. Wildung, *Imhotep und Amenhotep: Gottwerdung im alten Ägypten,* MÄS 36 (Munich, 1977). On the Litany of Sakhmet, see J. Yoyotte, *BSFE* 87–88 (1980): 46–75.
On the new intellectual tendencies of the period, see L. Kakosy, *ZÄS* 100 (1973): 35–41. On Aya as Akhenaten's tutor, see H. Brunner, *ZÄS* 86 (1961): 93–94. On the marriages of Amenophis III and other kings to their daughters, see B. van de Walle, *CE* 43 (1968): 36–54, and W. Helck, *CE* 44 (1969): 22–25, with stress on their purely ritual character; see also C. Meyer, *SAK* 11 (1984): 253–263.
Akhenaten, his successor, and the Amarna Period in general have been extensively treated in the catalogs of important international exhibitions. See, inter alia, C. Desroches Noblecourt, *Toutankhamon et son temps* (Paris, 1967); I. E. S. Edwards, *Treasures of Tutankhamun* (London, 1972); C. Aldred, *Akhenaten and Nefertiti* (New York, 1973); and *Nofretete, Echnaton* (Munich, 1976). See further the monographs of C. Aldred, *Akhenaten, King of Egypt* (London, 1988); D. B. Redford, *Akhenaten: The Heretic King* (Princeton, 1984); E. Hornung, *Echnaton: Die Religion des Lichts* (Zurich, 1995); and the critical survey by J. Vandier, *JS* (1967): 65–91. A bibliography of scholarship on the period has been published by G. T. Martin, *A Bibliography of the Amarna Period and Its Aftermath* (London and New York, 1991), and a prosopography has been offered by R. Hari, *Répertoire onomastique amarnien* (Geneva, 1976); there is also a helpful orientation by H. A. Schlögl, *Echnaton—Tutanchamun: Fakten und Texte,* 4th ed. (Wiesbaden, 1993). On the designation of the Aten religion as a heresy, see J. Assmann, *Saeculum* 23 (1972): 109–126, and idem in *Lexikon der Ägyptologie,* vol. 1 (1973), pp. 526–540; see further G. Fecht, *ZÄS* 85 (1960): 83–118, wherein, inter alia, the name forms Yati (for Aten) and Akhanyati (for Akhenaten) are proposed. The texts from the period have been collected in translation by W. J. Murnane, *Texts from the Amarna Period in Egypt* (Atlanta, 1995).
On the vizier Aper-El, see A. Zivie, *Découverte à Saqqarah: Le vizir oublié* (Paris, 1990), and idem, *BSFE* 126 (1993).
The monuments of Akhenaten's new capital, Amarna, have been published by W. M. F. Petrie, *Tell el Amarna* (London, 1894); N. de G. Davies, *The Rock Tombs of El Amarna,* 6 vols., MEES 13–18 (London, 1903–1908); J. D. S. Pendlebury, *The City of Akhenaten,* 3 vols., MEES 38, 40, and 44 (London, 1923–1951); J. Samson, *Amarna, City of Akhenaten and Nefertiti: Key Pieces from the Petrie Collection* (London, 1972); L. Borchardt and H. Ricke, *Die Wohnhäuser in Tell el-Amarna,* WVDOG 91 (Berlin, 1980); G. T. Martin, *The Royal Tomb at El-Amarna,* 2 vols., MEES 35 and 39 (London, 1974–1989); and W. J. Murnane and Ch. C. Van Siclen III, *The Boundary Stelae of Akhenaten* (London and New York, 1993).
The Amarna archive of cuneiform texts was published by J. A. Knudtzon, *Die El-*

Amarna-Tafeln, 2 vols., VB 2 (Leipzig, 1908–1915; rpt. Aalen, 1964); see also A. F. Rainey, *El Amarna Tablets 359–379* (Neukirchen-Vluyn, 1970). A new, complete translation has been made by W. L. Moran, *Les lettres d'El-Amarna* (Paris, 1987), published in English as *The Amarna Letters* (Baltimore, 1992).

Smenkhkare: On his coregency with Akhenaten, see P. Munro, *ZÄS* 95 (1969): 109–116, and W. Helck, *CE* 44 (1969): 203–208. The question continues to be debated. According to a hypothesis of J. R. Harris, expressed in *AO* 35 (1973): 5–13 and 36 (1974): 11–21, Smenkhkare is to be identified with Nefertiti. By way of contrast, R. Krauss supports the opinion that after Akhenaten, Meritaten succeeded to the throne with a brief sole reign, only after which came the reign of Smenkhkare, whom she married after the failure of the Zananza affair; see *Das Ende der Amarnazeit: Beiträge zu Geschichte und Chronologie des Neuen Reiches,* HÄB 7, 2d ed. (Hildesheim, 1981). On the controversy regarding Nefertiti's fate, see R. Krauss, *MDAIK* 53 (1997): 209–219.

The reign of Tutankhamun lasted at least nine full years; see J. Černý, *JEA* 50 (1964): 39. His Restoration Stela was published by J. Bennett, *JEA* 25 (1939): 8–15. The Zananza affair has been reinterpreted by R. Krauss, *Das Ende der Amarnazeit,* and connected with a sole reign of Meritaten after the death of Akhenaten. The burial treasure is still not entirely published; see the exhibition catalogs listed previously and the publication of individual groups of objects in the "Tut'ankhamun's Tomb Series," beginning with 1963. There is a comprehensive volume by N. Reeves, *The Complete Tutankhamun: The King, the Tomb, the Treasure* (London, 1990). On the high priest Parennefer and his tomb, in which the chief theme is the return to Thebes of the cult of Amun, see F. Kampp and K. J. Seyfried, *AW* 26 (1995): 325–342; on activities at Thebes revealing the first reactions to Akhenaten, see M. Eaton-Krauss, *MDAIK* 44 (1988): 1–11.

Aya: O. J. Schaden, *The God's Father Ay* (Ph.D. diss., University of Minnesota, 1977); on his tomb, idem, *JARCE* 21 (1984): 39–65; and on his connection with Akhmim, see K. P. Kuhlmann, *MDAIK* 35 (1979): 165–188.

On Haremhab, see R. Hari, *Horemheb et la reine Moutnedjemet* (Geneva, 1965); E. Hornung and F. Teichmann, *Das Grab des Haremhab im Tal der Könige* (Bern, 1971); and J. M. Kruchten, *Le Décret d'Horemheb: Traduction, commentaire épigraphique, philologique, et institutionnel,* ULBFPL 82, (Brussels, 1981). On the controversy regarding the length of his reign, see J. van Dijk, *GM* 148 (1995): 29–34, favoring a brief reign, and J. von Beckerath, *SAK* 22 (1995): 37–41, in favor of a long one. In January 1975 his Memphite tomb was rediscovered by an English and Dutch expedition; see G. T. Martin, *The Memphite Tomb of Horemheb, Commander-in-Chief of Tutankhamun,* 2 vols., MEES 55 and 60 (London, 1989–1996).

The chronology and genealogy of the Ramesside Period are treated by M. L. Bierbrier, *The Late New Kingdom in Egypt* (Warminster, 1975). On the institution of kingship in this and the following periods, see N.-C. Grimal, *Les Termes de la propagande royale égyptienne de la XIXe dynastie à la conquête d'Alexandre,* MAIBL 6 (Paris, 1986), and on internal politics, see P. Vernus, *Affaires et scandales sous les Ramsès* (Paris, 1993).

On Sethos I, see S. Schott, *Der Denkstein Sethos' I. für die Kapelle Ramses' I. in Abydos,* NAWG 1964/1, and R. O. Faulkner, "The Wars of Sethos I," *JEA* 33 (1947): 34–39; on his activity in the eastern delta, see L. Habachi, *ZÄS* 100 (1974): 95–102. See also E. Hornung und E. Staehelin, eds., *Sethos—Ein Pharaonengrab: Dokumentation zu einer Ausstellung des Ägyptologischen Seminars der Universität Basel im Antiken-*

museum (5. Dezember 1991 bis 29. Marz 1992) (Basel, 1991). On the king's most important monuments, see H. Frankfort, *The Cenotaph of Seti I at Abydos*, 2 vols. (London, 1933); A. M. Calverley and M. F. Broome, *The Temple of King Sethos I at Abydos*, 4 vols. (London and Chicago, 1933–1958); G. Haeny, *Basilikale Anlagen in der ägyptischen Baukunst des Neuen Reiches*, BÄBA 9 (Wiesbaden, 1970) (hypostyle hall); and E. Hornung, *The Tomb of Pharaoh Seti I / Das Grab Sethos' I.*, (Zurich and Munich, 1991), based on the photographs of H. Burton, *The Battle Reliefs of King Sety I, Reliefs and Inscriptions at Karnak*, vol. 4, OIP 107 (Chicago, 1986). On his possible coregency with Ramesses II, see W. J. Murnane, *JNES* 34 (1975): 153–190. On the Book of the Heavenly Cow, see E. Hornung, *Der ägyptische Mythos von der Himmelskuh*, OBO 46, 3d ed. (Freiburg and Göttingen, 1997).

Ramesses II: K. A. Kitchen, *Pharaoh Triumphant: The Life and Times of Ramesses II, King of Egypt* (Warminster, 1982), and Ch. Desroches-Noblecourt, *Ramsès II: La véritable histoire* (Paris, 1996); see also the exhibit catalog *Ramsès le Grand* (Paris, 1976), as well as E. Bleiberg and R. Freed, eds., *Fragments of a Shattered Visage* (Memphis, Tenn., 1991), and J. D. Schmidt, *Ramesses II: A Chronological Structure for His Reign* (Baltimore, 1973), with the critical remarks of K. A. Kitchen, *JEA* 61 (1975): 265–270. On his mummy, see L. Balout and C. Roubet, *La momie de Ramsès II* (Paris, 1985), and on his deification, see L. Habachi, *Features of the Deification of Ramesses II*, ADAIK 5 (Glückstadt, 1969).

For a discussion of Pi-Riamsese in the eastern delta, see M. Bietak, *Avaris and Piramesse: Archaeological Exploration in the Eastern Nile Delta*, PBA 65 (Oxford, 1979).

Battle of Qadesh: The texts were published by Ch. Kuentz, *La Bataille de Qadech*, MIFAO 55 (Cairo, 1928–1934) and translated by A. H. Gardiner, *The Kadesh Inscriptions of Ramesses II* (Oxford, 1960); see also Th. von der Way, *Die Textüberlieferung Ramses' II. zur Qadeš-Schlacht: Analyse und Struktur*, HÄB 22 (Hildesheim, 1984), and H. Goedicke, *Perspectives on the Battle of Kadesh* (Baltimore, 1986). On Ramesses II's policy of peace, see J. Assmann, in *MF* 83/84 (1983): 175–231.

On relations with the Hittites and the treaty with them, see E. Edel, *Die ägyptisch-hethitische Korrespondenz aus Boghazköi in babylonischen und hethitischen Sprache* (Opladen, 1994), and idem, *Ägyptische Ärzte und ägyptische Medizin am hethitischen Königshof* (Opladen, 1976).

The tomb of Nofretari has been published in its entirety by G. Thausing and H. Goedicke, *Nofretari: Eine Dokumentation der Wandgemälde ihres Grabes* (Graz, 1971), and in part by E. Dondelinger, *Der Jenseitsweg der Nofretari: Bilder aus dem Grab einer ägyptischen Königin*, 2d ed. (Graz, 1977); by way of supplements, see E. Hornung, *BO* 32 (1975): 143–145, and H. C. Schmidt and J. Willeitner, *Nefertari, Gemahlin Ramses' II.*, special issue of *ZAW* (1994). Ramesses II's mother, Tuya, also received a tomb in the Valley of the Queens and a mortuary temple of her own. His chief wife, Isisnofret, is treated by Ch. Leblanc, *BIFAO* 93 (1993): 313–333.

On Khaemwese, see F. Gomaà, *Chaemwese: Sohn Ramses' II. und Hoherpriester von Memphis* (Wiesbaden, 1973). The problem of the succession is treated by Jac. J. Janssen, *CE* 38 (1963): 30–36.

Temple of Abu Simbel: To date, only the smaller temple of Nofretari has been published in its entirety; see C. Desroches-Noblecourt and Ch. Kuentz, *Le petit temple d'Abou Simbel* (Cairo, 1968). On the moving of the temple to higher ground, see C. Desroches-Noblecourt and G. Gerster, *Die Welt rettet Abu Simbel* (Vienna and Berlin, 1968), and T. Säve-Söderbergh, *Temples and Tombs of Ancient Nubia* (London, 1987).

The Ramesseum is now published by the Documentation Center in Cairo; see *Le Ramesseum* (Cairo, 1973–), and see further W. Helck, *Die Ritualdarstellungen des Ramesseums*, vol. 1, ÄgAbh 25 (Wiesbaden, 1972).

On Merneptah, see H. Sourouzian, *Les monuments du roi Merenptah*, SDAIK 22 (Mainz, 1989). He probably reigned only about ten years; see M. L. Bierbrier, *The Late New Kingdom in Egypt (c. 1300–664 B.C.): A Genealogical and Chronological Investigation* (Warminster, 1975), p. 15. His career before he ascended the throne has been treated by L.-A. Christophe, *ASAE* 51 (1951): 335–372. On his worship at Memphis, see E. Otto, *ZÄS* 81 (1956): 118, and on his mortuary temple there, see W. Helck, *JNES* 25 (1966): 34–35; the sarcophagus reused by Psusennes I may stem from his cenotaph. On his aid to the Hittites, see G. A. Wainwright, *JEA* 46 (1960): 24–28.

There is a survey of the Sea Peoples by A. Malamat in *The World History of the Jewish People*, 1st ser., *Ancient Times*, vol. 3 (Tel-Aviv, 1971), chap. 2. Of the many further works, reference here will be restricted to G. A. Lehmann, *Die mykenisch-frühgriechische Welt und der östliche Mittelmeerraum in der Zeit der "Seevölker"-Invasionen* (Opladen, 1985). There is much new material in W. A. Ward and M. S. Joukowsky, *The Crisis Years: The 12th Century B.C.* (Dubuque, 1992).

On the location of the battle against the Libyans (under their leader Marayu) and the Sea Peoples in the western delta, see H. de Meulenaere, *BIFAO* 62 (1964): 170. On a contemporary, terrible judgment against the Nubians, see A. A. Youssef, *ASAE* 58 (1964): 273–280. For a recent translation of the Israel Stela, see M. Lichtheim, *Ancient Egyptian Literature*, vol. 2, *The New Kingdom* (Berkeley, 1976), pp. 73–78.

On Amenmesse and the royal succession at the end of Dynasty 19, see R. Krauss, *SAK* 4 (1976): 161–199 and 5 (1977): 131–174; Amenmesse had no sole rule, but temporarily occupied Nubia and Upper Egypt during the reign of Sethos II. On further monuments of Amenmesse, see A. Dodson, *JEA* 81 (1995): 115–128.

On Twosre and Siptah, see A. H. Gardiner, *JEA* 44 (1958): 12–22, and J. Vandier, *RE* 23 (1971): 165–191; on Twosre and Sethnakhte, see H. Altenmüller, *JEA* 68 (1982): 107–115; on the tomb of Twosre, see idem, *GM* 84 (1985): 7–17; on Bay, see J. Černý, *ZÄS* 93 (1966): 35–39, and H. Altenmüller, *SAK* 23 (1996): 1–9. On Sethnakhte, see J. von Beckerath, in *The Intellectual Heritage of Egypt*, ed. U. Luft (Budapest, 1992), pp. 63–67, and on his stela from Elephantine, see H. Goedicke, *MDAIK* 52 (1996): 157–175.

Ramesses III is treated by Jac. J. Janssen, *Ramses III* (Leiden, 1948), and P. Grandet, *Ramsès III: Histoire d'une règne* (Paris, 1993). On his mortuary temple, see the exemplary publication by the Oriental Institute Epigraphic Survey, *Medinet Habu*, 8 vols., OIP 8, 9, 23, 51, 83, 84, 93, and 94 (Chicago, 1930–70), and U. Hölscher, *The Excavation of Medinet Habu*, 5 vols., UCOIAS 21, 41, 54, 55, 66 (Chicago, 1934–54); there is a summary by U. Hölscher, *Die Wiedergewinnung von Medinet Habu im westlichen Theben* (Tübingen, 1958), and the historical inscriptions from the temple are translated by W. F. Edgerton and J. A. Wilson, *Historical Records of Ramses III: The Texts in Medinet Habu*, SAOC 12 (Chicago, 1936). On the tombs of the princes, see F. Abitz, *Ramses III. in den Gräbern seiner Söhne*, OBO 72 (Freiburg and Göttingen, 1986).

On the battle against the Sea Peoples, see R. Stadelmann, *Saeculum* 19 (1968): 156–171, and the works cited previously under Merneptah. On the Philistines in particular, see K. A. Kitchen in *Peoples of Old Testament Times*, ed. D. J. Wiseman (Oxford, 1973), pp. 53–78.

Important portions of the material from Deir el-Medina have been appraised by J. Černý, *A Community of Workmen at Thebes in the Ramesside Period*, BE 50 (Cairo,

1973) and Jac. J. Janssen, *Commodity Prices from the Ramessid Period* (Leiden, 1975); see also D. Valbelle, *"Les Ouvriers de la tombe": Deir el-Médineh à l'époque ramesside*, BE 96 (Cairo, 1985). There is a selection of texts in S. Allam, *Hieratische Ostraka und Papyri aus der Ramessidenzeit* (Tübingen, 1973).

On the workmen's strikes, see W. F. Edgerton, *JNES* 10 (1951): 137–145; P. J. Frandsen in *Studies in Egyptology Presented to Miriam Lichtheim*, ed. S. Israelit-Groll (Jerusalem, 1990), Vol. 1, pp. 166–199; and Jac. J. Janssen, *BSEG* 16 (1992): 41–49. On the assassination of Ramesses III, see A. de Buck, *JEA* 23 (1937): 152–164, and H. Goedicke, *JEA* 49 (1963): 71–92.

The text of Papyrus Harris is published by W. Erichsen, *Papyrus Harris: Hieroglyphische Transkription*, BA 5 (Brussels, 1933); see also the edition by P. Grandet, *Le Papyrus Harris I (BM 9999)*, BE 109 (Cairo, 1994).

On Ramesses IV, see E. Hornung, *Zwei ramessidische Königsgräber: Ramses IV. und Ramses VII.*, Theben 11 (Mainz, 1990); and A. J. Peden, *The Reign of Ramesses IV* (Warminster, 1994). On the great stone quarrying expedition, see L.-A. Christophe, *BIFAO* 48 (1949): 1–38; it was under the command of Ramessesnakhte, the high priest of Amun.

The still uncertain genealogy of the late Ramesside monarchs has been repeatedly discussed; see K. A. Kitchen, *JEA* 58 (1972): 182–194 and *SAK* 11 (1984): 127–134.

The tomb of Ramesses V and VI has been published by A. Piankoff and N. Rambova, *The Tomb of Ramesses VI*, 2 vols., BS 40/1 (New York, 1954), with a translation of all the texts; see also F. Abitz, *Baugeschichte und Dekoration des Grabes Ramses' VI.*, OBO 89 (Freiburg and Göttingen, 1989). Papyrus Wilbour, an important economic document, belongs to the reign of Ramesses V; see A. H. Gardiner, *The Wilbour Papyrus*, 4 vols. (Oxford, 1941–52). On the end of Egyptian sovereignty in Palestine, see M. Bietak, *MDAIK* 47 (1991): 35–50.

On the administration in late Dynasty 20, see M. L. Bierbrier, *JEA* 58 (1972): 195–199. For the texts regarding the tomb robberies, see T. E. Peet, *The Great Tomb-robberies of the Twentieth Egyptian Dynasty: Being a Critical Study, with Translations and Commentaries, of the Papyri in Which These Are Recorded*, 2 vols. (Oxford, 1930); and further, J. Capart, A. H. Gardiner, and B. van de Walle, *JEA* 22 (1936): 169–193. On the strikes, see above under Ramesses III.

On the high priest Amenhotpe, see E. F. Wente, *JNES* 25 (1966): 73–87, and on the thefts at Karnak, see O. Goelet, *JEA* 82 (1996): 107–127. For the events that followed and on the controversy regarding the transition from Dynasty 20 to Dynasty 21, see A. Niwiński, in *Gegengabe: Festschrift für Emma Brunner-Traut*, ed. I. Gamer-Wallert and W. Helck (Tübingen, 1992), pp. 235–262; idem, *BIFAO* 95 (1995): 329–360; and idem, *BSFE* 136 (1996): 5–26; and K. Jansen-Winkeln, *GM* 157 (1997): 49–74, reaffirming the sequence Piankh-Herihor. A translation of the report of Wenamun can be found in M. Lichtheim, *Ancient Egyptian Literature: A Book of Readings*, vol. 2, *The New Kingdom* (Berkeley, 1976), pp. 224–230.

Late Period

On the Third Intermediate Period (Dynasty 21 to Dynasty 24/25), see K. A. Kitchen, *The Third Intermediate Period in Egypt*, 2d ed. (Warminster, 1986), and also M. L. Bierbrier, *The Late New Kingdom in Egypt* (Warminster, 1975), and M. Römer, *Gottes- und Priesterherrschaft in Ägypten am Ende des Neuen Reiches: Ein religions-*

geschichtliches Phänomen und seine sozialen Grundlagen, ÄAT 21 (Wiesbaden, 1994). See also the richly documented survey by H. Jacquet-Gordon, *Textes et langages de l'Égypte pharaonique,* vol. 2 (Cairo, 1974), pp. 107–122. On illustrations and religious papyri, see A. Niwiński, *Studies on the Illustrated Theban Funerary Papyri of the 11th and 10th Centuries B.C.,* OBO 86 (Freiburg and Göttingen, 1989), and on the coffins, idem, *21st Dynasty Coffins from Thebes,* (Mainz, 1988).

On the political history of the actual Late Period (Dynasties 26–30), see F. K. Kienitz, *Die politische Geschichte Ägyptens vom 7. bis zum 4. Jahrhundert vor der Zeitwende* (Berlin, 1953), and M. F. Gyles, *Pharaonic Policies and Administration, 663 to 323 B.C.* (Chapel Hill, 1959). On the institution of kingship, see U. Rössler-Köhler, *Individuelle Haltungen zum ägyptischen Königtum der Spätzeit,* GO 21 (Wiesbaden, 1991), dealing with Dynasty 21 to the Roman Period.

The royal tombs of Tanis were published by P. Montet, *La Nécropole royale de Tanis,* 3 vols. (Paris, 1947–1960). On the type of the Late Period royal tombs, see R. Stadelmann, *MDAIK* 27 (1971): 111–123. On the finds from the tombs at Tanis, see the catalog *Tanis, l'or des pharaons: Paris, Galeries nationales du Grand Palais, 26 mars–20 juillet 1987, Marseille, Centre de la Vieille Charité, 19 septembre–30 novembre 1987* (Paris, 1987). On the reburial of the royal mummies, see K. Jansen-Winkeln, *ZÄS* 122 (1995): 62–78.

The stela in Paris regarding banishment to the oases has been studied by J. von Beckerath, *RE* 20 (1968): 7–36.

On Gezer as the dowry of Siamun, see A. Malamat, *JNES* 22 (1963): 10–17, and A. R. Schulman in *Egyptological Studies in Honor of R. A. Parker,* ed. L. H. Lesko (Hanover and London, 1986), pp. 122–135. On further contacts between Egypt and the monarchy of David and Solomon, see A. Malamat, *Das davidische und salomonische Königreich und seine Beziehungen zu Ägypten und Syrien* (Vienna, 1983), and on possible Egyptian influence on the administration of the new state, see T. N. D. Meltinger, *Solomonic State Officials* (Lund, 1971).

For the Libyan Period (Dynasties 22–24), in addition to the works cited at the beginning of this section, see J. Yoyotte in *Mélanges Maspero,* MIFAO 66, vol. 1 (Cairo, 1961), pp. 121–179; F. Gomaà, *Die libyschen Fürstentümer des Deltas vom Tod Osorkons II. bis zur Wiedervereinigung Ägyptens durch Psametik I.* (Wiesbaden, 1974); K. Jansen-Winkeln, *Ägyptische Biographien der 22. und 23. Dynastie,* ÄAT 8 (Wiesbaden, 1985) and A. Leahy, ed., *Libya and Egypt c. 1300–750 B.C.* (London, 1990). On the chronology and the sequence of kings, see also K. Baer, *JNES* 32 (1973): 4–25, and M.-A. Bonhême, *BSFE* 134 (1995): 50–71. On the annals of the priests at Karnak, see J.-M. Kruchten, *Les Annales des prêtres de Karnak (XXI–XXIIImes dynasties) et autres textes relatifs à l'initiation des prêtres d'Amon,* OLA 32 (Leuven, 1989).

Shoshenq's campaign to Jerusalem is discussed by S. Herrmann, *ZDPV* 80 (1964): 55–79, and the stela at Gebel el-Silsila by R. A. Caminos, *JEA* 38 (1952): 46–61 (on pp. 60–61 there is also a discussion of the date of the erection of the first pylon at Karnak, which has not yet been determined precisely).

H. K. Jacquet-Gordon assumed an essentially shorter reign for Osorkon I in *JEA* 53 (1967): 63–68; but see now Kitchen, *Third Intermediate Period,* §89. On an attack on Judah and defeat by King Asa, see Kitchen's §268, and on a brief coregency with the high priest Shoshenq (II), §269.

The tomb of Osorkon II was published by P. Montet, *Les Constructions et le tombeau d'Osorkon II à Tanis* (Paris, 1947), and his *sed* festival hall by E. Naville, *The Festival Hall of Osorkon II in the Great Temple of Bubastis,* MEEF 10 (London, 1892). On the high priest Harsiese, see K. Jansen-Winkeln, *JEA* 81 (1995): 129–136.

On the Egyptian finds in Spain, which stem in part from this period, see I. Gamer-Wallert, *Ägyptische und ägyptisierende Funde von der Iberischen Halbinsel*, BTAVO 21 (Wiesbaden, 1978), and J. Padro i Parcerisa, *Egyptian-Type Documents from the Mediterranean Littoral of the Iberian Peninsula* (Leiden, 1980), with supplement (Montpellier, 1995). For the Egyptians' participation in the Battle of Qarqar against the Assyrians, see Kitchen, *Third Intermediate Period*, §285.

On the crown prince Osorkon's intervention at Thebes, see R. A. Caminos, *The Chronicle of Prince Osorkon*, AnOr 37 (Rome, 1958), and Kitchen, *Third Intermediate Period*, §§291–293. The installation of Bakenptah at Herakleopolis did not occur until Shoshenq III; see Kitchen, §300. On the controversy regarding the order of the monarchs of late Dynasty 22 and Dynasty 23, see D. A. Aston, *JEA* 75 (1989): 139–153; A. Leahy, ed., *Libya and Egypt* pp. 155–200; K. Jansen-Winkeln, *JEA* 81 (1995): 139–149; and J. von Beckerath, *GM* 144 (1995): 7–13 and 147 (1995): 9–13.

Osorkon III, Takelot III, and the Divine Adoratrice Shepenwepet I decorated a small chapel to Osiris in the eastern portion of the temple of Karnak; see the preliminary report by D. B. Redford, *JEA* 59 (1973): 16–30.

On Kashta in Egypt, see J. Leclant, *ZÄS* 90 (1963): 74–78, and K.-H. Priese, *ZÄS* 98 (1970): 16–32.

The name Piankhi has been read as Piye for some time; see R. A. Parker, *ZÄS* 93 (1966): 111–114; K.-H. Priese, *MIO* 14 (1968): 166–175; and J. von Beckerath, *MDAIK* 24 (1969): 58–62. See now, however, G. Vittmann, *Orientalia* 43 (1974): 12–16, and I. A. Katznelson, *Meroe* 3 (1985): 112–117. On his campaign, see A. Spalinger, *SAK* 7 (1979): 273–301; and H. Goedicke, *Pi(ankh)y in Egypt: A Study of the Pi(ankh)y Stela* (Baltimore, 1998).

On the Ethiopian Period (Dynasty 25), see J. Leclant, *Recherches sur les monuments thébains de la XXVᵉ dynastie dite éthiopienne*, 2 vols., BE 36 (Cairo, 1965); G. Vittmann, *Priester und Beamte im Theben der Spätzeit: Genealog. u. prosopographische Untersuchungen zum thebanischen Priester- u. Beamtentum d. 25. u. 26. Dynastie*, BÄ 1 (Vienna, 1978), and E. R. Russmann, *The Representation of the King in the XXVth Dynasty* (Brussels, 1974). The most important historical sources, including the victory stela of Piye, are collected in H. Schäfer, *Urkunden der älteren Äthiopenkönige* (Leipzig, 1905–1908); see also M. F. L. Macadam, *The Temples of Kawa*, 2 vols. (London, 1949–1955), and N.-C. Grimal, *La stèle triomphale de Pi('ankh)y au Musée du Caire, JE 48863–48866*, MIFAO 105 (Cairo, 1981). On different results for the chronology from Piye to Shebitku, see L. Depuydt, *JEA* 79 (1993): 269–274.

On archaism in the Late Period, see H. Brunner, *Saeculum* 21 (1970): 151–161; P. Der Manuelian, *Living in the Past: Studies in Archaism of the Egyptian 26th Dynasty* (London, 1994); and S. Neureiter, *SAK* 21 (1994): 219–254.

The institution of Divine Adoratrice is treated by C. E. Sander-Hansen, *Das Gottesweib des Amun* (Copenhagen, 1940), and its administration by E. Graefe, *Untersuchungen zur Verwaltung und Geschichte der Institution der Gottesgemahlin des Amun*, ÄgAbh 37, (Wiesbaden, 1981). On the predecessors of Shepenwepet I, see J. Yoyotte, *BSFE* 64 (1972): 31–52. The *sed* festival and other royal features of their rule were probably fictive in character.

Bocchoris is treated by Jac. J. Janssen, "Over farao Bocchoris," in *Varia historica aangeboden aan Professor Doctor A. W. Byvanck ter gelegenheid van zijn zeventigste verjaardag* (Assen, 1954), pp. 17–29, and G. Hölbl, *GB* 10 (1981): 1–20. He was also recognized as king at Tanis, and thus in the entire delta; see J. Yoyotte, *Kêmi* 21 (1971): 44f. On the date of the conquest of the delta by Shabaka (712 B.C.E.) see A. Spalinger,

JARCE 10 (1973): 95–101. K.-H. Priese, *ZÄS* 98 (1970): 19, and K. Baer, *JNES* 32 (1973): 23–24, reckon on a continued existence of the defeated dynasty and an uninterrupted transition to Dynasty 26.

The Asian policy of the Ethiopians was peaceful under Shabaka, while his successor, Shebitku, the beginning of whose reign has been established as 702 B.C.E. by Kitchen, became embroiled in fresh battles. In 701 B.C.E., an Egyptian army under the command of the young Taharqa was defeated by Sennacherib near Eltekeh; see Kitchen, *Third Intermediate Period,* §346.

On Mentuemhet, see J. Leclant, *Mentouemhat, quatrième prophète d'Amon, prince de la ville,* BE 35 (Cairo, 1961), and H. Kees, *ZÄS* 87 (1962): 60–66.

For the extraordinarily high flood during the reign of Taharqa, see V. Vikentiev, *La haute crue du Nil et l'averse de l'an 6 de Taharqa: Le dieu "Hemen" et son cheflieu "Hefat,"* UERTFL (Cairo, 1930), and J. Leclant and J. Yoyotte, *Kêmi* 10 (1949): 28–42. On Taharqa at Karnak, see R. A. Parker, J. Leclant, and J.-C. Goyon, *The Edifice of Taharqa by the Sacred Lake of Karnak,* BES 8 (Providence and London, 1979). On the stela at Dahshur, see H. Altenmüller and A. M. Moussa, *SAK* 9 (1981): 57–84, and W. Decker, *KBS* 13 (1984): 7–37.

On the Assyrian conquest of Egypt, see Kitchen, *Third Intermediate Period,* §§352–354, and A.-U. Onasch, *Die assyrischen Eroberungen Ägyptens,* ÄAT 27 (Wiesbaden, 1994).

On Dynasty 26, in addition to the works by Kienitz and Gyles already mentioned, see H. de Meulenaere, *Herodotos over de 26ste dynastie (II, 147–III, 15): Bijdrage tot het historisch-kritisch onderzoek van Herodotos' gegevens in het licht van de Egyptische en andere contemporaire bronnen,* BM 27 (Louvain, 1951). On the Saite royal family, see G. Vittmann, *Orientalia* 44 (1975): 375–387. On the institution of kingship, see A. Spalinger, *Orientalia* 47 (1978): 12–36, and D. A. Pressl, *SAK* 20 (1993): 223–254. On Asian policy, see D. B. Redford, *JAOS* 90 (1970): 474–484, and A. Spalinger, *SAK* 5 (1977): 221–244. Brooklyn Museum, *Egyptian Sculpture of the Late Period 700 B.C. to A.D. 100* (New York, 1960) is a fundamental work on the art of this dynasty and of the entire Late Period.

On the last mention of a Great Chief of the Libyans, whose name was Padikhons, see F. Gomaà, *Die libyschen Fürstentümer des Deltas vom Tode Osorkons II. bis zur Wiedervereinigung Ägyptens durch Psammetik I.,* BTAVO 6 (Wiesbaden, 1974), pp. 99–100. On Sematawytefnakhte, see H. S. K. Bakry, *Kêmi* 20 (1970): 19–36. On the internal politics of Psammetichus I, see V. Wessetzky, *ZÄS* 88 (1962): 69–73.

On the adoption of Nitocris, see R. A. Caminos, *JEA* 50 (1964): 71–101, and J. Vandier, *ZÄS* 99 (1972): 29–33. The most important document on the administration of Thebes in this period is published by R. A. Parker, *A Saite Oracle Papyrus from Thebes in the Brooklyn Museum,* BES 4 (Providence, 1962). Ibi, the first Saite administrator, is treated by E. Graefe, *CE* 46 (1971): 234–244, and idem, *SAK* 1 (1974): 201–206; on his tomb, see K. P. Kuhlmann and W. Schenkel, *Das Grab des Ibi, Obergutsverwalters der Gottesgemahlin des Amun (Thebanisches Grab Nr. 36),* AVDAIK 15 (Mainz, 1983), and E. Graefe, *Das Grab des Ibi, Obervermögensverwalters der Gottesgemahlin des Amun (Thebanisches Grab Nr. 36): Beschreibung und Rekonstruktionsversuche des Oberbaus, Funde aus dem Oberbau* (Brussels, 1990).

Private sources for religion in the Late Period are treated by E. Otto, *Die biographischen Inschriften der ägyptischen Spätzeit: Ihre geistesgeschichtliche und literarische Bedeutung* (Leiden, 1954). On the mortuary cults of former kings, see D. Wildung, *Die Rolle ägyptischer Könige im Bewusstsein ihrer Nachwelt,* pt. 1, MÄS 17

(Munich, 1969). The tomb of Petamenophis is especially important for the textual tradition of the Books of the Afterlife; see A. Piankoff, *BIFAO* 46 (1947): 73–92, and F. W. von Bissing, *ZÄS* 74 (1938): 2–26.

On the division of Egypt by the Assyrians, see the fundamental study of D. J. Wiseman, *Chronicles of Chaldaean Kings (626–556 B.C.) in the British Museum* (London, 1956). On ensuing events until 586 B.C.E., see. A. Malamat, *IEJ* 18 (1968): 137–156, and idem, *The Twilight of Judah*, Supplements to *VT* 28 (Leiden, 1975), pp. 123–145. Relations with Babylon and the new Egyptian naval power are treated by A. Spalinger, *SAK* 5 (1977): 221–244, and for Psammetichus I, see idem, *JARCE* 15 (1978): 49–57.

On the canal from the Nile to the Red Sea and on the circumnavigation of Africa, see the critical study by A. B. Lloyd, *JEA* 63 (1977): 142–155.

The Nubian campaign of Psammetichus II is treated by S. Sauneron and J. Yoyotte, *BIFAO* 50 (1952): 157–207, and H. Goedicke, *MDAIK* 37 (1981): 187–198. On his erasure of the names of Ethiopian kings, see J. Yoyotte, *RE* 8 (1951): 215–239. His construction work on the island of Philae is treated by G. Haeny, *BIFAO* 85 (1985): 197–199.

Kingdom of Meroe: For surveys of the history and culture, see P. L. Shinnie, *Meroe* (London, 1967); F. and U. Hintze, *Alte Kulturen im Sudan* (1966); and L. Török in *Aufstieg und Niedergang der römischen Welt: Geschichte und Kultur Roms im Spiegel der neueren Forschung*, ed. H. Temporini, vol. 2, 10, 1 (Berlin, 1988), pp. 107–341. See also I. Hofmann, *Studien zum meroitischen Königtum*, MRE 2 (Brussels, 1971), and L. Török, *The Birth of an Ancient African Kingdom*, (Lille, 1995).

On the controversy regarding the exact date of the conquest of Jerusalem, see A. Malamat, *IEJ* 18 (1968): 150–152 (opting for 586 B.C.E.), and E. Kutsch, *Biblica* 55 (1974): 520–543 (preferring 587 B.C.E.).

On the Jewish colony at Elephantine, see B. Porten, *Archives from Elephantine* (Berkeley, 1968); P. Grelot, *Documents araméens d'Égypte* (Paris, 1972); and B. Porten and A. Yardeni, *Textbook of Aramaic Documents from Ancient Egypt*, vol. 1, *Letters* (Jerusalem, 1986).

The coffin of the God's Wife, Ankhnesneferibre, which is today in the British Museum, is an important source for the religion of the period; see C. E. Sander-Hansen, *Die religiösen Texte auf dem Sarg der Anchnesneferibre* (Copenhagen, 1937). On her adoption by Nitocris in December 595 B.C.E., see A. Leahy, *JEA* 82 (1996): 145–165.

On Amasis, see H. de Meulenaere, *JEA* 54 (1968): 183–187,and A. Leahy, *JEA* 74 (1988): 183–199. On his reforms, see E. Jelinkova-Reymond, *ASAE* 54 (1957): 251–287. Relationships with Greece in the sixth and fifth centuries B.C.E. are treated by P. Salmon, *La politique égyptienne d'Athènes*, 2d ed. (Brussels, 1981). On Siwa Oasis, see K. P. Kuhlmann, *Das Ammoneion: Archäologie, Geschichte, und Kultpraxis des Orakels von Siwa*, AVDAIK 75 (Mainz, 1988).

The Instruction of Ankhsheshonqy was published by S. R. K. Glanville, *The Instructions of Onchsheshonqy* (London, 1955); for a recent treatment, see H. J. Thissen, *Die Lehre des Anchscheschonqi* (Bonn, 1984). See also M. Lichtheim, *Late Egyptian Wisdom Literature in the International Context*, OBO 52 (Freiburg and Göttingen, 1983).

With regard to Psammetichus III and attempted resistance to the Persians, J. Yoyotte, *RE* 24 (1972): 216–223, reckons with a pretender, Petubaste III, in 522–520 B.C.E.; and on an Egyptian rebellion at the transfer of the throne, see V. V. Struve, *PS* 63 (1954): 7–13. For an example of the piety of the last Saite kings, see J. Vercoutter, *Textes biographiques du Sérapéum de Memphis: Contribution à l'étude des stèles votives du Sérapéum*, BEHE 316 (Paris, 1962), pp. 37–43.

For Egypt as a satrapy of the Persian empire (Dynasty 27), see G. Posener, *La pre-mière domination perse en Égypte: Receuil d'inscriptions hiéroglyphiques*, BE 11 (Cairo, 1936; rpt. 1980), and E. Bresciani, *SCO* 7 (1958): 132–188. On dating practices, see L. Depuydt, *JEA* 81 (1995): 151–173. The Persians probably made Memphis the seat of their rule; see J. Yoyotte, *BIFAO* 71 (1972): 1–10. The reaction of the Egyptians is treated by D. Devauchelle, *Transeuphratène* 9 (1995): 67–80. On the "collaborator" Udjahorresnet, see A. B. Lloyd, *JEA* 68 (1982): 166–180. On Persian influences on Egyptian art, see J. D. Cooney, *JARCE* 4 (1965): 39–48. A nuanced picture of the mea-sures taken by Cambyses is drawn by G. Burkard, *ZÄS* 121 (1994): 93–105 and 122 (1995): 31–37, dealing with both textual tradition and archaeological finds.

Darius: A larger-than-life-size statue of the king, which was prepared according to the Egyptian model and bears a hieroglyphic inscription along with a trilingual cuneiform text, was discovered at Susa in December 1972; see J. Yoyotte et al., *JA* 1972: 235–266; and J. Leclant, *Orientalia* 43 (1974): 218–219. On the temple of Hibis, see W. D. van Wijngaarden, *ZÄS* 79 (1954): 68–72; and E. Cruz-Uribe, *Hibis Temple Project*, vol. 1, *Translations, Commentary, Discussions, and Sign List* (San Antonio, 1988).

On Greek military assistance and on the revolt of Inaros, who defeated a Persian army at Papremis in 459 B.C.E., see Salmon, *La politique égyptienne d'Athènes*, cited above.

Herodotus has been treated by, among others, J. A. Wilson, *Herodotus in Egypt*, SABMD 5 (Leiden, 1970); M. Kaiser in *Die Begegnung Europas mit Ägypten*, ed. S. Morenz, 2d ed. (Zurich and Stuttgart, 1969), pp. 241–304; and A. B. Lloyd, *Histo-ria* 37 (1988): 22–53. The temple archive discovered in 1988 at Manawir in el-Kharga Oasis sheds light on the transition from Persian rule to Dynasties 28 and 29; see M. Chauveau, *BSFE* 137 (1996): 32–47.

Dynasty 29: C. Traunecker, *BIFAO* 79 (1979): 395–436, and J. D. Ray, *JEA* 72 (1986): 149–158. On Hakoris's mercenary army and his especially close relations with Cyprus, see J. Barns, *Historia* 2 (1953): 163–176, and 0. Masson, *BSFE* 60 (1971): 37–40. On the first coinage in Egypt, see J. W. Curtis, *JEA* 43 (1957): 71–76.

Dynasty 30: On the last native royal family, see H. de Meulenaere, *ZÄS* 90 (1963): 90–93. For the chronology, see J. H. Johnson, *Enchoria* 4 (1974): 14–16, treating de-tails in the Demotic Chronicle. On art, see H. W. Müller, *Pantheon* 28 (1970): 89–99. Nectanebo I's lively building activity in the temples of Karnak and Luxor, including the avenue of human-headed sphinxes linking the two temples, has been discussed by M. Abdel Razik, *MDAIK* 23 (1968): 156–159. On Nectanebo II, see T. Holm-Rasmussen, *AO* 40 (1979): 21–25, and idem in *HCPHA* 10 (1985): 7–23; his sarcopha-gus is treated by H. Jenni, *Das Dekorationsprogramm des Sarkophages Nektanebos' II*, AH 12 (Geneva, 1986).

Second Persian occupation: On the preceding pacification of Phoenicia, see D. Barag, *BASOR* 183 (1966): 6–8. A statue at Memphis renewed the memory of the chief physician Udjahorresnet, the Egyptian "collaborator" under Cambyses and Darius; see R. Anthes, *Mit Rahineh 1956* (Philadelphia, 1965), pp. 98–100. On Udja-horresnet's newly discovered tomb at Abusir, see M. Verner, *ZÄS* 118 (1991): 162–167. On the native (Nubian?) counterking Khababash, who probably belongs in this period, see A. Spalinger, *ZÄS* 105 (1978): 142–154, and W. Huss, *SEL* 11 (1994): 97–112.

One of the generals of Alexander the Great issued an order, preserved in the orig-inal, for the protection of the sacred places at Saqqara; it is the earliest Greek-language papyrus document in Egypt: see E. G. Turner, *JEA* 60 (1974): 239–242.

The tomb of Petosiris is published by G. Lefebvre, *Le tombeau de Petosiris*, 3 vols. (Cairo, 1923–1924).

On the world of the late temples, see S. Sauneron and H. Stierlin, *Derniers temples d'Egypte: Edfou et Philae* (Paris, 1975), and F. Daumas, *Dendara et le temple d'Hathor: Notice sommaire*, RAPH 29 (Cairo, 1969). On Edfu, see D. Kurth, *Treffpunkt der Götter: Inschriften aus dem tempel des Horus von Edfu* (Zürich, 1994).

The worship of Egyptian deities in the Roman empire is dealt with in the series edited by J. Vermaseren, *Études préliminaires aux religions orientales dans l'Empire romain* (Leiden); volumes have been appearing since 1961. See also H. Temporini, ed., *Aufstieg und Niedergang der römischen Welt: Geschichte und Kultur Roms im Spiegel der neueren Forschung* (Berlin, 1972–).

On the continuing influence of Egypt down to the present time, see S. Morenz, ed., *Die Begegnung Europas mit Ägypten*, 2d ed. (Zurich and Stuttgart, 1969).

On the history of the Ptolemaic Period, see A. K. Bowman, *Egypt after the Pharaohs, 332 B.C.–A.D. 642: From Alexander to the Arab Conquest* (Berkeley, 1986); and G. Hölbl, *Geschichte des Ptolemäerreiches* (Darmstadt, 1994).

INDEX